A
Love Affair
with
Life

A Compelling Look
at Choice and Change

Barbara Hyde

Advance Reader Comments

"Wherever you're coming from, whatever challenges you have faced, there is a story or commentary in this work to help you reconnect with who and how you are and to offer you insights that will help you move towards living the life you truly desire. This extraordinary work will change a great many lives for the better."

. . .

"Powerful and riveting, this book leaves every reader closer to having a love affair with their own life."

. . .

"Searingly honest, Hyde gives her readers nowhere to hide—and no reason to—as she offers a unique perspective on life that leaves them choosing to regard themselves and others with greater acceptance, respect, and love."

. . .

"A few years ago my son stopped talking to me about his life and I couldn't understand why. 'Vicki's Story' still takes my breath away. For any parent wanting a more meaningful relationship with their children, *A Love Affair with Life* will assist you in your change to make that happen. An important and brave work."

. . .

"*A Love Affair with Life* offers a skills kit of ordinary concepts—the *life* skills— for building a better life."

. . .

"The most incisive book I have ever read on relationships, first and foremost the one with myself. A manifesto. Simple...profound...responsible."

. . .

"The wisdom offered in this book follows the unfolding of Nature. It is as plain as the dirt under our feet and as awesome as the stars in the night sky. This is not philosophy or psychology based; it is elemental."

. . .

"We need a new narrative, resplendent with more opportunity, autonomy, and choice. *A Love Affair with Life* delivers it in spades...a must read."

"Guaranteed to shift your perspective on humanity, *A Love Affair with Life* offers a most remarkable foundational shift in how we view our lives, including our responsibilities. This book will profoundly impact every reader's life and the lives they touch."

• • •

"If you want to enhance your life, then settle in with this book and prepare to be stimulated and encouraged by its unconventional thought. Sometimes startling, always provocative, it's a must read."

• • •

"I came away from reading this book feeling as if I had been set free to choose, to act—responsibly—on my own behalf...without guilt, shame, or a 'good reason.'"

• • •

"Hyde both invites and challenges us to choose the life experiences we really want, to resist the forces around us that would steer us in directions that are not in our best interest, and to become truly self-reliant in order to maximize our potential to make better choices for a satisfying life. A groundbreaking work that will transform lives."

• • •

"All my years of therapy about forgiveness, and it took this book to realize that I was 'jousting with windmills,' fighting a fight that had no enemy. A great weight has been lifted."

• • •

"*A Love Affair with Life* is a beautiful reminder of the greatest experiment in recent history—the founding of America on the principles of freedom of choice. How can we unite to help one another to build a better America? To quote the work: 'When each one comes to care for one's self, all are cared for.' A timely and much needed book."

• • •

"At nearly ninety, I can say that *A Love Affair with Life* is about real life and love and is an essential read for everyone who wants to make peace with their lives *and* themselves before they die. It is a beautiful and tender book."

Publisher
Life is Action, Inc.
3980 Broadway
Suite 103, PMB 143
Boulder, CO 80304
rights@LifeIsAction.com
www.LifeIsAction.com

FIRST EDITION

Published in the United States of America

Cover design by Robert D. Vernon

Print ISBN 978-0-9884221-1-7
Ebook ISBN 978-0-9884221-2-4

Library of Congress Control Number 2014918206

Dedication

A Love Affair with Life – A Compelling Look at Choice and Change is dedicated to my supportive, inspiring, and dearly-loved family: My son, Nathaniel Leonoudakis, who courageously and confidently moves forward in the world, taking risks on himself and voting for others; my mother, Phyllis Hanus, who brings her family together with honest and reliable love; my father, Thomas Hyde, who never stopped boldly stepping into new experiences; my brother Tom Hyde—generous and strong— who dares to live his own life authentically and with gusto; my brother Steven Hyde, who, in everything that life brings his way, continues to show his fierce tenderness; my sister Peggy Miller-Peterman, who cares for others with her open-hearted kindness and warm sense of humor; all my family members down the line, who example the freedom to live their unique lives and in particular my thoughtful nephew Ron Hyde, who gently said to me, "Why not write your book now?" And of course, to all those who came before me—on up the line—surprising me daily with what they handed me from their back pockets, available to express in me…in my lifetime.

∽

This work is not intended to excuse ill, anti-social, or destructive behavior; and the concepts do not apply to anyone desiring to engage in these behaviors. *A Love Affair with Life* is, above all else, a love story about humanity, written for and dedicated to all people desiring to improve their lives, with no harm to others.

A Love Affair with Life
A COMPELLING LOOK AT CHOICE AND CHANGE

Contents

Special Acknowledgment
to
Karen Sontag

This work is a culmination of my observations, life experiences, and conversations with others shared in an anecdotal manner. I wish to acknowledge with particular gratitude, the many deep and richly rewarding conversations I have had with Karen Sontag, a cherished and trusted confidant of good counsel to me for many years. Her unending willingness to share her sagacity with me—on all manner and variety of topics that might distress or bring joy and peace to others—I now share with you to the best of my ability. Her wisdom added clarity to the stories and provided a deeper, richer, and more helpful understanding to the commentaries.

We all cross paths with different experiences of our choosing, and in doing so, our destinies unfold. My serendipitous crossing of paths with Karen Sontag now leads to your serendipitous crossing of paths with this book. It is my wish that you find fulfillment in reading these pages and that your life will unfold more in keeping with your heart's deepest desires. To experience the freedom, dignity, and wonder of living your own authentic life can bring you closer to a love affair with life.

We find that as we bring ourselves into harmony and move into a responsible way of life—therewith achieving personal peace—this influences the same in our environment and with those around us. This is love.

—Karen Sontag

A
Love Affair
with
Life

A Compelling Look
at Choice and Change

Barbara Hyde

1

Are You In Love With Your Life?

When you integrate awareness of your true nature with the necessary life skills to pursue your authentic desires, acting on your truth becomes an easier choice. A personal awakening to a love affair with life is then possible.

It's got to be easier, better, more satisfying than this!

How many of us have thought or said that? In our heart of hearts, don't we all long for a love affair with life?

We try to live the best life we can, of course, but many of us still find ourselves in a world we can't make work for us in the way we would like. We want to choose well for ourselves so we can create the life we truly desire. When our life experiences are connected to our innermost desires, we feel vibrant and healthy and happy, but we just can't seem to make that connection often enough. And so many of us are overly stressed, unhappy, discouraged, disappointed, or just simply not experiencing life as we imagined it would be.

A Love Affair with Life offers a foundation for viewing one's own life from a unique perspective. The stories and commentaries which follow present information and viewpoints for experiencing the world that invite our indestructible and unique spirit—our truth—to freely express itself in actions that reflect better choosing for each of us. You will meet individuals who work through their issues and challenges, use their chosen experiences to develop themselves, and learn to trust their own inner authority, their own voice. You will recognize how various life experiences may impact their sense of well-being as you observe who or what is calling the shots in their lives and the sometimes unknowing "life compromises" they make. You can learn from their personal evolution as they better prepare themselves to make informed decisions in pursuit of their true desires, "own" their lives and their decisions, and journey forward to a life well-lived, a life of their own choosing.

How did we lose our way?

If we are doing only what we believe we must and should do, rather than what we truly want to do, we are most likely living a contradiction. When we do not live authentically, we compromise and "pretzel ourselves around," creating excuses and rationalizations and becoming experts at deluding ourselves. Is it any wonder that eventually the cumulative effect could be that we become overwhelmed, disengaged, or perhaps even reach a point of pervasive sadness?

Disharmonious emotions can occur within us when we take on life experiences at odds with our true nature. Do we dislike our jobs or work-mates or find our marriages and relationships unsatisfying? Do we feel bullied into compromises? Are we at our wit's end with parental challenges? What happens when we have feelings of ineptitude that sometimes lead to panic, when we're frustrated, angry, experience distancing, or when we feel "less"? How many of us have had that feeling of disability where we just can't quite cope the way we wish we could, can't quite deal with daily life in a manner that makes us feel good about ourselves, can't quite feel the joy we want?

This stress can have a profound influence on our bodies and our lives. Often, we don't *want* to recognize that our discomfort has purpose—has value—and that our unhappiness can be viewed as a message from the body that something in our life isn't correct for who and how we are. But if we choose to pay attention to what the body is telling us, we will be able to discern and interpret these messages. Do we feel listless and fatigued, unmotivated, crabby, or short-tempered? Do we sense our own resistance? Are we jealous, judgmental, or constantly comparing ourselves to other individuals? Unhappiness and stress, while not a diagnosis for a disease, comprise many signs of an unfulfilled life—a life that isn't what we want it to be.

What if we feel stuck or we don't know what we want? What if unsuccessful past attempts at change have left us concerned about "failing" yet again? More importantly, what can occur when we believe we don't have choices or when we don't want to choose?

A lost life…

We may risk accepting the identity of victims of circumstance. Like vegetables in a garden, we wait, passively stuck in the ground, to see if we are watered for our thirst, if there is sunshine to fuel our growth and strength, or if we are lucky enough to be pruned for our development. If moles come and attack our roots, if beetles come and nibble at our leaves, or if a dog comes by and pees on us, we are susceptible to damage or injury. That's what happens when we don't ask ourselves, "What do I want and not want? What do I like and not like?" We may find our humanity has become distorted or obscured because we have surrendered—even if by habit—our self-reliance and our dignity.

What makes choosing well seem easier for some than it does for others?

We head out on this journey of life choosing an easier or a harder path. Once on a difficult path, some of us do not self-assess and self-correct so that we might change course to an easier path; it may be that no change is desired or perhaps different reasons exist to continue along a chosen path. Conversely, others of us, once we recognize the reality of any "incorrect choosing" for ourselves, begin with small steps to take actions toward experiences of better choosing. And then there are those of us who, once awakened to our reality, are equipped and able to bolt into action to cross paths with experiences we truly desire. We are all different, and we each find our own way. Uniquely.

Contained within our own selves—in our natures—are inherent, unwanted, and unwell behavior patterns; these come from our genetic history, our environments, and our experiences. Unique to each individual, these inhibiting factors can disable us from being who and how we want to be, from having the life we yearn for. We all have these behavior patterns, but some of us have more of them than others.

These unwanted and unwell behavior patterns can certainly mess with our lives. They are part of our character, that which exists in our nature *in this moment*. While wanting to be the better of ourselves and improve our lives, we can find the pursuit of our authentic desires disrupted; we may compensate, avoid, deny, rationalize, create excuses and stories, and allow ourselves to remain unconscious of our reality. When we restrict, limit, and compromise ourselves in this way, we minimize the expression of our full being. And in so doing, we may stumble or struggle in our efforts to make the choices and take the actions needed for a more satisfying and happier life.

So we try to stay positive, often quoting phrases to remind ourselves to be kinder, more upbeat, or to be this or be that; while helpful, many who have tried unsuccessfully to make significant changes using that approach still don't feel peaceful and at ease.

What can we do to become more equipped to make better choices?

To change these inhibiting factors in our nature, we want to encourage and pursue our own development. We cannot cease being who and how we are by simply willing it to be so. We may "manage our behavior," but in order to free ourselves from our unwanted behavior patterns that limit us in having the life we desire, this capability—this development of our character—must be pursued. Why is this so important? Because it is our character—the "who and how" of us—that most influences our choices. This is not about our morality within the context of society; this is about our individual integrity—our wholeness within our own being.

How, specifically, do we develop the "who and how" of us—our character? Simply, and yet by our own choices, we begin to take action for experiences we want, owning the responsibility for those choices, however they play out.

Choosing well—a treasured life skill—can be developed

Experiences just exist. It is we who imbue them with values. Some we view as being of desired quality, some not. Some lead us to a better life, some do not. While it is likely easier, more fun, nourishing, and rewarding to develop ourselves from joyful and satisfying experiences we want, *any* experience can be used to further our personal capabilities and life skills for making choices.

Understanding ourselves and what we want is key to choosing well. Our body—with its innate knowingness—tries to communicate our true desires within us. When we listen to and trust its messages, it can be easier to make choices and take actions for experiences that are connected to our innermost desires—our "whole selves." These experiences give us a sense of fulfillment, of satisfaction and harmony. We discover a freedom to choose more of those experiences that nourish us and make us smile. In this way, we come to better health and greater happiness and peace in our lives.

So, what's holding us back?

Much of my professional career has been spent in the field of choice and change. I have assisted both companies and individuals in their change initiatives as an organizational consultant, educator, worksite wellness specialist, and facilitator. In all arenas, I have observed the same two critical barriers that may contribute to the frustration of those who struggle as they seek to move from the life they are living to the life they desire to live. Identifying and overcoming these barriers that keep people stuck is the focus of this book, and these messages are discussed throughout the stories and commentaries. If addressed, many may find themselves better prepared to bridge the gap between what *is* and what *is desired*, thus improving the quality of their lives.

Barrier One: Difficulty in effortlessly determining what rings true for us

Reasons abound as to why we can't hear and act on our authentic desires as our body tries to communicate them to us, or why this information may have become muddled for us. Maybe we have relinquished our foundations for living to misguided sayings and clichés or unconscious habits. Perhaps we've allowed ourselves to be confused by society's arbitrary standards, social mores, "proper" protocols, religious doctrines, unquestioned dogmas, government interventions, image concerns, or advertising. Could it be we have overlooked examining the cultural views, presumptions, and notions that inform our approach to our life and our own self-care? External systems—as with all the other qualifiers on our choices—can be so confusing that we may find we have delegated or passively surrendered our life choices to a variety of external authorities, be they institutions, spiritual leaders, teachers, doctors, self-proclaimed "thought leaders" and "experts," parents, bosses, partners, or friends. Perhaps we have avoided taking on the responsibility of making our own choices and that has simply become—as a default—our preferred way of addressing life.

When matters need our attention, we want to be able to effortlessly discern what rings true for each of us, but it can be difficult to make clear choices when we haven't consciously looked at who or what may be influencing us and how.

Is it possible some of us haven't even taken a moment to consider that our previous choices may no longer be the ones we want and that we are free to make new choices in keeping with who and how we are today? Have we, in our search for sense, relief, or peace, simply forgotten we are our own best "experts" of ourselves?

Many of us simply have not learned how to make—and trust—our own choices and hold ourselves accountable.

Barrier Two: Underdeveloped skills of self-reliance

Inherent in our nature is a deep desire to be self-reliant—to be effective in our lives in any way we want. We, as a species, are compelled to move toward self-reliance in order to survive as our nature seeks its own fulfillment through our actions. As when a baby takes its first breath and its first steps, this self-reliance is developed as we learn to trust ourselves to pursue what we desire. Regardless of the actions we ultimately choose to take, we know we want to give ourselves a chance to try to figure it out. We give value to the word "try" as a positive expression of hope and find it rewarding and nourishing to attempt to take steps toward what we want; we experiment with various possibilities.

Operating from our own internal authority, we become involved in creating our own access—to people, to information, or to any other experiences that get us moving in a direction we value. Options are endless because we know that with the necessary life skills of self-reliance, we have the freedom to go for what we want, responsibly and with no harm to others. Naturally then, the byproduct of a self-reliant life is a sense of self-respect… that lovely manner of being where we tend to view ourselves, our lives, and all of humanity with more tolerance.

Many of us want to become well-equipped for this kind of life and may be baffled when we find we are not. We may be poised—ready and willing—to begin to pursue it, but we do not yet possess, or in some cases even have an awareness of what may well be a cornerstone of healthy human relations. This cornerstone is the important life skills of self-reliance and all that it comprises: a healthy self-interest, the capability to discern reality, a curiosity for self-discovery, the ability to operate from our internal authority, self-management, self-knowing including body knowingness, ownership of our choices and the responsibility for our actions accordingly, self-providing, self-awareness, self-expression, self-assessment, self-correction, and self-care.

And so, when we find ourselves *ineffective* in our relationships, with our communications, in our finances, dealing with emotions, in the management of our lives and in society at large, or in realizing our dreams, often all we know is that we are not having a love affair with life. We know we do not adapt with ease and we are not feeling optimistic or hopeful about life. Without recognition that we could impact our lives positively with more developed skills of self-reliance, we give no consideration to this option.

The outcomes

Only we can know what gives our life meaning. Whenever we suppress, surrender, or delegate our own internal authority, we compromise ourselves to something outside of ourselves, sometimes almost blindly so. In making this exchange, we deny ourselves the opportunity to develop the necessary life skills needed to prepare us for a life whereby we are curious, engaged, and have the mettle and motivation to care for ourselves. We deny ourselves the comfort to easily make choices to go for what we want, improving our own lives along the way. This puts the opportunity to have the life we truly desire at risk. How?

First, compromise is inevitable when we choose to remain irresponsible for our own self-care—incapable of supporting ourselves emotionally, physically, intellectually, financially, or in furthering ourselves in any manner that we desire—because, in reality, we have forfeited our autonomy.

Second, we hesitate to make any changes in favor of choices and experiences we may truly desire. We avoid taking risks on ourselves because we don't know ourselves well enough to trust that we can go for what we want, that we can figure it out, that we can handle the outcomes whatever they may be.

Many of us then enter the workplace, relationships, and other arenas, mistakenly hoping to extract from them what we cannot create in our personal lives. Without sufficiently developed life skills to manage our own experience regardless of what is presenting in any "less than perfect" environment, we attempt to manage the experiences of others. And when that doesn't play out the way we want, it seems reasonable to many of us to fault something outside of ourselves—not realizing that we cannot get from anyone or anything what we do not bring. And so, for many of us, our freedom of choice—and all the wonderful options that could be ours—eludes us.

We often spend our time, money, and talent endlessly ruminating over which choice is the better choice to make. In the process we may overlook asking ourselves a fundamental question: Am I prepared to take action for the experiences I want and own the responsibility for those choices, however they play out? The reality is that many of us are not likely to take a risk on ourselves—to go for what we want; we simply haven't equipped ourselves to do so. And therefore, decision making will remain difficult and many of us will stay stuck where we are…in that place where we know we don't want to be.

How do we pursue the life we want?

The pursuit of the life we want—of what we truly desire—is really a pursuit of our relationship with our own selves. We are an animated and evolving species, and everything that occurs with us occurs through action. We would cease to exist without movement and change.

All experiences inform us as we listen intently to our body's reactions to them. We want to awaken and engage with our body, developing an awareness of the way our own individual truth expresses itself from every cell of every part of it. We want to take an honest look at our current reality—to fully recognize it—and from that viewpoint, ask ourselves what we truly desire and whether our life is reflecting that. The body communicates; it is our partner in creating our life. Whether it is a whisper in our ear, a tap on our shoulder, or a knock upside the head, we want to fully respect and embrace the intelligence of our body as it speaks to us. It will not betray us.

We want to ask ourselves, "Do I want more or less of the experience I am in? Do I like myself in this experience?" If we do, we stay; if we don't, we go. We take a new action. We are calm, solid, peaceful. Choice is easier when we pay attention to our body's messages and take ownership of our choices, regardless of how they unfold; there is no argument. Our behavior comes into alignment with our heart's desires—our truth.

Is it really so difficult to own our choices and move on?

Throughout the stories and commentaries to follow, you may often find—as I have—something within you relates to something about them. How so? Many of us have fallen prey to the victim mentality, claiming someone "did it to me" when betrayed by a friend, a lover, a business partner, or a manager—all who were simply revealing their true natures. Looking back, we can see that those behaviors of theirs were in place when we entered the relationships. But we—without consideration—chose to ignore, excuse, or deny seeing the reality of a non-quality experience as it presented itself to us, preferring not to take personal responsibility for our own choices, but to instead play the victim when all was later revealed. And haven't many of us played "nice" and followed the rules when everything inside of us was screaming to take other, more responsible action for something we did or didn't want?

How many of us have stayed too long at jobs and in relationships or hesitated to move on to something we wanted, when we knew—every part of us knew—that it was time to leave? Did we instead submit to a mental pro and con tally sheet, thereby compromising ourselves and dismissing or ignoring the accuracy and strength of our own genuine desires as they nagged at us? And aren't there those of us who, in the wee hours of the morning, have lain awake feeling the shame that comes with wanting do-overs in life, with everything from falling flat on our face at one-time-only golden work opportunities or parenting moments, to saying all the wrong things while sitting at the bedside of dying loved ones—reliving over and over again what, in retrospect, we wished could have been said or done differently?

A Love Affair with Life is, above all, a love story about humanity written for people seeking to improve their lives. In reading this work, you are offered an opportunity to have an authentic and respectful conversation with yourself, to give regard to your own sensibilities, your own truth, and to be the expert of your own life. You may find yourselves, as I did, sometimes surprised or amused, but often deeply touched—in spite of their individual vulnerabilities—by the amazing resilience of those whose life experiences, in bits and pieces, informed this work. And you may find that when you embrace your own humanity, it is really not so difficult to own your choices and move on.

A gentle reminder

If you identify with the material presented here and decide that you want to try to change some things in your life, be kind to yourself as you come to accept who and how you are today. We can't be more than "only" that in any given moment, and that "only" is a lot. There is enough suffering. While you will hear my opinions, you won't hear any shouting of directives at you to do, think, or be this or that so you will have success in your life. Haven't we been shouting at ourselves long enough to know that it may well be the least effective manner of approaching change? While straight-shooting messages may be helpful, I don't presume or profess to know what is best for you; and I'm not looking to arm wrestle with any individual, philosophy, religion, or opinion. I do not claim to know better than you do—better than your organism does—what your destiny is or ought to be. Your choices will determine that. Each of you is free to try;

each of you is free to choose; and I wish you every success in moving forward with your decisions, doing no harm to others.

A love affair with life is about
our own relationship with ourselves

It is a tremendous responsibility to live the life we want, the way we desire to live it. That is not to say it needs to be difficult. The responsibility of choice—the privilege of choice—exists in the real world, and we can delight in self-discovery. We are always with ourselves; the path is a singular one. We come into this world alone and we go out alone. Do we want to journey with our best friend, our dearest loved one? If so, we want to nourish, care for, love, and respect ourselves. Pursuing our authentic desires—our own selves—requires a deep realization that everyone has a unique nature; it requires compassion for all humanity. As we bring ourselves forward, some of us may be ready to take back our lives, the lives we are just now beginning to see differently from the compromised selves we have created.

We do the boldest things when living our authentic lives, pursuing responsibly what we truly desire, developing who and how we are through our chosen experiences. There is an ease to a life lived in this way, and it won't matter what any individual, any institution, any religion, any book, or any philosophy thinks we should want from or for ourselves. It will be felt in—and emanate from—our very being. When we recognize that the nature of mankind is to continually refine itself—that any species is compelled toward its own evolution—then we can put our trust in our own nature, our nature that wants to be self-reliant, to be effective in whatever it wants. When we stay conscious and listen to our body—where our truth resides—it will inform us of "correct choosing" for ourselves. We want to open our mind, follow our heart, and move our feet.

From a spark of curiosity to a step of action of any size in a direction more to our liking, all movement creates shifts—from the seemingly inconsequential to the profound. We want to know ourselves and always be mindful that our ultimate responsibility is to the life experience we are seeking from our true desires.

Uncover, be, and live your truth, with no harm to others.
—Karen Sontag

2

Dinah's Story

The Lioness Within

*I didn't know then that it isn't the negative or positive
experiences that make us who we are, but rather, it is the
choices we make of how we are going to try to use our life
experiences to move toward greater ease and happiness.*

It was the mid-sixties in a small, rural town in Indiana. I lived at
the end of the street in the last house in town, and my playmate Eva
Wagner lived one block away. Eva was two classes ahead of me, but all
the neighborhood kids played kickball together, shared sparklers on the
Fourth of July, and joined together for rousing games of hide-and-seek
after growing weary of smearing the glowing bodies of captured lightning
bugs all over our arms after sundown. I guess you could say we were a
tribe of sorts.

Eva and I had been friends since my family had moved to the town,
the summer before my third grade, almost two years before this story
takes place. We played cards and board games at each other's homes after
school and I always felt comfortable at her home. Weekend sleepovers
were frequent events. Her sunlit bedroom was off the living room; it had
faded pink wallpaper and tall windows with wispy lace curtains.

My favorite time at Eva's was 4 p.m. on the weekends when Mrs. Wagner served tea. Once summoned, Dieter, Eva's older brother, and Eva and I would wash up and race to the table. Dieter, who was in high school and rarely around otherwise, kept the conversations going, sometimes sassing his parents, who seemed old fashioned and backwards with their thick German accents, dour composure, and no-nonsense ways.

Teatime was a foreign experience to me. Even being allowed to drink tea was unusual; we only had coffee at home, and that was for adults. But this black tea from a whistling, rattling tea kettle—steeped to flavor in a flowered teapot, served with sugar from a glass sugar bowl and tiny spoon, and poured into gold-rimmed cups with delicate handles—was a delight. The ritual included a meal of cheeses, meats, and Mrs. Wagner's delicious, hard-crusted, homemade bread offered on beautiful platters. The tasty spread often included more than one dessert, and she made the best German crumb cake. I can still smell the cinnamon, and my mouth waters just remembering it. When finished, we would all inquire in unison, *"Das ist alles?"* and Mrs. Wagner would reply, *"Das ist alles."* That is all.

It was strange how it began. Dieter touched my foot under the table, and I moved my foot. Then his foot touched mine again. I adjusted my foot again, this time folding my legs at my knees and tucking my feet under my chair. I looked up at him as though to apologize with my eyes, and the look I saw was odd and unfamiliar to me. This happened a few more times at following teatimes. I became uncomfortable. At a sleepover, I was awakened in the middle of the night when he kissed me; he took my hand and led me into the kitchen. I told him I needed to go to sleep and to leave me alone. After that I did not want to go to Eva's house anymore. Dark came early in winter; and as I made continued excuses to Eva for declining her invitations and she moved into life in middle school, we grew apart. What had been a childhood friendship had changed.

I was no longer visiting the Wagner home, and Dieter began exposing himself to me from his corner bedroom windows upstairs, which was visible to me as I walked by to get to almost anywhere in town. He would either have his pants down or no clothes on at all. There was no sidewalk on the opposite side of the street, so whenever possbile I walked through neighbors' yards to avoid directly passing by his house. I averted my eyes when approaching near his house and I never walked home from school that way alone, even if it meant leaving early or staying late and watching for someone I could join in going my direction. I knew very little about sex, had never seen a naked man before, and had never touched myself "down there." I was very confused. I didn't know why he was behaving as he was and I desperately wanted it to stop.

One Saturday afternoon, heading over to a friend's home, I passed by their detached garage. There he was, standing naked inside, the sliding door slightly askew, motioning for me to come over. How did he know I would be walking over to Dorothy's house at that time? What was he doing in the garage? I wanted to throw up. Terrified and unable to make sense of what was happening, I bolted, fearing he would catch me and drag me into the garage. The close call only heightened my fears—even though I wasn't quite certain what I was afraid of.

～

That seemed to be the end of it. In the late spring, I went to Eva's house after school one day for a community project. We finished working at 5:00, the time I was due home. My mother served dinner promptly at 5:30 like clockwork. We were expected to be home for it without fail. I saw Dieter put on his coat and leave the house shortly before.

Every cell in my being warned me to be careful. The hair on the back of my neck stood up. I called home and asked if I could be half an hour late. My father answered the phone; that meant no grace period. I begged, but it was useless; he said that my mother had dinner ready and I was to come home. Why I didn't ask him to meet me, I don't know. It was one lousy block, but I knew—my body knew; everything in the all of me was screaming at me to protect myself. I asked Eva to stay by the back door, telling her it was icy and I wanted to be sure I got home safe. It was pitch dark. I was shaking. About three quarters of the way home, I yelled to Eva, "O-K-A-Y!"

Out of nowhere, Dieter attacked me from behind, covering my mouth with his hand, telling me not to scream or he would hurt me. He dragged me off the sidewalk to the yard between two houses. I fought and we both went down onto the wet, cold ground. He said, "I don't want to screw you—I just want to feel you up," as he pushed his hand down the front of my pants and jammed his fingers into my vagina. Searing pain shot through me. I didn't know what "feel you up" meant, but I was certain he was not someone who could be trusted. With his other hand he shoved my hand down to his penis and told me to rub it. I touched him tentatively. It was the first time I had ever touched a penis. It was warm. He said, "Rub it harder," and he placed his hand over mine to demonstrate what he wanted. At that moment, his cheek was right near my mouth and I took my opportunity. I bit him with all the biting I had in me. He yelled, and hit me. Hard. He flung me off. I scrambled up and ran like the wind toward the street. Ran toward the light.

Ran across the icy street to my home, toward the comforting glow of the small porch light my mother had left on for my safety.

Shaking uncontrollably, I snuck into the back porch. My mom yelled, "Is that you?" I called back, "Yes," stripped off my muddy coat, and headed directly for the bathroom. I sneaked past my father, who was visiting with a friend at the kitchen table—which I noticed hadn't yet been set for dinner; this meant I had a few minutes to clean myself up and calm down. I was covered with mud from head to toe, even in my hair, so I yelled to my mom that I had fallen and was going to clean up. I thought I might not have to say anything…until I realized my glasses must have flown off in the attack. After making myself presentable, I told my mom about my glasses and she grabbed a flashlight and said she would go with me to find them. All I could think was "Oh no! What if they are in the yard away from the sidewalk!" Noticing my wet and soiled coat, she offered me another one to wear.

Once outside, my mother asked what happened. I started to tell her I had fallen, but then some voice inside of me just spilled out the truth. She kept asking, "Did he touch you with anything but his hands?" My mother could not say the word "penis," she could not say the word "vagina," but she could make sure she got her point across. After finding my glasses, she announced we were going over to Dieter's house to speak with him and his parents. I had never seen my mother like this before—somehow calm but "on fire." She was a shy woman. While she laughed openly with her dearest friends and those in our family, in public I had never heard her open her mouth. What was my mother going to say? "We can't tell Dad," I said, apparently stating the obvious. She quietly and firmly replied, "Of course not." We both knew my father was a hothead, and no good could come from his involvement in this.

She looked straight ahead, kept walking, and quietly but firmly stated, "I can handle this." I thought, "How?" Nothing more was said, and it seemed like a very long walk.

What I didn't know at eleven years old was that within every one of us—male and female—there sleeps an animal of power, an awe-inspiring, ferocious animal that relies on instinct and cunning and strength. Some call it our "Lioness within." This animal owns an unearthly sound—like you have never heard before. This Lioness rises in those awakened by the call from others loved as their own, or even from the call within themselves—the call that beckons for protection—*for life itself.* It can surface from within all those who smell *even a threat* of temperance and who will not subject or acquiesce themselves to social mores or societies' needs for good manners and proper protocols. It knows no fear in the moment. And clearly, this Lioness can rise from within parents who face square-on the reality of what it means to protect their young.

~

My mother knocked on the Wagners' door. Eva answered. Quite matter-of-factly, my mother asked her if we could come in and speak with her parents. We entered the living room, and my mother asked Mr. and Mrs. Wagner if Dieter was at home and could he be called to the room. Mrs. Wagner asked us to take a seat. We did not sit. No words were spoken.

I remember it like it was yesterday. As Dieter entered the living room, my small-framed mother metamorphosed, rising up bigger than God herself. Enormous. Humongous. Staring directly at him across the ten feet of diminishing open space, she asked him, "Dieter, do you want to tell your parents what you did to my daughter tonight?" Casting his eyes downward, he said, "No." Transfixed and trembling, I then observed, in fear and awe, my mother—the Lioness herself—growing ever-larger, filling every vacant inch of the room with her vast presence. Although her shape was obscured in a shadowy white light, I could make out her massive gnashing fangs and long, sharp claws flailing as she looked squarely down at him and snarled in a voice I'd never heard from her before or since. *"Look at me, you dirty son-of-a-bitch. If you ever touch any of my daughters again, I will kill you!"* Then in the same even-paced voice, she low-growled, *"Do. You. Understand. Me?"* Dieter shrank to the size of an eight-year-old boy and mumbled, "Yes." We walked out.

~

Dieter was eighteen then, and shortly thereafter he must have graduated and left town. I never saw him again. Ever. Even though he lived a block away. I never had a conversation with Eva about it either. I don't know what she knew about it. My mother and I never spoke about it again for at least another forty years. My father died, our secret safe from him.

Of course I wished that it had never happened, but wishing doesn't make it so. I continued to try to make a more peaceful life for myself, as I desperately didn't want to keep feeling fearful and victimized, and that is exactly how I felt when reliving the memories. What I came to eventually realize is that it isn't the negative or the positive experiences that make us who we are, but rather, with all the cumulative happenings—planned and unplanned—it is the choices we make of how we are going to try to use our life experiences to move toward greater ease and happiness.

My experience that night gave me two of the most nourishing gifts I would ever receive, and acknowledging them has offered me a more peaceful life. The first was to always listen to my body—my body that communicates with me, *is* me—my nature, my truth, my partner—for its signals and to take action accordingly. To be receptive of its wisdom, to trust it. To encourage those I love to pay attention, to listen to their bodies as though their lives depend on it because it often does. The second gift came from witnessing my mother's actions. To see a ferocious Lioness, to witness someone who is so alive—so ready, so conscious, so responsible—is to know something very special about one's own nature. That nature that exists within us all.

Designing Our Lives by Choice and Action

Life comprises a multitude of possible experiences, available to us all the time. Through our choices and actions, our destinies unfold.

You may have heard people say that "things always happen for a reason." The first part is true: things happen. Of course they do. But when we try to find a reason, it is as though we are second-guessing the mysteries of life. Some things happen because we choose one way, and some things happen because we choose another way. Other experiences appear not to have been by choice, such as what occurred in Dinah's story.

All of us are vulnerable to being victimized. Even if it hasn't happened to us personally, we may know others who have dealt with painful experiences, some even horrific. However, we can observe that not all who have been victimized are victims. Taking upon oneself the *identity* of a victim is a choice, and cultivating this victimhood throughout one's lifetime is also a choice.

No one comes to earth the same as anyone else, but whatever we are dealt through circumstance or birth, we choose what we are going to do with our lives. We have the option to actively participate in our own betterment, and this can occur wherever and however we are. What if we have chosen and entered into experiences that are not satisfying, or as in Dinah's situation, happened to find ourselves in experiences that are even damaging? Suffering offers no virtue. All experiences—quality, non-quality, good, bad, pretty, or ugly—can be used to develop ourselves—to bring us to greater ease—if that is our desire.

Dinah knew this, most likely from witnessing her mother's strength and sensing it within her own self; and she made the choice not to live her life taking on the identity of a victim. She chose to design a different life, and from those choices, her destiny unfolded.

Skills for living the life we want can be developed

Some people seem to have the clarity and ability to make better choices. These people are able to more easily eliminate the dogmas, the fantasies, the illusions, the expectations, and the unquestioned rules that can bind us and imprison us—those inhibitors that keep us controlled and contained, unhappy and at risk for misuse by others. They are more readily able to act on their own behalf, regardless of who is watching or what anyone else might think. But any of us can develop the life skills to choose better. These life skills are the tools for designing and taking actions for the life we want.

Within each of us, uniquely as ever-changing organisms, an evolutionary and developmental process is taking place as we pursue our lives. Our genetic history, environment, experiences, and body knowingness all affect where we are on a developmental continuum, and many of us want to evolve and improve ourselves so that we can have a better life, a life that flows more joyfully and easily. We have the opportunity to influence where we are on our continuum by using our life experiences to develop ourselves further.

Everyone's life, from conception to death, encompasses a multitude of possible experiences available, all the time. Our task—should that be our desire—is to choose from among those possible experiences the ones we truly want. As we design our lives through our choices and actions, we want to observe and discover ourselves—to uncover and access our own truth—so that we can begin acting from it. In doing so we may begin to make choices that are better suited for who and how we are.

A rougher road or an easier road—which one?

Constant and continual exchange occurs in the universe. Both experiences—those of ease or contention—are always available to us. We can look for trouble and discord if that is what we want, consciously choosing experiences that take us down that particular path, or we can consider something more harmonious. If we make choices and focus on experiences of contradiction, difficulty, and discord, we may discover that we want to remain in those experiences—some of which may be inhibiting or even destructive—and the more we attend to those, the more we will get.

People may consider or portray themselves as victims—moping and brooding over an experience—but an exchange is occurring with the experience nonetheless. As our choices can either nurture or compromise our well-being, why would any of us choose a self-destructive path riddled with conflict? It may simply be lack of awareness that we have better options. Or maybe we have not seen healthy choosing exampled in our midst. We may have in our unique makeup, a predisposition to unwell and unwanted behavior patterns that currently keep us from being who and how we want to be. We may even be stuck in—and surrendering to—a reaction to an experience that was only meant to inform us *at that moment*, and not realize that we can learn to use that reaction to move us forward with new choices.

Perhaps it is from habit that we sometimes choose to keep reliving a familiar memory, or staying with a familiar situation, however unacceptable we may find it to be. Or we may be caught up in rationalizing an experience with stories or excuses to convince ourselves to stay. If that is what we want our life experiences to be—rationalizing and making excuses for a life of conflict, contention, limitation or even destruction—then our life will look that way.

On our path of self-discovery, we always have the option to shift gears

However, we may discover we prefer less difficulty and discord, not more; and if we want to choose to move away from destructive or discordant experiences, we may gravitate toward those experiences that are harmonious, nurturing, and supportive. We recognize what is happening, and we become consciously acclimated to noticing other experiences that are more to our liking. We begin to shift gears; we always have the option to shift gears. We may feel a sense of ease as we use these agreeable and pleasing experiences to support our healthy development—choosing them makes us feel good about ourselves—and we then design our bigger choices for continued harmony. In doing so, our life will begin to look quite another way—*indeed*. Yes, experiences of ease or those of contention are always available to us. We choose.

Aiming for imperfectly perfect

Living life is not about seeking perfection, nor do *we* offer it. Nothing is perfect. There are problems with all people, all jobs, but we try to choose the best we can. When seeking our best matches for ourselves, you might say that we aim for *imperfectly* perfect.

By our choices and actions, we also design how we address responsibly the complexities and complications that can occur and that are ours to own. These are not to be avoided; however, these may have varying levels of difficulty. Sometimes life presents challenges.

Just as in determining how we wish to choose and act, we want to respect the life choices of others and allow for the responsibilities that belong to them, to be theirs. We want to be mindful not to use our own life experience to trail after, revel in, or over-attend to the complications and problems of others, giving undue attention and focus to another's difficulties and making another individual our "project." If so, we may risk becoming indulgent to that experience—using up our own life—rather than creating our own life experiences that we may desire.

As an evolving species, we will not likely attain a life of no difficulty, but we try to have life experiences that offer the greatest match for what is satisfying to us. Most people want life experiences with the least amount of conflict and distress. Differences between or among people may exist, but differences don't have to be difficulties. We want variance in our lives. Variance provides opportunity for life expansion and richer personal development; it can provide a sense of engagement and anticipation. What most of us don't want is a life filled with melodrama, difficulty, contention, and agitation.

The body will be healthier than the mind will allow

In Dinah's story, we witnessed what can occur when we don't respond to, or act on, our body's messages in its attempts to communicate with us. Dinah knew—her body had informed her—that possible danger lay ahead if she stayed the course and walked home alone. Not being developed sufficiently, she did not persist to change that course. She succumbed to the unquestioned rules requiring her to get home by dinnertime, disregarding the danger she sensed. When we dismiss our own internal authority, we leave ourselves vulnerable to errors in thinking, in judgment, in deed, and in action. These errors do not represent failure, but rather they indicate learning opportunities, steps along the way in our ongoing development. Dinah chose to extract from the experience something that would guide her positively for the rest of her life. She made a choice that determined her destiny: she chose to integrate the experience and let it inform her as she sidestepped the option of victimhood.

Destinies unfold

You will hear people speak of destinies as though they are something mysterious and pre-ordained.

Consider this perspective: The word "destinare" means "to stand." By way of the choices we make on a daily basis, we all end up somewhere. A destination reveals itself after the fact; it is the cumulative effect of where the continuum of choices we have made along the way—those multitudes of choices we stood upon—brings us to a given moment. We can only know in the present moment, after the fact of choice and action, from the place we now stand, what our destiny is today. Through our chosen experiences, our destinies unfold accordingly. Multiple destinies are available to us relative to our choices acted upon. When we design our lives by choices and actions made from our true desires, greater connection is possible—things just seem to make sense—and life can be a lot easier.

All the cells of our body want the same thing—to express our truth

When we move into experiences that fulfill our authentic desires, our nature expands—it develops itself. With this movement, more accessing of our fullest expression of our genetic potential is possible, giving us better opportunities to be able to live the kind of life we want. When we are in integrity—whole and integrated—there is a harmony, an openness to life. We are living our truth—our truth that is our deepest desires. With increased well-being, we feel stronger, more capable, and more alive than we have ever felt before. As we decide what it is that we want and don't want, we seek out harmonious matches.

This doesn't mean we won't choose poorly at times. After all, we are developing ourselves through each new choice and experience. But we self-assess, self-correct, and we figure it out because we are moving forward living our deepest desires as we know them at this time. When we choose from our truth, our body responds by thanking us with improved health, laughter, real love, and genuine joy.

Our accessible body knowingness

Throughout our lifetime, there have been and will be more and different experiences available to us. With sober eyes, genuine hearts, and a respectful approach, we can clearly discern the reality before us, if we want to see it. We then simply ask ourselves, "Is this the experience I want?" and notice our body's reaction—our truth—and take new and different actions as our desires change. We have a partner in life, ready and accessible. A powerful and formidable Lioness exists within each of us, male and female—it *is* us—and we use this body knowingness to assist ourselves. This wisdom is reserved not only for times of possible danger; when we are conscious, we can hear ourselves concerning all awareness and alertness that prepares us for our unique "correct choosing" in the moment or many years later.

3

Henry's Story

The Body Is Determined
to Behave Its Truth

*For all of us desiring lives filled with greater happiness and well-being,
we have a partner. Our body—our nature—is determined to behave
its truth. It wants to thrive.*

Living on the reservation was a tough life for Henry. His home had no running water or electricity; it was heated with wood and lacked indoor plumbing. Getting to and from school was a major event, both in time and in logistics.

Henry always knew he wanted to be a doctor. In high school, it became clear that he needed access to better educational opportunities if he wanted to get into medical school someday. Both his family and his tribe made tremendous sacrifices so that he could go to college. There was much focus on Henry's potential. Some reservations had gambling casinos that provided funds to educate tribal members and even earn advanced degrees. That was not the case on Henry's reservation. Funds were tight.

Henry did go on to become a doctor, and it had been an arduous journey. He had varied experiences in the ten years he was away from the reservation. In his first year as an undergraduate, he had to take additional classes in the subjects he was lacking to bring himself up to par with his classmates. Upon completing his undergraduate work, it took him several more years to get into medical school, during which time he prepared academically and got more experience in the medical field. The competition was fierce, but he persevered with his dream.

Henry returned to the reservation to fulfill his obligation to work for three years as a doctor in exchange for the grants he had been given by the Tribal Council. He was happy to do so, as he felt he had chosen well for himself and enjoyed his work. The unspoken hope however—which at times felt more like an additional obligation—was that he owed the reservation more than just the three years agreed upon before he started school. They wanted desperately for Henry to continue his doctoring practice there. Indeed, the need was immense.

Henry knew he had been of value to his tribal community. He had worked hard at treating cases of diabetes, stroke, heart attack, and alcoholism. Many of the health problems were preventable, and he had started education programs that became very successful. During that time, he had been at the deathbed of two of his grandparents, and he was grateful for that. It was as though both had waited for him to come home. And now, his people were waiting for him to tell them he would stay; but staying wasn't what Henry wanted to do.

There were other places he wanted to live and other worlds he wanted to explore with his doctoring. At the same time, he could clearly see how his people were in need. Almost by default, Henry allowed others to influence his decision because he felt obligated and wanted to please them. He thought it would only be for a matter of months while he figured things out, but there were matters of newborn babies, deaths, disease, and more educational courses to attend to and time sped by. While Henry loved his work, he grew increasingly aware that remaining a doctor on the reservation still wasn't what he wanted to do. Staying longer wasn't changing that.

~

Well into the second year past his obligatory three-year commitment, Henry noticed he began to feel extremely weary, and he was perplexed by the extent of this feeling. It had all come on rather suddenly. Just three weeks earlier, he'd helped his cousins to load up a pickup with some heavy tires to sell at the flea market and he thought perhaps he had overdone it, but his condition worsened. He began to notice what seemed to be neurological problems. His legs felt heavier when he walked, and his left arm was tingling. A few days later, he noticed a metal taste in his mouth.

Saliva would accumulate and he would drool throughout the night. Within a week, his left arm was almost unusable. He began walking with a cane for additional balance to assist him with the lightheadedness he felt at times. He told himself it would pass, but by now his ears were ringing intermittently. When he breathed through his mouth, it was as though he were chewing mints because the coolness created by the strong metal taste made the air feel cooled. He could no longer climb stairs without reaching down and pulling one leg up after another. He felt so very tired and was so busy that it was all he could do to keep up with his work and he finally had to take a few days off because he simply could not get out of bed.

Henry was scared.

As a doctor, he understood that it was probably wise to get some testing done, but he also knew testing would take time. This was not anything ordinary, but he had witnessed it before in others. His body was shutting down.

Henry prayed. He prayed the prayers that thanked the ancestors who gave him his life, his history, his stories. He prayed the prayers of gratitude for the wisdom and the courage of his elders. He prayed the prayers of appreciation, of acknowledgment for the troubled journeys of those who had gone before him so he could have a better life. He then fell asleep. Upon waking a short while later in total darkness but for the sliver of a new moon, he began acting on a decision for an initial step of action. He would pay a visit to Nona, an elder of his tribe, a wise and unusual woman.

～

The sun was rising when he finally was able to get situated in his four-wheel drive vehicle. He had crawled from the house, used his cane to prop himself up, and drove the many miles over rough reservation lands, hoping she would be there. A few hours later, in bright sunlight, he arrived at her home. Scrawny chickens greeted him, and an old, broken windmill clanked in the light breeze. His energy was noticeably lighter. Oddly, he felt hopeful for the first time in a long time.

A wizened old woman, hunched over, propped up with her walker, and nearly blind, Nona greeted Henry at her door. As soon as her leathered and gnarled hand reached for Henry to guide him in, the tears began rolling down his cheeks. He could not stop them. It was as though floodgates were opened. She motioned him to a small, worn-out sofa with missing cushions. Lowering herself slowly into a straight backed chair that was positioned directly in front of him, she placed her walker to the side of her, spread her knees apart with hands folded in front of her and waited. Henry could see she had been shelling peas; the white dented and chipped wash pan full of peas was next to her on a wooden stool. But she didn't reach for them. Her eyes closed; she began to rock her body ever so slightly, breathing a constricted nasal breath and humming softly. Waiting. Henry's tears continued as though springing forth with a life of their own. Full-bodied, rolling tears. Henry lowered his face into his hands, sobbing and wailing like never in his life before. She began to whisper the words "yes" and "it's okay." As he continued sobbing, his wails grew stronger and more primal. Screams surged up through his body, demanding to be recognized, insisting on a life lived for his true self—shrieking, roaring—for inner peace.

When he left, he felt drained of every ounce of energy inside him but peaceful for the first time in many months. He smiled to himself. What had just happened?

Not a word had been exchanged. But he knew.

〜

Henry tried hard to disguise his condition. His mind was sharp since his visit with Nona, and he was clear that whatever was happening with his body had everything to do with his life satisfaction. He recognized that his current life and choices were in conflict with what he really wanted. How could he self-declare and live his truth, which was to move on to other doctoring opportunities, and yet still please everyone?

Henry knew it wasn't possible to please everyone else unless he stayed. What he was only beginning to realize was that it wasn't necessary to please everyone.

Resigning from his position as a doctor on the reservation would mean disappointing many people and leaving half-finished education projects and abandoning many good intentions. As is customary for medical doctors needing care, Henry set up a meeting with a therapist for a deeper conversation about these choices. This professional was fully aware of his tribe's culture and the deeply imbedded, unspoken expectations and hopes that weighed on Henry. When offered the routinely suggested medication to handle the anxiety that can come with figuring out one's life, he declined.

Henry recognized his body was not responding; he was dying. He wanted to be fully conscious of every single decision, every single thought that might be contributing to his deteriorating physical health, and every subtle and not-so-subtle message from his body's attempts to inform him. His very life depended on it.

〜

Within a matter of days, Henry resigned, believing the correct decision for him was to move on to other opportunities of genuine interest. At the banquet held in honor of the service he had given, several young men and women approached him. They, too, had considered accepting grants from their tribe, and some had been reluctant to do so out of concern that it would obligate them for longer than the agreement, perhaps even their whole lives. So, with no funds for further education, they had hesitated in pursuing their desires of becoming teachers and nurses and doctors and other professionals. They thanked Henry, as they now felt more emboldened to move forward with their dreams.

Henry's courage to allow his body to inform him gave him the freedom to pursue his own life in his own way, and his health noticeably began improving. Taking action for what he believed was "correct choosing" for him provided his people with much more than just a good doctor for his lifetime. His brave actions created a legacy.

The Body Speaks Loudly and Clearly

We take actions thinking they are a good idea at the time—a "correct choosing" for ourselves. We don't know how our actions will affect others' lives. We can't know.

Henry, like many of us, had never had to make a decision without the full support from everyone he knew and loved, including his tribe. When the decisions we make are also the decisions that everyone in our life wants us to make, life may be easier. But when we want to do something that others don't want us to do, or we want to do something that doesn't appear to serve others, making choices can present some challenges. The messages can be subtle—unspoken rules, wishes, expectations, and hopes others may have come into play. For Henry, it was all of that as well as the blatant, unmistakable need he saw on the reservation—his reservation—for a good doctor like him.

For whatever reason this might occur, we want to ask ourselves what we truly want, regardless of serving others. Whose rules are we following, and who or what is calling the shots for our life? We cannot live our lives tending to other's beliefs that they know what is best for us, or that they can control our destiny, or that we need to subjugate our lives for *their* comfort, *their* security, *their* need. Is that a life well-lived? Is that a life worth living?

If something gives us pleasure, then it is wonderful to do it. If it isn't what we want or we simply prefer another path, then that is our truth.

Pursuing what is correct for us

If others have difficulty with our decisions, we have a choice to make about how we want to handle that. Do we concern ourselves when they have difficulty with our decisions to the point that we modify our behavior? If we do, then we want to recognize it may limit how we live our lives. We want to act in our own better interests with any given choice and be true to ourselves. Another option is not to concern ourselves with their disagreement or discomfort. We were authentic in making those choices, and we can trust others will figure out how they can take care of themselves in light of our actions and make their own choices accordingly. If someone chooses to be hurt or to experience difficulty in response to our choices, that is a choice they make.

The same applies to us; we can choose how we wish to respond to the choices of others. We can feel hurt, offended, or surprised, creating cover stories to "image manage" the situation—any number of possibilities. Or we can simply accept another's authentic self as it is presented to us. We want to be true to ourselves and extend that same freedom to others. We want to ask ourselves this: "Do I want to stay in a relationship with this individual, stay at this job, continue on in this life experience; or based on the truth that has shown its face, do I desire something quite different?"

All we owe another is our authentic self.

Our body wisdom

Henry was a good student, a trustworthy man, and he fulfilled the obligations that he owed to his tribe. During that time, everything was in accordance with his true desires. He enjoyed his experience, and his health was strong. It was when he began acting outside of that accordance with his true nature—not doing what he was compelled to do, but rather doing what others wished him to do—that a schism (a separation in his body wholeness) was created, affecting his health. For some, this disconnect can take years to come to consciousness. For Henry, it didn't take long at all. His body knew. Fortunately, he had strong body wisdom, wise and helpful counsel, and the wherewithal to know he had to stay consciously aware through his experiences as he came to realize and respect that his nature, his "wanting" was not to be ignored.

When stepping into an experience, we want to check in with our whole selves, noticing if the experience feels like it is moving us toward what we desire. What does our body tell us? We may find we have robbed ourselves of this ability to develop discernment, and so we defer to outside sources and experts to the exclusion of our own body intelligence—even the glaring messages. Some of us may have loved ones or trusted advisors all giving us their opinions—some solicited and some not—on what we should do. Unless there are concerns for imminent danger, we may find no real need for such advice. We can trust ourselves—trust our body— and always stay conscious in our choices. And if we feel that someone is not wishing for us exactly what our best self is telling us—we want to take notice. Others have their own agendas, no matter how convinced they may be that our better interests are their only concern. And regardless of how kindly others' intentions may be, we are our own best "experts" of ourselves.

Each of us can only make our own correct choice

Henry's tribe—his employer—did not intentionally misuse him when they asked him to stay. Yes, there were those in the tribe who it appears would have—there often can be. But in Henry's case, it was Henry who made it difficult for himself. Sometimes fulfilling obligations and expectations gives us value in our society—it feeds an image we like to portray to others. Because Henry liked how the value he brought to his tribe fed his image—he made his choice more complicated than it needed to be as he ignored his body's wisdom to take an action for a different experience. But when we follow what is true for us, choosing can actually be effortless.

How many of us have found ourselves in situations similar to Henry's, when we have mentioned to others in a relationship or workplace that we were thinking of moving on and heard from others that they don't know what they would do without us and ask us to reconsider. They tell us all kinds of ways we make their lives easier and their companies better by being there and they try to convince us to align ourselves with their agenda for us. Sometimes, we may carry judgment about their attempts to do so.

Consider this: It isn't necessary to carry judgment because another individual or a company is pursuing what is correct for them, for their developmental path, however that may look to us. The tribe, our spouse, our friend, or our company all have an agenda; they are all pursuing their own desires—those which are correct for who and how and what they are.

What is important here to note is that no individual or company can make a correct choice for another individual. Each of us can only make our own correct choice. We tend to think we know what is in another's better interests—but that is not possible. Each individual comes into this life with thousands of years of ancestral history, each with a unique genetic code. Generation after generation, passing down through one's gene complex—enriched with one's own environment and life experiences—with options of multiple destinies depending on one's choices.

When we move through new choices, taking on new experiences, our lives take twists and turns and may go in directions that we never imagined. Not in our wildest imaginings could we foresee all the possibilities to come. And so, if what another is choosing for us doesn't satisfy what our true desire is, then that *is our truth*. It is up to each of us to give regard to our truth, and act on what is correct for us. That is what will ultimately serve everyone.

Healthy individuals and organizations understand and respect this. They simply hope we will stay, that there can be sufficient value in the exchange—in what they offer—for us to want to stay and choose to do so.

Serve others from your own desire to do so

We all choose what we want if we can, and in doing so we are first serving ourselves. Many make a choice to serve others because it gives them pleasure to do so. There is nothing wrong with serving the "collective"—helping others or serving an organization. The challenge comes when people decide that the good works they are doing for the collective is the answer—that it is the best thing—for someone else.

To attempt to second-guess others' destinies would be to find ourselves messing with the earth, the heavens, the stars, the oceans, the entire universe and beyond.

If we want to serve others, then let's go for it; but realize we do it because we enjoy it and not because we can presume to know better than others, what best serves them. We may ease their pain, we may keep them alive, we may bring them joy. But we can't know better than their organism knows, what is truly best for them.

A species develops continuously for its own survival

Our species, in its attempt to continuously develop, will seek out the new, the strange, the different, and the odd qualities. It evolves by taking all the complexity and flavoring from those qualities and compounds itself further for growth. That is how we secure our own survival and thrive as a species. What we want to respect is each individual's right to care for his or her own self in a way that speaks to him or her.

If each individual takes care to participate in his or her own betterment—the betterment of the self (regardless of how that appears to others) —then we all benefit our world. Always we are crossing paths with millions of experiences, and others may be sparked and influenced by examples—negative or positive—of who and how we are. As we recognize and identify our truth and transform ourselves, we bring that new, more developed self to society. Others, not always known to us, may use the opportunities we bring. Either way, the cycles repeat; we cross paths with millions of experiences and it is our choice to use them to develop ourselves, should that be our desire.

Henry's actions for himself created a legacy. None of us know how our actions will affect others. We only know we are compelled to take them; it feels right for us in the moment. When we cross paths with what we truly desire, and answer "yes," this perceived correct choosing for ourselves results in harmony and ultimately serves everyone.

Both a babbling brook and a rampaging waterfall
can transform the earth.

4

Unseat the King

The body rules. It is your partner in creating your life. The sooner you embrace your truth through listening to your body, the better you may find your life to be. Try to stay out of the logic of the conscious mind.

We may have heard people say something to the effect of "tell your chatterbox mind to shut up!" That is, generally speaking, good advice. The mind does not have the capacity to exchange information the way the body does.

The conscious mind—that verbal, reasoning "chatterbox" voice in our head—is limited in its awareness. It can only act on direct and limited instructions from the body; nonetheless, it tries to be the dictator; it tries to be the king. How? The mind tries to overrule the body by giving credence to other influences such as other people's opinions, the use of willpower, or rules established by external authorities. It tries to convince us that "positive thinking" is the means to eliminate "negative thinking"; that the opposite of "x" is necessarily "y." It tries to have us carry out dictates that hold no interest for us, that we'd rather ignore, or that we simply don't want to follow.

If successful, this effort creates a split—a schism—in the body's wholeness, creating a challenge to our enjoyment of the life we truly want. The messages that allow sound decision making based on one's truth are restricted from flowing freely and, as a result, the decisions made are not correct for one's self. When this occurs, we may experience a compromised life that shows up as excessive tiredness, diminishing vibrancy, and other symptoms expressing.

Our true desires are to be respected

Our true desires are not to be overruled and overridden; they are precious gems deserving of our highest regard. Each organism begins as a final combination of a genetic code passed down to us from our parents and our ancestors. What plays out in our life is the culmination of this ancestral history along with our own history and experiences…the choices we make for experiences as we say "yes, please" to this and "no, thank you" to that. The organism knows, and it directs the choices; it is not our will. Will is subjugation by the mind. Will has one job; it suppresses the whole—the body—and it has the body being the obedient servant to the mind. This is not the optimal way to make sustainable changes or to live out our desires. Lasting change occurs by following our body's wisdom, not by going against it and trying to discipline ourselves to continue on a path we no longer desire. Because of this, we want to cultivate our skills for self-management, not self-discipline. No, the mind is only second in command, not first. It does not have the capacity to be first. It is merely part of the whole.

We come to know our desires by listening to our body

The body—the whole—has the capacity to synthesize massive amounts of information—there is a knowingness that occurs as this information is absorbed, comprehended, internalized, and owned. The body exchanges it completely, efficiently, and correctly. The body's job culminates in a coming together with the self as a whole. It's as though the body is having a committee meeting in which it synthesizes information, decides what it wants, and then tells the mind to go figure it out—do the research, take a walk, fill out the application, book the flight, move the body, drive the car, and so on. The body rules and being fully conscious gives us the greatest chance to interpret our body's messages correctly. We want to be knowledgeable about ourselves—who and how we are. We want to trust ourselves so that as we take a step in a direction and listen, we will know if we want to stay with an experience or move in yet another direction, should that be our desire.

Our body will let us know what resonates with us. When we give voice to our truth—to our deepest desires—we confirm what we truly like or want, bringing everything back to the self. When we are aware of and actively notice what resonates with our body, then the body can calibrate to that truth and there is greater ease in taking action. The body won't be fooled; it knows reality. It is ordinary that our desires change—after all, we are a morphing organism—so we want to give ourselves permission to have new wants and likes and new don't wants and don't likes. In this way, everything in the whole of us will be in accordance with our next actions.

Learning to discern what rings true for us and to care for ourselves accordingly, is essential to a satisfying life. How can we design our environments to better support us or have deep and meaningful relationships with others if we don't know what is meaningful to us? It is not possible to know this when we have habitually given all of our authority to others. How can we determine what our attitudes and values are if we have never attended to them and cultivated them as our own? How can we possibly know where our integrity lies when it has never been developed? How do we speak to ourselves when we are solely dependent on the praise, affirmation, applause, and attention from outside sources that distract us from ourselves? How can we possibly begin to manage our time when someone else determines how we fill our hours, our days, and our lives without our questioning if those activities are meaningful to us?

We say we have priorities, but are they truly ours? How is it that what we claim as our priorities often don't seem to get lived? Has our internal authority been stripped from us, or have we given it away to the point where our life seems to be no longer our own? And what about whether or not we hold a belief or alignment in a God or absolute energy, possibly the most individual of all relationships for many? Have we allowed others to define or determine that for us?

Our truth—our deepest desires—is expressed outwardly in our actions

Our sensibilities are unique. Whatever we desire is a possible experience within us wanting to be satisfied, for all kinds of reasons or for no reasons at all. We are our own experts and want to provide ourselves with access to information, people, and experiences in order to move toward those things we desire. We want to try to shift from old habits where we "worry about…" and instead reframe our perspective as we begin to "wonder about…" We want to grant ourselves the freedom to want what we want and to not want what we don't want, and to know ourselves well enough to be honest about what they might be.

We may have heard it suggested that we go up to "God's level" and "think like God" and lead a selfless life. But "spirit"—truth—does not reside in the mind alone; all is within the whole body. We want to go down, down, down, and ask ourselves very simple questions: "Do I want? Do I not want? Do I like? Do I not like?" Then live that truth as we know it in any given moment. Others can see us exampling our truth and living the life we want, and others can make their own best decisions for themselves regarding their involvement with us. Yes, we may disappoint or upset people who want us—or who may try to influence us—to desire something other than what we actually desire…people who thought they could count on us in a way that worked for them. But when we live our truth, what we actually want is for people to count on our authentic self. And as we begin to behave our truth in all arenas of our lives, we wish with grace, for others to live their truth in the life they choose. If we care for ourselves and for others, how can it be otherwise?

The mind can interfere with our body wisdom

When we say "this is overwhelming," the mind tells the body it is overwhelming. This doesn't help us navigate the actions that are necessary in going toward what we want. Thoughts dictate chemical reactions, and thoughts of stress are harmful to the body. When our mind tells our body that something is overwhelming, it triggers the body to go through the experience with stress. Now the body has to focus on addressing the stress, diverting its attention away from what may be challenging situations. It is better to tell ourselves, "I don't know how I'm going to do this; but if I want it, my body will figure it out. I'm not going to allow my chatterbox mind to interfere." This way, the body is free to go through a situation with the least difficulty possible and the greatest sense of ability and ease. There is no constricted imagination when the body is no longer distracted by, and adhering to, the dogma of external influences and authorities. The cells of the body actually have intelligence and respond to ideas that resonate with our truth.

The body will re-energize us in our movement toward healthy choices

We know that thinking is not a path to self-discovery; it simply cannot get us there, nor can visualizing and wishing, asking others to behave in a way we want them to, or other forms of intense efforting. All knowingness is accomplished in the body. The healthier and more developed we are, the better our skills of discernment. Sometimes we won't even recognize an experience of "incorrect choosing" when it is right in front of us because we so very much don't want it. We just move right on past, not even taking the time to say "thanks, but no thanks." We're out of there before we even get in there. Life can be easier when we partner with our body in creating it. It will hold up its end; it is determined to thrive. It will begin to shut the mind chatter out. Pay attention.

When you feel yourself beginning to compromise—if your prosperity or your energy diminishes; if you feel unmotivated, disinclined to follow-through, symptomatic with repeated acute health conditions, or physically compromised—you will know that the experience you are in can't possibly be correct, regardless of what your mind chatter says. In this case, pull yourself together, recalibrate, reassess, and move to a different experience. The body will re-energize you in your movement toward choices that are in your better interests.

Sometimes, you will move slowly. Other times you will turn and run— fast and furious in your escape—as though a roaring, wind-driven wildfire blazing against your backside propels you toward whatever brings you joy.

5

Zane's Story

Love and Lunacy in Latin America

*A man mopping the floor wore a full bandolier with a 12 gauge
shotgun in the holster and enough ammo for a small war.
What had I gotten into?*

I was crazy in love with this girl, Lola. She had just graduated with
a degree in speech pathology and audiology and had taken a job at an
orphanage in Honduras. I missed her terribly, and so I did what seemed
natural to do. I ditched my apartment, quit my job, dropped out of college
yet again, and within days was bound for Honduras.

At twenty-four, I did not consider myself particularly sheltered and
felt prepared to make the journey. In college, I had been in ROTC and
had completed the paratrooper's jump course at the Airborne School,
taken combat courses and weaponry, and was physically fit. I was text-
book fluent in Spanish and had a good understanding of the culture. My
college fraternity had been largely Latino, and I'd been with my family on
vacations in Mexico. Being Meticcio myself—I was adopted; my biologi-
cal father was Mexican of Italian descent and my mother was French and
Cherokee Indian—I looked Latino. I couldn't imagine anything I needed
to worry about.

After arriving in the capital city of Tegucigalpa, Honduras, the night before, I was waiting for the bus to take me to the orphanage the next morning when a deafening shot rang out within a few feet of me. The sound exploded in my ears. I watched a police officer fall to the ground, bleeding to death from a shot in the head, his hand still twitching. Around me I could hear people whispering, *"¿Era Bueno? ¿Era malo?"* (Was he good? Was he bad?) Good or bad, he was dead.

Nothing could have prepared me for either that or the onslaught of dangers that had preceded it. I had heard the term "Magical Realism" before in reference to life in Latin America; and now, looking back, I know I will never see life the same as before my experiences there. Never.

～

Everything seemed ordinary and familiar enough traveling through Mexico. It was after that where life as I had known it began to change.

Heading south into Guatemala, we hit torrential rains, and the highway filled with water. The bus could not make contact with the road and the driver pulled the bus over to a concrete divider to assess the situation. Just then, the entire side of the mountain gave way, with mud and rocks coming down on cars on the other side. There was no time to think. Only act. The driver screamed the commands at us. Everyone who could, got out of the bus and pushed it with all our might through the two feet of water up to the existing road where we could escape, leaving behind cars filled with people buried in the mud slide. Once inside the bus, people were crying and praying. No one spoke. We all looked back. We could see nothing through the rain, but we knew what we had left behind. We knew that if we had taken the risk to try to save them, the water may have then been too high for all of us. The rain continued thundering against the bus.

～

In Guatemala City, the bus stopped at an overnight transfer spot in what I began to realize was a high crime part of the city—Zone One. Sensing unrest, fellow travelers Manny and his nine-year-old son Oscar and I took a taxi to a hotel. Within moments of arriving, a gang tried to break into the hotel. The hotel owner locked all the doors and we turned off the lights. Manny told Oscar to barricade himself in the bathroom and not to unlock it until he heard the magic password from his father. The hotel owner gave Manny and me bats to defend ourselves, suggesting we lock ourselves in our rooms, and he did the same.

We could see through the bars on the windows that lined the street. The gang had gone on to bust into a nearby building. We heard windows breaking and people screaming. Then there was silence in the early hours of the morning. At three o'clock, we planned our escape. Manny gave Oscar the magic word and Oscar emerged from the bathroom, his eyes huge with fear. I could see he had been crying. Reaching for Oscar's hand, Manny opened the front door slightly, and we all eased out, running as fast as we could in the opposite direction of where the gang had gone.

But not fast enough. The gang spotted us and the chase began. We could hear their voices and the sound of their feet hitting the street as they twirled their arsenal of bats, saws, and knives at us. Just as they were gaining on us, a police patrol truck pulled up and someone yelled, "Jump in now!" I remember thinking, "Oh no, worse luck, the real criminals!" But what were we to do? There was no alternative. We kept pace with the moving truck, threw our bags and Oscar on, and hoisted our bodies into it. Thankfully, it turned out they were "good guys," at least for us. Later, upon boarding the bus to El Salvador, I slept from exhaustion until we reached the border.

〜

Once in El Salvador, I managed to grab a taxi with a driver who claimed to have contacts in the city of San Salvador to help me navigate getting to Honduras safely. Thinking that Manny and Oscar would be welcomed also, I quickly discovered that there was great divisiveness and hostility within the country surrounding the recent political coup that resulted in ousting the president of Honduras, Manuel Zelaya. My new friend, the taxi driver, was a supporter of Zelaya. Manny was not. Manny, Oscar, and I quickly said our goodbyes. Such are the short-term allegiances and alliances in countries in conflict.

The cab driver drove me to a hotel, where my bags were searched for drugs. A man mopping the floor wore a full bandolier with a 12-gauge shotgun in the holster and enough ammo for a small war. What had I gotten into? I was next escorted into the bar by a gentleman with guns and holsters on each hip and asked if I wanted a drink. Relaxing with a drink didn't even register in my mind. I was not in a party mood; in fact I was beginning to feel like I had been transported to some dystopian society in a Mad Max movie. Surely, thugs riding motorcycles would crash through the doors at any time. This couldn't be my life. I said, "No thanks," bought a phone card, and reported in to my folks that I was fine. I told them nothing more. Really, how could I?

The next day, arriving at Tegucigalpa, Honduras, I was greeted at the bus station by a couple who offered me a room in their home. At this point, I didn't know who to trust. It was a crap shoot. All I was interested in was reducing contingencies for death. I didn't want anyone to see me mixing with the enemy, and I was unable to distinguish between friend and foe. I accepted their offer, but sleep eluded me due to the level of domestic conflict that went on into the wee hours of the morning. Fearful to leave my room, I pissed in my water bottle.

Waiting at the bus station the next morning to head for the orphanage, was where, not three feet from me, the police officer was shot in the head. I hadn't even had my coffee. My God, whose life was I living?

I was still in shock by the time the bus driver dropped me off at the side of the road, telling me to hike on down to the orphanage. Once there, I met up with Lola and stayed a few days to decompress. I could make no sense of it and finally decided that's just how it was. There was no cause and effect; everything seemed independent of anything else.

At the orphanage, the children ranged from small babies to kids almost eighteen years old. Beautiful children, each with heart-wrenching stories and a great deal of laughter to share. Speaking their language, I instantly had over a hundred new best friends.

I took a job teaching fourth grade in a school in Tegucigalpa. In spite of the violence, it is a colorful, bustling city of over one million people where no one seemed to be strangers. Military personnel appeared everywhere, along with open air markets, adobe homes, laughter, and kids playing in the streets. I worked for room and board and not much more. Lola was working around the clock, both at the orphanage and in town. The need for speech therapy and her audiology training was great. She was exhausted. I thought it was from the heavy work load, but it was more.

In my spare time, I volunteered at the orphanage every weekend, all weekend. I loved it—far more than my teaching job. If not for my own adoptive parents making the choice they did, I would have grown up in an orphanage. I wanted to help these kids learn to believe in themselves. The orphanage, with its great reputation, may have been the only break in life that some of them would ever get. For this day, anyway, they were safe. They could be educated and receive health care. Given the unlikely event they would ever be adopted, they had to learn how to be proactive in making their way. They needed to learn the truth about life in Honduras outside the orphanage so they could be better prepared to do just that.

Lola had not fared well in this environment. While she enjoyed her work and the children, she was not prepared for what she encountered. Her upbringing in the States had been upper class and protected. Her Spanish was only basic, and salsa dancing was pretty much the extent of her exposure to the Latino culture. She was neither experienced nor equipped to handle what was needed to navigate in this developing world culture. She had come with assumptions and expectations that did not fit the reality. She mistakenly thought that her perception of trust and accountability and responsibility was the way it should be for everyone. Murders, government oppression, and never-ending drug problems weren't what she had expected.

The tipping point for our relationship came after a particularly stressful event when Lola just completely lost it. She had mistakenly thought that staff members would let her know when paperwork for visas needed to be completed. Because that wasn't the case, the paperwork was overdue, and she needed to get it finalized in town. With the long lines, only part of the process was completed by closing time; she was escorted to the door without her papers and passport and was told to return the following morning. With her level of Spanish, this was confusing and frightening to her. She rented a room, and outside her hotel, a government teachers' strike and gun fighting went on throughout the night. The violence and noise terrified her.

A big heart simply wasn't enough to sustain Lola. Without understanding the culture, she stopped listening; she fell back on her understanding of North American culture, creating even more of a disconnect for her. The next day she came storming in to my room. I had no idea what had happened. She was pissed off at the culture, the situation, people's laziness, their selfishness, their idea of time, their craziness with always wanting to kill each other, her lack of Spanish that she wasn't told she needed, and her whole situation. She began yelling obscenities at me, blaming me and calling me all kinds of names. I was told the Latino culture was damn stupid and slow and ridiculous and on and on. She told me this was my f*cking culture and it was f*cked up. And how I was f*cked up just for being Latino, too.

I tried to calm her down, but it seemed to me that maybe most of all she was pissed off at herself because she knew on some level that she just wasn't hacking it. Finally, I got so angry I told her to get the hell out, afraid of what I might be capable of saying or doing if she stayed. I was shocked that she had turned on me; I mean I hadn't dragged her down there. I'm an American, not a representative of the circumstances in Honduras.

As far as she and I were concerned, she had neither the nerves nor the capacity for continuing our relationship. When I went there, I wasn't expecting anything. Definetely hoping, yes. Why else would I have never considered returning to safety instead of continuing on to see her? But after that incident of her "losing it," we both knew it was over. I tried to make amends for my part anyway, but she wasn't going to own up to any of her own stuff. She seemed numb about everything. I didn't know how to fix anything for her. I guessed she just had to work it out and I told her I admired her courage for taking the job on.

After licking my wounds, imbibing a bit too much drink, and smoking way too many cigarettes, I returned to the States with no regrets. Latin America was a good experience for me. I saw the same problems everywhere I went—the malnutrition, the issues in gender roles, the lack of education, and the struggling political issues. But I also witnessed the care about family and the sense of community that was so strong there. I liked the social support people gave one another—the awareness of their neighbors. It is Latin America and part of my cultural heritage, also.

～

I had discovered I really liked working with youth in need and once home, I began attending night classes to finish my degree and got a job as a case manager, helping Latino high school kids overcome difficult challenges. These kids came from homes with bad living situations, poverty, abuse, and psychological disorders. I advocated for them, finding out what they wanted to do, assisting and teaching them skills to manage their lives better in spite of their circumstances. I learned to be very resourceful and to assist the kids in learning better skills of resourcefulness as well. Some were homeless; others had home environments that were not supportive. Some needed difficult illnesses diagnosed so they could be referred for medical care.

Often, I just had to wait while the kids determined if I could be trusted, while they decided whether or not to tell me what was going on with them. Waiting was okay if they were not a danger to themselves or others and if their welfare was good enough. Always if I could, I avoided guessing. Guessing was not in their better interests.

At one point I had fifty kids from every major religion and every continent. Many of them deeply affected me with their resilience and drive. I was amazed by the parents, also. While some parents were on drugs, had mental illnesses, were in jail, or just simply weren't available much due to work schedules or other reasons, I never met a parent who didn't deeply care about his or her child. Regardless of what they were able to do, or could do, they all definitely wanted the best for their children. These parents were voting with their hearts and souls for their children, even if they were unable to parent the way they wished they could.

The job suited me well—I liked the movement with the work, going to different sites, and meeting with different kids—and I stayed three years because I wanted to. And when I wanted to do something different, I moved on.

With All Life Choices There Are Outcomes

Be sincere with your heart, speak your truth as it really is for you in this moment, and others will either want or not want. Let the outcome emerge as you move through life experiences.

Here were two people taking risks of choice. Neither could predict how things would turn out. Sometimes, we don't look as good as we thought we would when we make a choice. It can be embarrassing, discouraging, and humiliating all at once. When things don't turn out as we expected, our world can seem topsy-turvy. Unfortunately, we tend to deny our own selves the patience, love, and tolerance we would offer to others in these circumstances. We can get caught up in how we looked when we came unglued; and this sets us up for a train wreck if we internalize the outcome as personal failure. We might blame and compare ourselves to how others would have handled things better, making ourselves feel bad. Or we might try to justify our reactions by stating how awful someone or something else was—even though that may have been true—when what is really bothering us is that we don't like the way we behaved. This kind of self-recrimination is pointless, and clearly self-defeating. It is important to appreciate who we are and acknowledge the value of taking a chance at something.

If we are involved in situations or relationships where we really don't like the way we are behaving, it is time to get clear about what we truly want and not judge the past, rationalize, or compare. We can appreciate the opportunities to learn and grow, apologize if we want to, and steer clear of getting caught up in image. If we want to feel better about our behavior, we might want to consider a different situation, friendship, relationship, or job, and let our reactions inform our next experience.

Zane was open to influence, but with discernment he recognized his relationship with Lola was over. While he wished she had been better able to cope with the situation so that they could have seen what was possible between them, the relationship wasn't going to be more than what it was.

There is no obligation to connect

Lola was embroiled in her commitment to do what she started out to do. She had embarked on a journey with tremendous courage and a lot of naiveté, but clearly she was in over her head and had some decisions to make about what she wanted to attend to. She came from a protected environment with limited exposure to the larger world. In Honduras, she was forced to quickly learn skills of discernment, judgment, and survival. We don't know whether Lola will stay or leave, whether she will act out of obligation or from her growing realizations. She may even choose different experiences while there and end up improving her situation that way. She will want to ask herself, "Is the experience still satisfying for me? Is this experience still connected to me? What can I do to make it better, or is it simply an experience I no longer want? If I no longer want to continue, will I have the courage to leave responsibly, to terminate my commitment; and if so, can I feel good about the chance I took?"

It happens to most of us that sometimes the game changes, or sometimes it turns out we just weren't prepared for the game in the first place. Either way, we want to check in with ourselves and ask if it is the experience we still want. It is possible to say "no thank you" without becoming judgmental or huffy about it. Of course, that ability to discern comes after we are informed by our initial reaction to that situation or experience.

Have you ever been to a farmer's market in your local community? You see three stands, all selling tomatoes and other vegetables. You go to one of the stands and buy your tomatoes. You don't really know why you chose to buy from that particular stand, given the tomatoes all looked and were priced the same, but you made a choice. After buying your tomatoes, you start walking away, and someone from that stand runs up to you and wants you to buy cucumbers and carrots from them, also. Because you bought your tomatoes from them, they tagged you as a potential customer—*their* customer—and may pursue you in the hope that they can compel you to buy more items. You can simply decline the offer.

There is no need to feel obligated to engage further with an experience that we simply no longer connect with. There will always be needs we are asked to satisfy. For those prone to fulfilling the needs of others, it is important to recognize it isn't our job to oblige others.

As Lola's Honduran experience progressed, something shifted— either within her or between her and something or someone else. Perhaps she was fine at the orphanage, where she was not exposed to violence or drug activity; but she allowed herself to be talked into agreeing to extra work in an environment where she was not comfortable.

Again, this can happen to any of us and probably has. How many of us have found ourselves in a volunteer or work situation where we felt we wanted to "do the deal"—perhaps even went to great strides to get the chance to do the deal: a rigorous interview process, extra schooling, a transfer for ourselves and our family to another location, or a pay cut to keep or get a job we wanted. Whatever it was when we did the deal, we thought we were getting what we wanted. Then perhaps our company management changed, our circumstances or interests changed, or the job grew in scope and responsibilities that we never would have wanted in the first place. Things do shift, within us and around us. The question to ask ourselves always is what decision we want to make today, in light of today's realities.

Numerous resolutions exist to any given experience, but they all begin with knowing what it is that we want—want to give, want to experience, even whether we want to take the first step. Without that understanding of knowing what we want, it may be better not to do the deal or leave it responsibly if we are already engaged. Because if our heart is not open to the experience, our well-being will reflect the life lived in compromise or conflict of true desires. We will want to be loyal to ourselves.

Doing life

Both Zane and Lola moved in directions they wanted for themselves. We all take risks of choice every day—we never know how things will unfold. Each time Zane changed course with colleges or jobs as his desires changed, he was exploring consciously and responsibly. He made himself available to new options that interested him at the time. While this isn't to suggest we take on double digit, near-death experiences (as unexpectedly happened in Zane's adventures), we could consider taking a small step even if we don't know where it will lead. We could just trust ourselves that we will figure it out as opportunities present. Life can be quite an adventure when we—with peace, passion, and no harm to others—participate by taking steps of action toward what we desire at the time. We simply connect and do the deal until we no longer want to.

6

An Exploration of What You Want

Is it being suggested that your life is only valid if it serves a purpose?
This troublesome notion can restrict the life that wants to be lived. It
can steal one's dignity. Each and every moment offers opportunities
to explore what you want.

What is your purpose in life?

This question has caused unnecessary confusion, stress, and consternation for many people. While some people seem to come out of the womb knowing what they will do or be in this lifetime, it certainly isn't that way for most of us.

Many of us have been told that we will die unfulfilled if we don't identify our life's purpose and then set about making goals and action plans to achieve it for the express reason of serving the world. We are told we have to, we must, we need to, and all this is urged on us at a young age so that we can go about our assigned mission of beginning to achieve that purpose as quickly as possible. Other people want ready answers from us, and there are a multitude of programs and workshops to help us get those answers. This troublesome notion, if adhered to, can create an unnecessary life struggle as it places a focus on an approach to life that is restricting, thereby robbing the joy and the sense of discovery from a life not yet lived, from a potentially exciting life journey.

What is all the hoopla about anyway?

We hear of the so-called "immutable truths" proclaimed by many who tell us that we must be clear on why we are here and that we need to identify, acknowledge, and honor our purpose in life. Then we are told to pursue—with passion and enthusiasm—whatever it is we were put on this earth to do. We are told that without knowing our life's purpose, it is easy to get sidetracked on life's journey; it is easy to drift. We are told we must hurry up and figure out what our life purpose is so that we can design and organize all around it. Ideally, it should not only happen as early as possible in life, it should also be something we are good at. We are told we must be clear why we are here and that clearly everyone is here on this earth for a purpose.

Then, after we know why we are here—including our true purpose and right livelihood—we are encouraged to inject passion into every activity we undertake. It doesn't matter if it is what we want in any given moment. No, no, no. What is important is that we are good at it and that we do it with passion; therefore, it is what we should do, because our actions serve others and the world ought to benefit from our gifts. Consideration of what we might want, separate from what our "purpose" might be, was never part of the equation or it got lost somewhere.

Are you feeling the pressure yet?

Once we determine our life purpose for being on this earth, then if we haven't yet defined our idea of success and our desires in clear and compelling details, we are told that we risk not getting what we want. Under such circumstances, we may begin to feel that we are wasting valuable time. So we seek out counsel and programs, and we listen to CDs to help us figure it out.

Our instructions are to write it down and read it every day, paint a symbol, make a sign, and hang these on our refrigerators in order to keep us focused on our purpose. Goals and vision aligned with our purpose are also to be written down. Time for reflection is essential and must be set aside so we can always stay focused on our unique role in the universe… on our reason for living. This is just in case we forget it in all these gyrations we're going through. But not to worry, if we've written down all our goals, we should be able to stay right on track.

If we become stumped, we may be told to figure out what brings us joy and makes us feel most alive. Now that could be helpful were it not meant to be approached as the means to an end—to give us insight to our life purpose so we could serve others.

Who is suggesting that your life is only valid if it serves a purpose?

Whoa! First of all, whose immutable truths are we listening to? This is pure craziness. Many genuine, kind, hardworking, earnest people are frazzled with anxiety as they race against the clock to determine what they "should" do with their lives. They feel the stress of struggling to find their calling, feeling clueless—or even guilty—because their life purpose is eluding them.

Many of us desire to serve the world, but it is important to recognize that those of us who do so are first serving ourselves. If it is what *we want* to do and we go for it, then we get to experience a more satisfying life. That is a choice, *our* choice. But it is not necessary to find a life purpose quickly, immediately—or ever—so that all our goals are aligned in such a way that we can serve others.

Naturally, we want to ponder and examine those things that nourish us and make us feel alive and try to find a way to bring more of those experiences into our lives, even making a living doing them. No one is suggesting that we don't want meaning and purpose in our lives. But the suggestion that we need to have a "justification,"—a "reason"—for why we are on this earth, for why we exist, is restricting. And these proposed methods to uncover and access what we value for our experiences create a distraction. How can incessant worry, feeling stress, making lists, and repeating slogans ad nauseam *not* create a distraction?

Consider this:
"Your life purpose is to have life experiences, nothing else…and everything else. Make them yours!"

– Karen Sontag

So here you are, you and all the other billions of people. What do you want? You've got now; you've got this lifetime. Do you want an experience of misery or do you want an experience of joy? Do you want to have choices, take actions, be the director of your own life, or do you want someone else to call all the shots? Do you want to uncover and follow your truth, live in integrity, or do you want someone else to determine for you how you live, what you believe, what you want and don't want, like and don't like?

If you had passion and purpose for something that was important to you, would you need a neon sign telling you what your purpose is? Of course not, because you would be living it fully and robustly every single day; it would consume you. And you wouldn't need to inject passion into every activity. You would be living passionately because you would be happy with what you were doing—compelled to do it by your nature.

Consider these six possibilities on this life journey:

First: There is no right way or wrong way in our life pursuits—just what is right for each one of us in a given moment.

Second: What mistakes? How is it possible that someone pursuing her own life could be considered by another to be making a mistake? A mistake becomes a mistake when an error is not corrected, not cleaned up responsibly. Action in the pursuit of life could indeed result in what others may regard as "errors." And those, like every chosen experience taken on responsibly, become part of an evolutionary and developmental process.

Sure, we can say all kinds of things about that choice once we step away or look back afterwards. But that isn't how choice works. Choices—chosen experiences—are made and lived in the context of a given moment.

Third: We are told that we need self-discipline, but what we really want in moving forward with our authentic desires is self-management. That will help to guide us. We want to participate in creating our own access to what we want and to check in with ourselves to assess if something is still relevant and important to us. When we get the signal from our body that we no longer desire something, we want to self-correct and choose again. This is not an act of discipline, but rather it is a process that requires self-awareness, with attention paid to how our body's reaction informs us. We then act from a place of self-accountability. This is what we call self-management. If we truly want something, we will figure out a way to work toward it through choice and action. We will be compelled to do so if it truly is our desire. We all know the feelings of passion, engagement, being motivated and compelled. Desires have their own movement. Discipline is not needed when we are acting on true desire.

Fourth: "Should?" How about we reserve the word "should" for how to prepare our taxes correctly rather than referring to anything having to do with our life choices? There is no "should" in figuring out life.

Fifth: Struggle? There is no need to struggle if there are no "shoulds."

Sixth: We are told our life purpose will guide us so that we don't drift. What's wrong with drifting? Other words for drifting might be "exploring" or "pioneering." Instead of being considered as something positive, some have associated the word drifting with aimless and irresponsible movement. Hold on a minute! Let's not confuse the two. An individual can drift, explore, and pioneer and still be responsibly active.

Sample the flavors and tastes of different experiences

How do you begin to take life experiences and make them yours? For those inexperienced in this regard, be good to yourself. While it is easier when you believe you can, it isn't necessary. You don't even have to believe you will figure it out at this stage. With *any* movement, things will begin to shift—they always do. You can simply move in a direction and pay attention to your body's reactions. Ask yourself, "Do I want more or less of this experience?" Notice your reactions. There is no need to try to change them; simply let them inform you. Allow for that; be aware and open to the messages.

There is no need to push for choice; just let possible choices percolate. Try to stay out of the logic of the conscious mind; it tries to set up rules. The body chooses according to truth. Listen to the whole body as it communicates with you and, when you are ready, move your feet. The conscious mind will catch up.

You don't have to have a preference; you don't have to act as if you had any thoughts other than those that are genuinely yours. There is no need to rush, no need to hurry. Take care not to go digging. Your body will tell you what to do. There is no horse race and you are no one's racehorse. Just keep moving through your life and allow yourself the dignity and the right to pursue your own life, your own happiness, your own choices—in your own time. However, when you have a desire, action is necessary. If you do nothing, you may still be sitting with that desire, waiting for something magical to happen while you make lists and plans. No substitute exists for living a full out life of taking action—even small steps—each action informing the next desire. What you want can change at any given moment, perhaps even dramatically. An hour later, a day later, ten or fifty years later. So what? Your life purpose is to have life experiences.

Each and every day is an exploration of what you want

The suggestion that your life is only valid if it serves a purpose is a notion that can restrict the life that wants to be lived. It can steal one's dignity. Each moment offers an opportunity to discover and explore whatever it is that you now may desire. Is everything still a match for you? If not, why kid yourself? You may not be able to end the experience you are currently living at this exact moment, but you can begin steps of action that will lead you out of the situation. Of course, you want to be responsible in the way you end your commitments or agreements as you move on with other interests and desires.

What if everyone all chose to embrace the loving idea: "Your purpose in life is to have life experiences, nothing else…and everything else. Make them yours!"? Then no individual would become a project for someone else. There would be no need—no opening—for anyone to be someone else's life director. All could sample the flavors and tastes of different experiences themselves. And all would be healthier for it because a life of health and well-being is far more than just a life absent of injury or disease.

How different might it feel to you when asked,
"What is your life purpose?" to smile and respond,
"To have life experiences that I choose based on my true desires."

Success is taking joy—with a capital J-O-Y—in accessing
the experiences you truly desire.

7

Rodney's Story

No Right Choice,
No Wrong Choice

*I couldn't change or control either "Uncle Sam" with his draft
or my daddy with his ways. So I made me the best choices I could,
given what I was dealt.*

It would be convenient to think that we have total control over
calling all our own shots in life, but sometimes there are limits put upon
us that require great thought, some premeditation, and a whole lot of
luck. While I'm all for acting spontaneously, at age nineteen that wasn't
the option that life presented me. It was 1970, the US military was in
Vietnam, and my draft number was 146. In June the count was at 142.
I had me a decision to make, and foremost in my mind was making the
decision that I felt would keep me most alive. I really didn't wanna die.

I assessed the situation to the best of my ability. My research was
limited by the nightly news and the stories from the returning soldiers
who I knew. And the dead soldiers, of course. What my research told me
was that the men in the army seemed to believe they was not well trained
and not well led by people who had any idea what they was doing. The

men in the Marines told me that they did feel well trained and well led by men who knew what they was doing. With four numbers away from being drafted, I made my decision to take a step in the direction I wanted, which was to become a United States Marine and hopefully increase my odds for staying alive. I came in from the fields at lunchtime, left a phone message for a Louisville Marine Corps recruiter to bring me by the paperwork, and before sundown, me and that recruiter was standing amidst forty acres of knee-high tobacco completing the forms on the hood of my 1957 Chevy. It was the second time I'd made a good decision to keep from getting myself seriously hurt, and I figured there'd likely be more. I was right.

～

The first time I made a good decision to protect myself as best I could was when I was fifteen and left home.

See, the thing is, me and my daddy didn't see eye to eye. He wanted everyone to be just like him, think like he thought, and believe like he believed. My daddy thought there was just one way of seeing anything, including race, religion, and politics; and that would be *his* way with his biases and prejudices. None of us kids ever grew up learning it was okay to have differences of opinions, have discussions, or say what you thought about something different from the way my daddy thought. Nope, we wasn't raised comfortable with disagreement; we'd all get nervous and tense if one or the other of us spoke up against what my daddy thought. He had a way of just shutting us down if we said anything contrary to his viewpoint.

Well, that went for the house rules also, which I was found to be breaking from time to time. So the last time it happened, I was thrown so hard up against the kitchen wall that the shingles fell off the outside of the house. It was clear to me then that my mama was not capable of interceding between the two of us. The police officer found me at a friend's home down the road a piece the next day and gave me a choice to go back home to Winchester or go to a state home for boys. I said I didn't care where I lived as long as it wasn't with my daddy. I wasn't interested in getting myself beat up no more for living my own life. My family participated in making arrangements for me to live with a farming family, working as their farm hand when I wasn't in school.

Thing is, see, it wasn't ever personal with my daddy. It was just who he was. My daddy had a hard time accepting the true nature of anyone. He just took offense and got hisself all mad and crazy. Like with our dog, Leroy. We kids gave him a bath in the tub one spring night because he'd muddied hisself up outside. While we was drying him off, Leroy got loose and ran into the kitchen and did just what a dog does when he's all wet. He shook hisself. Well, that water sprayed all over the kitchen. My daddy was so pissed off; he picked Leroy up, took him to the front porch and kicked him just like a football way out into the yard. That was my daddy—short-fused.

$\sim$

He was just three years old when his parents divorced, and his grandmother raised him until she up and died. He was fifteen then, and the Depression had gone on awhile. Both his folks had gotten themselves remarried and had more kids. My daddy went to both of them, asking and begging for a place to live and a meal, but got turned away. There just wasn't enough to go around. So after rambling around for a bit, he was placed in a state home for boys, where he lived until he went into the Army. With Pearl Harbor, he ended up having to stay for the duration. His temper then had him promoted and demoted more times than you can imagine in them five years. He was tough, and he was wounded. Don't make it right, him being how he was; there's no reason for someone to beat on their kid the way he did with me. Fact is my daddy had a problem managing that temper of his. Yep, we all get dealt what we get dealt with our folks. I decided I wasn't going to walk around letting it ruin my life. Folks are just who they are, and it was clear to me I needed to take care of myself.

How interesting would life be just reliving something that we couldn't change? What a waste of a life that would be. And how interesting would life be trying to control things we couldn't control? There's just no sense in it. I couldn't change or control either "Uncle Sam" with his draft or my daddy with his ways. So I made me the best choices I could, given what I was dealt.

Like with my work. I just figured there's something to that saying about if you go out and get yourself a job you actually like, you'll never work a day in your life. Thing is, see, you wanna figure out what you like and just do it. For me, that wasn't difficult. I liked living a full life, just the way I wanted to—and a job was just part of it. That's it in a nutshell. Still do. After the job with the Marines, I tried working for someone else; got me one of them office jobs. It wasn't as though I couldn't follow orders. I can assure you I could follow orders without question day and night and night and day, as long as they was given by men who knew what they was doing. I just wasn't interested in working for someone who was giving out orders that didn't make no sense to me. And well, turns out I prefer getting stabbed in the front where as I can see it coming, so I decided self-employment would likely suit me better.

I'd had a hankering to follow in my daddy's footsteps of being a truck driver since I was maybe seven or eight when we'd have us some fun going on some short runs together. And I couldn't have been more than thirteen or fourteen when I was helping hook up the flatbeds and moving things around. I was comfortable in the truck; same with working the big machinery on the farm.

So I took me a job as a truck mechanic for a spell so I could learn all about the repair end of things. Now that wasn't a huge leap for me. I'd been rebuilding cars all through high school. I did like to drag race, so I'd rebuilt more transmissions than I care to admit. In my exuberance of youth, with more horsepower than sense, I crashed out of control and broke my neck. If it wasn't for the police officer mentioning to the paramedics that seeing as how there was no blood gushing from the cut in the crown on my head that maybe it was likely my heart wasn't beating, I'd probably still be dead. But they put the cables on me and jump started my heart. That would be the luck I mentioned earlier that is awfully welcomed when making choices, particularly stupid ones.

Some choices just seem to work out better than others; becoming a mechanic before starting to drive truck was a great decision. It likely saved me a lot of money right from the get-go because as you can imagine, folks think they can hoodwink a twenty-three-year-old rookie kid driving a big rig. And well, over the years, those savings added up to a lot of good times.

~

Yep, I like my work; it's a good fit for how I do my life. Why, I think it might have been about ten or twelve years ago, just one day I was out riding me one of my motorcycles that I had parked in Lodi, California. My truck was in a shop. It would be a few days before she was ready, and, well, it was just a series of whims actually. I decided I wanted to head to a great seafood buffet there in Reno. After that tasty feast, I decided to go visit a friend a few hundred miles up the road a piece. I guess just through a series of lefts and rights, the next thing I knew I was gone for twenty-nine days on my bike, traveling near about six thousand miles. Visited me a Blues festival in Wisconsin and did me a bike week in Sturgis and, well, what can I say? I could do it. My truck, my time, my rules.

I get to sit in a class-act, long-tail Peterbilt semi-truck all day long in my air conditioned office, looking out a big window, mess with a few gauges, and turn a wheel. I can work as much or as little as I want. For me, that depends on what's grabbing my fancy at the time. After the kids was grown, the wife got her license and started trucking with me; and that suits both of us just fine.

We're still working; probably will a few more years, at least until the truck dies. She's got over a million miles on her now, so we'll see. My health is pretty good. I quit me them cigarettes years ago. Went to the doc with a problem with my pecker, and he told me I wasn't ever gonna be able to play full out again unless I quit. That was that. Just another good choice for me, for who I am. I have very few complaints about my life. My work and my life have both been a good match for me. I've lived it the way I've wanted most of it; and when I didn't, I made the changes that needed made. Never was afraid of making decisions—just figured I'd work it out one way or another just like those two decisions years ago.

The way I figure it is this life is my one shot. I'm still out making my own messes, having my own good times. And when I don't have any years left in me, it's like I always say, "The winner is not who dies with the most toys, it's who has the best stories to tell in the nursing home." I hope to be collecting stories for as long as I can.

Choose as Though No One Is Watching

What makes decision making more stressful for some and not for others?

Most of us like to see our choices and actions manifest in satisfying productivity or in being effective in a way we desire. And so it can feel disabling when we can't seem to choose well. When was the last time we simply walked away from something we didn't want and took action toward something we did? Often, when everything in us is screaming for us to act and we don't take action, it isn't even the actual doing that can seem complicated. In our hesitancy or inability to respond to our own needs, we can feel frozen, like a "deer in the headlights." As we consider the possible ramifications of new choices and changes, we may suffer if we fear that we lack the capability to take effective action. What may look like resistance, however, may actually be constraints imposed by the mind as it attempts to ignore or override the body's messages.

This hesitation is a result of being "trained" in a certain manner of being and acting. This keeps many of us from just going forth with what we truly want, being responsible with our choices and for our actions.

People who were raised to trust themselves as they took on experiences, sometimes making errors, have learned to trust their own ability to respond or self-correct. They do not have the same level of hesitation as those without this experience. We want to check the source of our desires. If we find we are pursuing something recommended by a trusted individual in our life, we may find we have reservations because it was never our own desire to begin with, or we may hesitate because something about it doesn't resonate for us.

Not taking actions, or having others decide for us, are still choices

So many people become stressed when making decisions, and this can keep them from making any choice at all. While not taking action appears to be a consequence-free, passive path, it is not. Not taking action is still a choice. If we desire the situation, the job, the career, or the relationship to be different from what it is, and if we choose not to act on that desire, then we want to be honest with ourselves that we made that choice.

Sometimes we approach decision-making with mixed emotions because we may not *want* to make choices and take actions. Actions obligate us to the responsibility for those actions, however they play out. Some of us may be more comfortable when someone else makes our decisions for us. In this way, we feel absolved of all responsibility for what went well and what didn't. We get to be the victim, the martyr, and sometimes even the hero. This is a personal choice; and frankly, giving away our life director responsibilities and having someone else make our decisions for us can have payoffs in attention, in money, in excuses. Perhaps, when we get real with ourselves, we may realize these payoffs are worth it.

Taking responsibility for your choices, regardless of the outcome

In learning to choose and discern better, we won't always have all the answers. That doesn't matter. We want to lighten up a bit. Many of us remember the first time we made macaroni and cheese and didn't drain the water, the first time we cut our own hair, the first time we prepared our mom breakfast in bed. Some of these experiences may not have turned out as we thought they would. As we got older, the outcomes were not any more predictable as we chose a lemon of a car, a mismatch in a marriage partner, a poorly planned financial decision or business partnership, and the list goes on.

If we've always been self-responsible, chances are we will always be able to figure out a way to be responsible with any choice we make. We see this with Rodney. From a very young age, he was willing to take responsibility for his actions. And because of this, he easily moved through making all kinds of decisions in his life, playing in any playground his heart desired.

This is not to say that making a choice that is correct for us—that is comfortable for who and how we are—is without challenges. There may be some anxiety, some exhausting schedules, and so forth. But we are still genuinely wanting to move forward with it, it is still want we want until we no longer want it.

Learning to support ourselves in our choices

Parents, partners, and well-meaning friends often want to fix what they believe to be out of balance or unhealthy for our well-being and long-term growth. They may even tell us that we are wrong. They may want us to explain to them what we are doing and what we are thinking because they want to be made comfortable with decisions we are making. However, doing so often works against our desires and rarely gives us the outcomes we were hoping for.

We may communicate to death about every single detail or possible scenario or possible outcome, none of which we have any idea how will actually turn out. We waste time and energy asking others to support us, involve themselves, or buy into our ideas unnecessarily. Often, these "life strategizing sessions" can impede any organic way of choosing. And it often ends up being guesswork anyway—made up stories—since most of the plans we make inevitably change in the doing.

Some people do understand and accept our reasons for something, but often the people we want to, simply don't. We wait, we explain, we justify, we plead, we pretzel ourselves around until we are blue in the face—and if they then understand and decide to support us in our choice, we feel great.

But what happens if they don't? Often, when we don't get one hundred percent permission from others, we may, in fact, override our natural inclinations that would otherwise guide us to the choices that are right for us. Do we proceed as we were originally inclined with what we want? Do we abandon our choice altogether? Or do we go against our own truth to remake and adjust our choice—a choice in part then determined by someone else?

How many of us, when we weren't successful in trying to convince others of our decision, simply became indignant about how wrong they were? Or how many of us were surprised or offended when someone chose not to discuss the details of an impending decision with us before making it? Who knows? It doesn't matter. Each does life his or her own way, and in that same way, we, too, need to move forward in our own choices, taking care of ourselves.

Although not necessary, if we choose to enlist the support of family and friends, we want to remind them that the most beneficial support they can give us is to encourage us in the pursuit of our life. Taking it over from us is not a supportive behavior.

However well-intentioned others may be, we want to guard the path to figuring out our own life—whether it is our first step or our millionth step. It belongs to us.

We all know that there is no right or wrong choice, just the choice that's correct for each of us in the moment—the one we are comfortable enough making that we can live with it.

When asked, what further explanation can be offered for a decision made?

Trying out our desires, even with very simple and small steps of action, may reveal itself to be an easy and enjoyable experience. Curious and innately motivated, often we find it to be an exploration of life itself. But when questioned about how our plans are progressing for something we thought we were going to move forward with but didn't, we may start creating all sorts of justifications, rationalizations, excuses, and stories in order to let others know why this is so. A healthier and easier response might be just to say (if we've already told them and were excited about it at one time): "Oh yes, I wanted that then, but I don't now." or "Oh, I haven't pursued it yet. Maybe I will sometime down the line, but there doesn't seem to be much desire around it at the moment." End of story. We didn't do it. We may never do it. People may think there is a right way or wrong way to do life and attempt to extract reasons from us for why we made the choices we did. We want to retain our authenticity, stay loyal to our own desires, and move on—not wasting precious moments on rationalizations and stories in order to make ourselves look good or make others comfortable.

Is it still what you want?

Many people find decision-making stressful because they anticipate failure. The process of achieving goals is often attached to specific outcomes and accomplishments; if they are not achieved, those who aspired to them feel they have failed or may tend to see themselves as failures. To be myopically focused on one specific outcome can leave no room for necessary adjustments.

Maybe it would be helpful to substitute the word "desire" for the word "goal" in reference to what we want. Perhaps it can seem easier for us to change direction on our life journey—and make the necessary corrections—when our *desires* are allowed to evolve as we change as people. We have no need for a sense of failure when we do not achieve what we no longer desire. If we still truly wanted it, we would still be going for it.

Pursuing desires can be easy and fulfilling, as the only expectation we have of them is in the experience they offer. We want to set ourselves free from the concepts of immutable goals with their consequent judgment of failure and success. After all, we aren't a business or a corporation or a cause; we are individuals having life experiences. We can simply allow our true desires to guide us to the experiences we want and then move on when we no longer find them satisfying. While we may need to arrange the details in order to responsibly change course, that's usually not nearly as difficult as might be imagined. When we no longer find those experiences satisfying, it is organic and natural to move on to something else. We can be authentic in this process.

It doesn't matter if what we want is called a goal or a desire or a dream or a whim. What matters is that if, regardless of how challenging or easy the path becomes in the pursuit of it, that it is *still* what we truly want... that moving toward it is still our truth.

Appeasing one's instability

Perhaps you have heard something to the effect that "our greatest fear is that we would be powerful beyond belief." This troublesome cliché is self-serving. Let's try to be real here. When we deny that it is our concern about being inadequate—not about being successful—that keeps us from learning and trying new things, we set ourselves up to wonder why we have trouble handling an experience that hurts like the dickens. Sometimes we just look less than perfect at something while we figure things out and self-correct. When we feel we must get it "right" coming out of the gate, this need for "image management" can interfere with acting on what we really want.

Sometimes we don't rely on ourselves, looking instead to others and our environment to appease our instability. We can't seem to simply move forward. We tell our friends, "Oh, I just don't have the confidence to do this or that," and our well-intentioned but misguided friends are right there—building us up—because our concerns of inadequacy make them uncomfortable. They may perpetuate yet another troublesome cliché when they respond with, "Oh, you are just afraid of being successful." This is commonly said to children.

Lack of confidence and fear of being successful as reasons for not moving forward are two erroneous notions that can interfere with our ability to see reality. So what might be really going on when we can't seem to move forward and we look instead to others and our environment to appease our instability?

Consider this: Many of us, when confronted with decisions to make, feel as though we are at some sort of crossroads where we hesitate, we ask friends, we ask "why," we spin…in confusion and non-movement. Without sufficient experiences and information, we simply don't "sense" a desired action. We feel we should, so we ask everybody else what we should do, we put stress on ourselves and deride ourselves for not acting, none of which is helpful.

We do not need to ask "why we are not getting it." This "mind chatter,"—this habitual language—is distracting and stunting as it interrupts healthy thoughts from developing. We can instead relax. The questions we might ask are: "*What* do I find compelling and *how* do I proceed in that direction?"

Our inability to act simply means that our senses haven't sufficiently integrated information from different experiences into the free-flow of a choice, so we stay indecisive. We want to take on more and different experiences so that we *do* have sufficient information. When this integration occurs, we more readily make a decision to go for whatever we want. We act efficiently and with our own desired timing. There need be no confusion that we don't have the confidence. If we feel we need practice, we find ways to practice. This is the value of acting on our natural inclinations as we try out new experiences—even in just small steps of motion, of practice. It brings us to the point where we *do* have integration, and we can easily move forward.

What can we say to ourselves and others that may be helpful? *Consider these:* "You'll figure it out one way or another, so go for it." Or "Good for you for taking a shot!" Or "Have yourself an adventure—what have you got to lose?" Or we may make any number of comments of encouragement to try something desired.

We risk ignoring our own unique genetic and historical differences, our own individual makeup when we ask others to appease our instability by giving us our "answers" for who and how we are. We want to trust that we will know, our body will let us know, when there is sufficient information for us to take decisive action on our own.

In any case, it is not likely that any of us are afraid of being successful; it is far more probable we are concerned about stubbing our toes, falling on our butts, or making a huge mess of things. We've probably all been through times we just wanted to curl up and disappear because we were feeling so inadequate or unprepared or embarrassed—times we knew we were wrong and didn't know how to make it right; times our faces were flaming red; times we were so disconnected from the truth and yet all the while mightily defending ourselves; times our words or deeds left us with egg on our faces and later we relived those moments over and over in shame. And we know it just might happen again.

If the word "try" has a negative connotation for us, it could be we're limiting ourselves with a mistaken notion of the word "try." Perhaps we have fallen into a habit of judging it as an effort and a struggle to accomplish that which we don't really want to do. But many of us can remember being encouraged as children to taste something new or to "put our toe in to check things out," and so forth. "Try!" was an encouraging word. When did it change that we began to hear that it wasn't good enough to "only" try or that we "lacked commitment" with only trying? We may want to begin to reframe "try" for ourselves into an expression of forward movement. Practice in making choices prepares us for a new and different experience next time. Learning to make ourselves more comfortable comes with practice.

So, go ahead. What the hey. Let's try, let's taste and sample. Let's check out what might be available and satisfying to us. It's called "doing life."

Image Management interferes with our true desires

We choose an experience, and then as we come back out of that experience, we ask ourselves, "Did I handle that the way I wanted to?" It may be that upon reflection we realize we might have handled it differently. There will be times when we dearly wish we would have acted in another way, or that things would have played out differently as a result of our actions, but reality is what it is, and there's no need for excuses. We want to become intolerant of illusions. If we are making excuses for our behavior—and for that of others—we may be living our lives as one big excuse.

We may desire to apologize and do so. It is helpful to bear in mind that others are responsible for their own reactions; that is not our territory. Others made the decision to engage with us, and how they are affected is their responsibility. We are only responsible for ourselves, and nothing is gained by continuing to feel bad. It is rarely possible to undo what we did, and we want to show ourselves the same kind of compassion others would give another who acted in a way that was less than perfect.

We may want to ask ourselves this question: "Do I care more about my life experiences, or do I care more about how I look to others?" Oftentimes, we tend to live our life like performers, as though our every decision and every move is reviewed and judged through the lens of our perceived audience. That audience can be at our jobs, in our towns, through social media, or with our families and friends. Or the lens might be the rules we think we need to live by. When image management is the priority, we may construct all kinds of experiences to protect that image. Our choices can become focused on creating an illusion, but this only leads us further away from who we are and what we want. Our basic authenticity always serves what we want. If we act otherwise, everything is compromised. Our life becomes a compromised life.

What would you be doing at this very point in your life if you truly believed no one was watching?

Rodney has it knocked

How we synthesize each experience is key. We want to try to stay out of fantasy and stay in reality by listening to our body knowingness. That is the value of practice. Yes, oftentimes we may appear awkward or look bad for some time before we become proficient or even have a clue. Before we had that experience, we simply didn't know what we didn't know. But afterwards—after that messy, god-awful, image-destroying experience where we were yelling out of control, got fired, or whatever it was—we were more experienced and wiser in choosing. Maybe that's a good reason not to be judgmental when others look a certain way. They are just practicing, too. They may never improve—maybe no more serves will ever go over the net—and they may make what we perceive as messes of their entire lives. We can choose to be around them—or maybe not—but it is a good argument for the importance of considering others with compassion. In these instances, certainly there can be no denying that life experiences are happening.

People are often surprised at how quickly they cease to fret as they transition to new experiences when they aren't concerned with what others think. Do any of us think that Rodney, for even a moment, concerns himself with that? No, Rodney has it knocked; it doesn't matter to him what others think. He moves forward with the grit and curiosity of a man fully engaged in doing his life, his way—responsibly and with no harm to others.

Choice is for the moment

Those looking for permanence will often put a lot of energy into a choice, but choice is for the moment. We don't want to overthink our choices, but rather just move beyond any restrictive dogma, tenets, or rules and into creativity. Any doing is creativity, as one action simply leads to another. We begin with small, simple, easy ones taken at our own comfort level—as we wish.

We want to ask ourselves what truly brings us satisfaction—what delights us and brings out our passion. If we take time to do what we love to do, our enthusiasm for life will show up in our work and in everything we do. When we choose something that is our true desire, we can enjoy our lives in its pursuit. We can then let it go and trust our body to figure it out as we responsibly stay focused on taking steps of action. We want to be loyal to ourselves, stay in reality, and be able to freely change course as our experiences inform us, accessing what we next desire.

> *The life that is lived when an individual dares to live his or her moment—each and every moment—knows no greater gift.*
>
> *What is your desire, what is the choice you want to make that you can live with, regardless of the outcome, regardless of how it all plays out? That is the question to ask when you want freedom from the stress of making decisions. And generally, that choice is the better choice for you. That can't happen unless you take authority over your own life. This life that is yours alone to live.*

8

Elaine's Story

Wake Up! Follow the Whim

Desire is a direct expression of your inner being; try on hats and costumes and roles and determine "that's the one I want at this time." Then go for it and enjoy. Today, tomorrow, in fifty years.

For close to thirty years, every morning when I left the house to go to work, I'd look toward the eastern sun thinking I'd really like to explore New York City and see who I might become if I lived there.

To say I was a shy child would be an understatement. I couldn't open my mouth if my life depended on it. I barely could whisper a "hello" in most situations. I grew up in a family where the norm was an absolute dearth of expression. The five of us children were isolated under the pretense of being homeschooled. The problem was not in homeschooling or having the free reign to pursue our interests; the problem was our family dynamics.

We had a "say nothing, speak nothing, do not offer an opinion, do not make commentary that is not exactly mimicking my mother's opinion" sort of policy. We'd go back to Twin Oaks, Ohio, to visit her family some summers, and there again, no one disagreed with her. If my aunt offered an opinion or made a statement that my mother didn't believe, want to discuss, or even listen to, my mother had unique ways of dismissing it and changing the topic. Later in the car, she would make sure that we all knew her reality of what was said, how wrong someone was to have held an opposing viewpoint, and no one dared utter a word otherwise. No questions were ever seriously entertained.

There never was any encouragement to explore a notion, pursue a whim, be inquisitive, ask questions, engage in lively discussion or dialogue or any form of self-expression. There was very little joy, rarely any laughter, and, oddly, no allegiances built among us children. I couldn't tell you what any of my brothers or sisters really thought. We never learned to write a paper or defend a position. It was just year after year of my mother filling the empty air with her judgments, criticisms, opinions, and biases—sort of thinking out loud as she ruminated. It wouldn't have mattered if we had been in comas (and sometimes it seemed as if we were). It's just what she did. Obedient child that I was, I never said anything.

My mother had no idea what we read. We were dumped off at the library and left on our own. In retrospect, other than her ramblings of how the world should be—should work, what people should believe, how they should act—it was okay, except it certainly didn't prepare someone like me for the world.

～

I loved learning about art and theater. I read historical fiction, watched movies of plays, attended live performances, and at an early age, began drawing replicas of fantastic costumes and elaborate set designs. I taught myself to sew, both machine and hand stitching. While then, I hadn't taken any formal art courses, years later I got my degree in commercial art in college. I never developed my own sense of creativity, but I became quite skilled at reproducing. To have created something would have meant using my own "voice." I didn't have a voice. And my body, although it knew it wanted to express itself artistically, could only "copy."

New York City embodied both theater and an artistic life vibrancy for me. My yearnings to live there had everything to do with my desire to be somewhere that I could begin to move myself in a direction where I could draw my own life, where I could simply draw my own breath, while exploring what held my interest. Perhaps, somehow, my living inside circles of protection, staid opinions, and repression influenced my desire for a place that held an almost fictional allure. I believed New York City offered it all for me. With its theater district, tall buildings, and chaotic energy, it represented a place of contrast and depth. But was it only for the daring? How about for the cowardly like me?

For my fortieth birthday, a few girlfriends of many years surprised me with a collage they had made up of photos from college days, including ones of me with the costumes I'd sewn. While I pretended to be delighted with their gift, they couldn't have known that this was yet another reminder that never living in New York City was one of my biggest disappointments in myself. We all laughed gaily at the "fantasy" I had had many years before—twice when plans had been well underway to move to New York City with a friend and those plans had been aborted because of a change in my friends' lives. So it had never happened. At the party we all commented that it was too bad it hadn't worked out. Nobody even so much as whispered the idea it still could happen. I kept mum.

～

At some point in my early fifties, working at a job I'd held for over two decades that had nothing to do with my interests in theater and art, I became increasingly aware that I'd never stopped looking to the east every morning. I'd never stopped wondering what it would be like to experience living and working in New York City. I wondered how exploring and delving into new things would enrich my life. Yes, that was it, wasn't it? Life enrichment. I wanted life enriching experiences to awaken, to arouse me. For the first time in my life, I asked myself what was holding me back. Why was I still just wondering? Why hadn't I ever gone? Was I just acting like a silly old woman to still even be entertaining such thoughts? And just exactly when had I become so "old" that I even questioned myself for dreaming about going there? I casually mentioned my thoughts to a few different people, and everyone seemed to want me to consider all I was giving up rather than all I would gain should I go. The comments were focused largely around my knowing precisely how everything would play out before pulling the trigger by quitting my job to go. I said nothing more, but did not deny to myself that the dream was still alive in me.

I didn't mind my job; and although things changed from time to time with differing government contracts, I knew I could probably grow old and retire from this job eventually. I could work there another fifteen years if I wanted to. I worked in the back office, I didn't have to handle people much, and I never had contact with clients. I was a good, solid worker—dependable, quiet, thorough, and organized. I made enough money to live comfortably, had a home, a few friends I saw occasionally, but mostly I was still the quiet, shy person I'd always been who never opened her mouth.

I began to vividly daydream about what it might be like to work and live in Manhattan—to ride the metro, eat lox and bagels at a real deli, and dash among traffic. I wondered about work in the business of theater or art, even temp work helping out. I accepted that I wasn't extroverted, that I had unfounded worries and concerns, that I was timid. But I certainly was a good worker and definitely resourceful. Maybe there were things I could do. I'd have to talk to strangers, find and figure things out, and be questioned. All this in a big city. Oh, but what a city. New York City.

⁓

The yearnings didn't stop. I began to feel stuck. Life didn't feel full, nor did it feel fun. I knew it was me who needed to do something differently, begin living a more engaging life with some texture to it. I just didn't know how to start it. So I decided I would just take some sort of action, any action. I researched a few extension courses and checked out design magazines from the library and bought a book on New York City. I took two short courses, one in textiles and one in weaving. I began walking daily, sometimes only for fifteen minutes. I started taking social dancing lessons, which forced me to be social and to dance with a partner. The walking and those classes were the first surges of life—of motion—that I had felt in over twenty years, and the movements invigorated me. I began drawing again and doing crafts with my hands. Something was shifting. I was becoming unstuck.

During these explorations, I found coffee shops, fabric stores, and a community theater in a town nearby where I volunteered to help with the costumes for a play. Often I would discover something unexpected and delightful. With all of the actions of doing—just tiny steps—I began to notice I was feeling better about myself.

What got into me, I can't say for sure, but on my walk one Saturday morning, I didn't just cruise on past the travel agency like usual. I went inside. Fifteen minutes later, I walked back out with an airline ticket for a weekend trip to New York City.

The experience left me spinning. It was a thunderbolt weekend.

⁓

Within six weeks of returning home from the weekend, I knew. I guess I realized that I didn't have to stay anywhere. Here or there. If I didn't like the experience, I could move on to something else that I might find more satisfying. But I wanted to go. The condo sold. I gave notice at my job. My colleagues at work had asked me how I could possibly leave after twenty years at a good job for something so uncertain. When I told them I wanted to give this a shot—that I had often wanted to—and my worst case scenario was that I could always return to similar work some-where, I realized I was already living my worst case scenario. That reality was hard to hear, even from me.

There was nothing I needed to prove, to show I had "made it." This adventure was not about having to be part of a Tony-winning production on Broadway. Quite simply, I wanted "to do" New York City and the theater scene there. I wanted to do what I believed only young people did in their twenties when they went off and had an adventure…so little did I know that age has nothing to do with passion and pursuits and taking on new experiences.

I left a few keepsakes with friends, gave the rest away, and drove my car part way, parking it at my sister's farm for an indeterminate period of time. I didn't know if I would go for one month, six months, or two years. I didn't know anything except that this was what was next in my life. I was past fifty, and it wasn't going to be past time for me. It was now time, and this was my life. For the first time since I had gone to college, I was pursuing something I really wanted to experience.

I had found lodging through the Internet; and although only stay-ing there a week, I was able to then secure a room in an apartment in Manhattan near Gramercy Park. It was a share situation, so the kitchen, bath, and living room were shared with an older Korean couple who lived in the other larger bedroom. They spoke broken English, but through their actions I sensed kindness and hospitality. I tasted kimchee and bul-gogi for the first time; and much to my surprise, I really enjoyed the flavors and textures of this new cuisine. At one of our first of many home dinners together, I attempted to use chopsticks. My food flew onto the white tablecloth. I looked up at my sweet hosts, aghast at my error. What started as a hidden smile behind their hands at their face, turned into full-bellied laughter among all of us.

It was the beginning of something very new to me—trying new things, making messes or looking bad somehow, and ending up laughing.

Sure enough, after settling in, I just had to go to Katz on Houston to get a pastrami sandwich with their fabulous pickles—and of course a toasted bagel smothered in cream cheese, heavy on the lox at Zabars. I checked out all the theaters on and off Broadway. I was constantly asking strangers for directions. I'd read about these places for years, and I wanted to experience the real or at least the tourist version of the real New York City. If I was going to run out of money, some things just had to happen first. I had no idea how things would unfold.

I got right to work. I took inexpensive extension classes and worked in internships. I was a production assistant several times at different theaters, which meant I was a "gopher." To me, that was exciting as I ran errands for getting props, brought in food or coordinated with the caterers, took visitors on tours of the theater, made all kinds of arrangements for random needs—really I did whatever needed done. There was always a lot of variety. I also worked on artistic set designs for the theater productions and assisted in designing costumes—thank goodness I knew all about each era of the past, the colors, the fabrics, the textures. I worked for sane people and a lot of crazy people.

I laughingly called myself a "free-lance artisan," which meant I worked almost for free. I never had enough money, and most others didn't either. We all found ways to make ends meet to stay in Manhattan. For me, this meant office temp jobs and working at an all-night copy center a few times a week. Any work I could get meant I could stay. I walked the entirety of Manhattan's neighborhoods, parks, and over the Brooklyn Bridge. I explored all the boroughs. I tried on hats at Sax Fifth Avenue and stood in line for hours to get cheap tickets for whatever was playing anywhere and visited museums on free days. New York City was everything I thought it would be and more. So much more.

~

My experience there lasted four fabulous years, and I wouldn't trade a moment of it. When it was over, it was time to move on. No huge explanations, no big deal reasons. In so many ways, living there brought me out of my shell. I'll never be who I am not; my nature for a work life is diligent and behind the scenes. I like my life that way. But I'm no longer paralyzed to express myself, to try new things, to take a chance. Laughter is now second nature for me. Most importantly, I feel great about myself and my life.

And my next adventure? What's my whim, my desire? Hmm…It's percolating, and I'm guessing it might be just around the corner. I can feel it in my bones. And you can bet I'm now paying attention to those bones!

Only Because We Live Our Truth
Do We Have a Unique Life

We want to learn to be our own matchmaker,
to find our "fit" in work, love, and play.

When we sense we are unsettled in ourselves because we are not pursuing our desires and moving toward some new experiences, we want to observe what is impeding our movement and try to dance our way past anything that holds no true value for us.

This call within is the only support and approval we need

Elaine had this idea that, at over fifty years old, maybe her time was past for following the call—that whim that had popped up off and on all her adult life as it often can do. Twice before, she had made serious attempts to take action and move toward the larger, more colorful and self-fulfilling experiences she desired, but it hadn't worked out. She had attached the pursuit of what she wanted, to the mistaken notion that others would need to participate. She wasn't developed enough to know that this was not necessary.

Elaine's life pursuits had always been structured around supporting others; she hadn't thought about giving herself support for her own desires. As a young adult, she saw those around her taking steps on their own and flourishing, but somehow she had bought into a notion that it was different for her. For the most part, she had never questioned how those assumptions were working for her. After all, even as a child, she had stepped into a role of satisfying the expectations of others with her support of their lives; that had worked well for them, so no one was interested in that changing.

Many of us, as with Elaine, find we don't really give credence to our whims. By their very nature, they are whimsical—something we fancied at various moments in time—and so we characterize them as frivolous, as lacking substance and weight. We may devalue them as having no real meaning. They "pop up" off and on—sometimes for years, now and again—and often we ignore that the possibility that the pursuit of them may be of interest, may be correct for us. When we follow our whims, however, the more we are prepared to listen when presented with something big—even crucial or life critical. Yes, compelling dreams have immense value, as do whims. They may not come to light; they may just die out. But we want to give them our full regard.

Too much "thinking" can be hazardous to our health and well-being

For many years, Elaine had felt a stirring. But even as that wake-up call persisted and demanded to be acknowledged, she still felt conflicted because she thought she needed to be younger to have such dreams. She also bought into her friends' and colleagues' idea that she needed all the details worked out before letting go of her current situation and embarking on something unknown. She had a lot of "thinking" going against her. At jobs, she had often been praised for her ability to think and rationalize and figure things out in her head, and she did it well. But what she had going for her now was a newfound realization that she had nothing to prove to anyone, even herself.

For anything she had ever wanted in her life, Elaine had figured it out, and she reminded herself that she believed that about herself. Something in her had changed and she knew it. This time she was paying attention to the nagging, gnawing feeling in her body that wouldn't go away, to that call inside her.

Elaine came to recognize that all that external noise and misdirection wasn't going to keep her from going, from taking action in response to that stirring. Not this time. Not anymore.

When you know that you are the one responsible for what happens in your life, regardless of the outcome, and you feel confident you can figure things out for yourself, a growing freedom to take chances in your own life occurs.

You then choose your own experiences, self-directed and self-accountable. You come to understand that "figuring it out" comes from all within you: your heart, your stomach, your head—everything. Once you experience this wholeness, you realize —innately—that you are equipped to play in any playground you want.

Remember what happened in the story of Little Red Hen when Hen went around the farmyard, asking the duck, the cat, and the dog to help her plant the grain of wheat she had found? When all three said, "Not I," she did it herself. Their answers were the same when it came time to cut the wheat, thrash it, take it to the mill to be ground into flour, and then make the bread. They all said, "Not I," and so she did each task herself. When she inquired who would help her eat the bread, of course the duck, the cat, and the dog all said, "I will." Little Red Hen said, "No," and enjoyed the bread all by herself.

How does this apply to living our own truth? If we try to solicit help and are met with obstacles, we may or may not get the encouragement or offers of assistance we think we need. But if it really is the time for us to take action, we will act anyway.

In Elaine's case, two different times her friends bailed on plans with her for their own reasons. That's okay; it was their life to live, and they were making their own choices accordingly. Elaine didn't have an attitude about their decisions, but she did assume that she couldn't pursue her desires without support and approval from others. That's how she saw things then, and that perspective and any choices relative to it, belong to "her yesterday." What is stopping her or any of us from paying attention to our whims, from following the call within today?

Friends often unknowingly, and often with good intentions, may question us about our journey, about our life yet to be lived. Sometimes, they want to be made comfortable, to be sure we have everything figured out so we'll be okay. And we want people to think we are grounded and that we know what we're doing; so we try to give them reassurances or answers for all the possible scenarios that could or might happen, but in fact, we don't know. How could we? Isn't that part of the mystery of life? But with our response to their inquiries, we can begin second-guessing ourselves or possibly put ourselves at risk to partner with them to disregard or dismantle our inner choice. Take caution—the fact is, we *are* grounded when we live an authentic life because the one thing we trust is ourselves. We trust ourselves to check in with ourselves, figure out our next steps, and be responsible in the end. We really do know that regardless of how well we plan, eventually things are bound to happen that are not part of any plan. We don't kid ourselves about that.

If the action feels correct, energy will mobilize

Once Elaine was open to taking some new actions, it was easier for her to recognize all the possible ways she might actualize her deep desires. One by one, she removed the prejudices and restrictions around her options that would otherwise have seemed impossible for her. She knew what she wanted, but she didn't force her actions. She simply began noticing what energized her and then sought more of that. Her body knew. She was learning to pay attention and to trust that.

All the cells of our body want the same thing—to express our truth in actions. For Elaine, it was happening with each small movement as her body energized; it did not shut down. She allowed this energy to propel her forward. She moved, she walked, she got physical, she took small actions, and her mind reordered itself.

If there is something in our past we didn't do and we look questioningly into the rear view mirror, perhaps it simply wasn't the correct time for us to do it. We need to learn to respect the fact that when the body knows *sufficiently*, movement will happen. It can't help itself. The body can't override itself, and that's a wonderful thing. If there is no movement, if we are not animated, it could be it was just a random thought that had no energy behind it, no impetus from the body. Maybe it took on energy for a while and then just sort of died out. It could be that the idea was still germinating, but at that time the body didn't compel us to begin taking even baby steps toward it. Perhaps we had an idea such as to go back to school; we expressed that, and then lost the drive. There was no animation, no movement behind the initial idea, and we didn't move toward exploring programs, getting applications completed, and so forth. Maybe at a later point there would be energy for it. Maybe not.

Quell the chatter, perhaps test the waters, see what resonates within

If the timing of something feels okay, we do what we can to make it work and then see what mobilizes around that. That "doing"—those steps of action—looks different for everyone, depending on ability, development, and desire. It is another life experience we're stepping into. If the action feels correct, energy will mobilize and we'll feel compelled to move forward—maybe even propelled forward—to take further action. We do our part by choosing and owning our choices, recognizing and responding to time and place, and then checking for harmony with that movement. If we find agitation or panic, then that is the movement; sometimes those feelings awaken us or act as an alert bell for us to consider and choose accordingly. If that movement is joy and peace, then that is the movement. We carry out what needs to be carried out, being mindful and listening closely to what the body is telling us. If there is no movement, it's okay. It is important not to concern ourselves with what others may say or think if movement doesn't occur. We want to practice taking experiences, perhaps testing the waters and seeing what resonates within.

Elaine could not deny the energy. Each action led to a new experience, which led to yet another new experience. These energized movements created an opening for her to choose the long-awaited New York experience.

We are often presented with situations that we know offer us any number of possible choices. We contemplate and say to ourselves, "Well, things could go this way or that way." But we've never done this before—we have no experience—so we may not know what to do. Elaine admitted she was already living her worst case scenario by staying at her current job, all the while wishing she were on an adventure working and living in New York City; so her conclusion was that she had everything to gain and nothing to lose. Taking that approach, she was able to overcome the issues, prejudices, and self-imposed restrictions impeding her. She quelled the chatter, both internally and externally, put one foot in front of the other, and made her unique life her own.

Ask yourself, "Do I like myself in this moment, in this experience?"
When you believe a choice is the better choice for you—you like yourself in that choice and you are willing to live with it regardless of how it all plays out—then you have created an atmosphere of acceptability for the self. Many, as did Elaine, have found this to be foundational to their development because this atmosphere of acceptability can then expand *beyond* the self. "Your people"—people with whom you resonate—harmonize with you and your actions. You may not yet have even met them, but you know you will.

Any choice that brings you into a moment or an experience in which you find you like yourself in that moment—really like yourself—can be liberating. Responsible, self-accepting, and enjoying her heart's desire… that's how it was for Elaine with her New York City experience.

9

Appreciating Each One's Unique Individuality, Including Our Own

Another individual's life is his or her own;
we don't have to judge it or fix it.

Our "business" with another individual's life is for us to choose to engage with it or not—and to do so while maintaining our own dignity and self-care. We want to prepare ourselves with the life skills to be able to manage our own experiences.

Getting Comfortable with Disagreement

When children grow up in families where they have not learned to carry on open and explorative discussions, or have not had exampled for them the importance of respecting differences and differing viewpoints, their social development may be impeded. Even when discussion concerns a contentious issue, children can learn to become comfortable with disagreements. There may or may not be resolution, but the experience of disagreement and the expression and sharing of differing viewpoints and opinions will not likely threaten the child's comfort; the child becomes accustomed to these truthful interactions.

It is important to assist our children in finding a comfortable way of listening to people in disagreement. In a healthy family, this is ordinary and welcomed. We found that in Chapter 7 for Rodney and in Chapter 8 for Elaine, self-expression was not tolerated. In Rodney's family, he and his siblings were diminished and shut down in their attempts at expressing disagreement. In Elaine's family, spontaneous conversation was stifled; the boundaries of acceptable expression were clear, even though they were never stated. Everyone just knew. Little signals kept everyone in line: a frown or a "look" or an under-the-breath utterance was all it took. Elaine became an expert at self-editing; she automatically ran everything she expressed through a filter—she knew what would be accepted and what would not. Her thoughts and feelings were self-censored before they even reached her lips.

Healthy, open discussion and conversation is not inherently debate; it is a simple sharing of differing viewpoints through dialogue that preserves the dignity of each participant.

Every family has its own dynamic. In some families, the result of crossing the boundaries of acceptable expression—that which is not allowed—is met with a withdrawal of love, a severing of affections, or even rejection of the individual. Regardless of how it plays out, when discussion isn't open, a child will feel that she has to "please" or she will be at risk for expressing ideas and concepts that she senses are not acceptable or comfortable for others nor welcomed by them.

Similarly, if a child is exposed only to the prejudices or biases of the parent, the child's thinking becomes severely limited. When she then meets and interacts with another individual, these pre-programmed parental viewpoints and generalizations can get in her way. When children are not able to approach their *own* experiences unencumbered and with an open mind—and therefore can't be openly receptive to the experiences of others—their ability to make their own observations and assessments is affected. Something akin to an intellectual and emotional invisible fence stops them where the set borders and lines of acceptable thinking and expression are drawn; this may render them unable to engage in critical thinking processes. At this point, they remain isolated in their own experience. Even when desiring to be open to influence, their skills for discernment are limited. They can't receive—process and integrate—the experience of the other individual; they are unable to engage freely with others and unable to assimilate new information. It is as though a script were written for them, a response predetermined, and a conclusion decided.

These prejudices inhibit children—*or any of us*—from an appreciation of honest expressions that are free from the encumbrance of pre-conceived ideas.

Managing our own experience

In an open, healthy, and trusting environment, a child feels free to express her true self, her true feelings and ideas. She senses that her opinions are valued and honored. Having that exampled for her gives her the ability to do the same for others. Generally, in the comfort of those conversations amongst family and friends, no offense is taken; in fact, often greater liberties are taken to openly share opinions without the existence of the "social police." These exchanges are authentic.

What is the value in preparing our children with their initial development in this way? It prepares them for a more global existence. How? While we want our workplaces and our relationships and all our situations to be what we want them to be, the reality is, they are what they are. Out in the world, often we find that we are not in a "trusting, open, and healthy environment." It doesn't matter. The child who is raised in the comfort of healthy environments won't be disabled should she sense any nervous tension with others or with her own ability at self-expression as she moves forward into her adult life. No tension felt will stop her.

All of us carry a "culture of one" that evolves with self-discovery. While seeking experiences with a "cultural fit"—a match—is a worthy pursuit, we begin this pursuit by operating from a strong sense of our own internal authority. Others may attempt to shut us down, "correct us," bully or manipulate us, or engage us in unhealthy dialogue. Managing our reactions, thoughts, emotions, language, and communications with and within any experience is key to self-care. We then can make responsible decisions that are ours to make, taking actions we want relative to the experiences we want. There is no need to "manage" others' behaviors, to ask others to respect our boundaries or to reframe something more kindly, or to be this or to be that. People are who they are. It doesn't matter what they say...sooner or later, everyone behaves their truth. Personal culture eats proclaimed strategies, tactics, and goals for breakfast and character—well-developed or not—trumps rules. The child or adult who has sufficiently developed the skills of healthy and respectful discussion and expression will not rely on the "perfect" environment; he or she will manage his or her own experience regardless of whatever is presenting and make choices to stay or not stay in any given situation, job, relationship, or environment.

When we have the skills to manage our *own* experience, we can choose to engage with someone or something or not...and do so while maintaining our own dignity and self-care. That is our "business"—our interaction—with another's life. Our life is not about managing someone else in *their* experience but managing ourselves in *our* experiences.

Care for the self involves respecting that others live as they choose

How many individuals and organizations are attempting to be what another wants them to be because they think that is what is required to get engagement from others? This feeds an expectation that it is someone's duty to create the perfect environment or persona for another. It is not. Individuals and organizations are who and how they are and offer what they offer, and others are free to participate or not.

No one needs to stay, to leave, to offer, to buy, to borrow, to give, to accept, to reject, or to participate in any thing for any reason. No one needs to create for another. We are each responsible for making our own life work. With this understanding, we may become more comfortable in letting others live their own choices and their own lives, and offer what they wish to offer. That being said, we want to prepare ourselves with greater abilities at observation, awareness, and articulation so we can choose better for ourselves from what is offered.

Suspending Judgment—Keep Your Feet to Yourself

It can be difficult for us to have the life we want when we carry judgments of ourselves or others. Often we become frustrated with someone's behavior at work or with an individual we are around, and of course we don't spare ourselves, either. We may find it difficult, or perhaps we are unable, to be tolerant and simply appreciate someone as an individual. Maybe he or she brings opinions that we completely disagree with. They have ideas about who should marry who and when and why, when someone should go to college and which college, how someone should pursue this or that, how some company should do their business, whether or not someone should stay in a relationship. No topics around race, religion, and politics are exempt and they act like know-it-alls with their strong opinions that they are always expressing. These people may be our neighbors, associates, in-laws, colleagues, other people's children, the cashier at the grocery, our boss, the homeless individual in front of the bus station, or maybe we don't even have contact with them—they might be the people we read or hear about in the news. But something about them and their life drives us wacko or otherwise keeps us from feeling good about our day, about our life. It's as though they have all the answers about how everyone should be and should choose.

It's always a subjective assessment as to whether you believe another is choosing well or has their head on straight about their opinions. The fact is, just as we do, they speak from the experiences they have had and from who and how they are. They make assessments and apply conclusions drawn from and relative to their unique life—just as we do from ours. Those same conclusions may simply not apply to our life, to our way of thinking or being.

We are each a product of our unique genetic makeup, history, and experiences. Our opinions are correct for us and the opinions of others are correct for them. We may prefer not to engage in respectful dialogue with others, but if we do so anyway, we want to respect and give regard that their opinions are correct for them until or unless they determine they want to change them.

What is not helpful

While we want to use our skills of discernment and assessment about others so that we can determine how to best care for ourselves and those we love, judgment of others, or even ourselves, isn't respectful. We don't get to be judge and jury of the life of another or the decisions they come to. The fact is, we may not like that individual, we may not want to be around him or her. He or she may not make choices satisfying to us or be "our type of people." Often when others are behaving a certain way, we experience feelings of intolerance; we go into that judgmental mode where we hold ideas about how that individual "should" or "should not" choose to be or act. This judgment breeds a sense of illness in our own well-being.

But even when we want to have compassion or empathy for others, we may default to the way we are told to accomplish this, which is to "try to put yourself into their shoes." So we try it. While possibly well-intentioned, it is not helpful or respectful advice. We think we will have more tolerance and acceptance and understanding by "putting ourselves in someone else's shoes" and by presuming we can know what it would be like to live their experience through our imaginings. But what happens is *we* become judgmental, which was not our intention.

What might be helpful

Consider this: It is a misdirecting of our intention to have tolerance and acceptance of others when we try to imaginarily insert ourselves into another individual's life experience. It is difficult to access compassion or empathy for humanity in this manner. We cannot possibly fathom what makes others behave as they do. We can't know other people's genetics, their history, their experiences, their natures and wants and desires—everything that makes them who and how they are. To attempt to do so will always involve an act of judgment as long as we "create a story" about another individual. It may sound like compassion, but it isn't; it is story-telling—an attempt to construct another individual's experience in our heads. We create a "story," a "justification," in order to make it "okay" (in our eyes) for these individuals to act as they do and be who they are. Somehow we think, if we can imagine ourselves in others' experiences, we can understand why we find them as we do; and this will somehow make their behaviors or traits more "tolerable" or "acceptable." This notion is offensive and injurious as it disregards another individual's very life. Divisive and polarizing, it creates a "them" and "us" setup.

What we can do is have tolerance and acceptance for the *right* of others to choose for themselves, with no harm to others, and we can always take care of ourselves. Do we all have the right to have an authentic reaction about their choices? Do we all have the same right to have our own strong opinions? Of course we do. Things appear to have gotten out of control, however, when we got into the habit of offering our opinions with an attitude of right and wrong. Opinions are not to be superimposed onto others; they are not for the purpose of determining standards for others. They are for each of us and our life. It isn't necessary that others either agree or disagree with our opinions. Opinions with an "attitude" of right and wrong are what we call judgment.

What we can do also, is be an example. It is not by discipline nor force that change is most likely to occur. Yes, we can bring forth our opinions and ideas in respectful dialogue and conversations. But it is by our example that we can offer the greatest possibility for sustainable change.

Characterizing others often becomes a habit

We assume that all people want to or are able to or are ready to develop themselves so they can choose better, but that is an erroneous assumption. Some may not now—or ever—seek to develop themselves.

There is no need to convince, manipulate, or judge others because we believe they should want more for themselves or because we've decided they have so much potential. If they want to live it in a way that appears to us to be lacking in interest in their own development, and they are able to make their way in life without laying their lives on others for support, that is what they have chosen. Perhaps they don't have more within them at this time. Perhaps they never will. Perhaps they are developing themselves through the experiences they are currently in, and you simply can't see that. It doesn't matter. Their life and development is theirs to own.

Many people are content with themselves, even if that puts them on a path that leads them to their own destruction. Some may simply choose unconsciously without taking ownership of their choices. Some people believe that life happens to them and, as victims, they may complain, deny, and avoid taking any ownership of their own life. Who is to say that is not the best they can be or want to be? If others are satisfied with who and how they are—even if that is to be a complainer, to be a victim, to be unconscious, or simply not to develop themselves—that is their right.

Our genetics, our history, our experiences, our natures, and our desires can influence second by second, how we show up in the world. So we want to be mindful not to superimpose characterizations onto ourselves or others. All we can see through our own filters is who and how people appear to be in a given moment. We may catch ourselves saying things such as "I'm a person who…" or "she's a person who…" We are an evolving species; we see behavior at a moment in time, and we don't know five minutes, five months, or fifty years later what may have developed for that individual. It is important to always allow for transformation. While characterizing others may simply have become an unthinking habit—one we have seen exampled many times—it is an inherently disrespectful behavior.

Compassion for humanity comes with a deep realization that everyone has a unique nature. We are not the same. We co-exist in this world, and each of us has an individual path.

Our "business" with another's life

It is for each of us to determine our own choices. How is it possible to have tolerance and acceptance for others when we assess every life based on an arbitrary determination and want them to do the same for us? If someone's nature does not mesh with ours and we don't want to be around him or her, all we need to do is figure out a responsible way to maintain our own personal preferences; but in doing so, not disregard another's life.

Chasing and pursuing answers as to "why" others choose as they do cannot yield compassion. Another individual's life is his or her own and he or she gets to choose how that life will be lived. With tolerance and acceptance, there can be more peace on the planet. We don't have to like something or someone—and of course, we always want to take care of ourselves so that no harm comes to us and those we love—but it is easier to feel good about ourselves when we appreciate the unique individuality of those around us *and our own.*

10

Danielle's Story

Destinies Unfold from Choices

My boss called me into the conference room without any witnesses. He told me, "I don't appreciate the way you look. You didn't look this way when we hired you two years ago, and we don't like your kind here."

Even when I was a small boy, I loved hanging out with my mom, my aunts, and my mom's girlfriends more than anything else. I loved women and girls. I loved their gossip, their laughter, and their easy banter. I loved being in the kitchen and playing board games and brushing their hair. I played with the boys because I didn't want to be teased, but I was happiest just visiting with the girls and the ladies. I knew I was peculiar, that there was something different about me. However, I learned early on what I could get away with and what I couldn't. I learned to stay within the confines of what was expected of me. I wore cowboy boots and hats and played with guns and went fishing. It wasn't until I was in junior high and high school when my mom and dad were both at work that I had the opportunity to explore another side of me.

I began to play "dress up" with my mother's clothes and walk around in her shoes. I didn't dare risk putting on her perfume, but I wanted to. I held the bottle up very close to my nose and inhaled deeply. I put on makeup and different lipsticks, always very careful to put everything back exactly how I had found it. I knew I was an oddity, but I couldn't help myself. I was compelled to explore. I wanted to look on the outside how I felt on the inside. I wanted with all my heart to not just look like a woman; I wanted to *be* a woman.

～

About this time, my grandmother on my father's side of the family decided that I should accept her offer to send me to an all-boys military academy boarding school in Virginia. She was a graduate of Smith College and believed in the value of a very proper education. Information for several schools arrived in the mail, and my parents pored over the options. It was a wonderful opportunity, and I had the aptitude for it and was a good student. But I knew that I was peculiar enough, oddball enough that I did not belong at an all-boy boarding school. That school didn't want a young man who felt he should have been born a woman. With their stated goals of instilling a "strong moral code" in their students, there was no way that who I was would ever pass muster in their eyes. More importantly, I knew I couldn't accept such an offer even as I was figuring my life out myself. I would have to find a more suitable way to get an education. I greatly disappointed my family by declining this generous opportunity, but they fortunately backed down in their efforts to convince me.

～

I married right out of high school and had a daughter the following year. Within two years my wife left, and it was just my daughter and me. It was several years later, in the mid-80s, strolling down the Walk of Stars in Hollywood on vacation, that I saw the magazines. I was shocked and thrilled to see photos of men who had actually become women! I had no idea it was possible. I knew about men dressed like women—transvestites—but that was of no interest to me. I wanted to learn, to read everything I could about men who had become women. They were called trans-genders or transsexuals. I was astonished and overcome with joy to know that others felt the same way as me. There were special doctors that performed surgeries for men who wanted to become on the outside what they knew to be true for them on the inside. That's what I wanted, and now I knew it was possible. I returned to Oklahoma, where no such magazines existed, where no library contained such information. I told myself it was just a whim and I needed to be practical and live with what was before me. I was a man—with a job to work, a daughter to raise, and obviously a very big secret to keep.

Half a decade later I met my second wife while working overseas for a brief time. We married and had three beautiful daughters together. She wanted a John Wayne husband; when I would get emotional and cry, she would tell me to stop it, that she did not want me to openly express my emotions. She left thirteen years later, and again I was left to raise my children. While she sees our daughters only monthly, that is sufficient time for her. She knows they are safe with me…with the "real mom."

～

With my second divorce behind me, I knew I had yet another opportunity to explore again my secret desire. I got the names of medical specialists who performed sex reassignment surgeries and researched more detailed information, reading over and again the same warning; the path for those embarking on this surgery holds huge obstacles to overcome. The real challenge was not the sex change itself, but what could happen throughout the process of changing from a man to a woman. I was cautioned that my life as I knew it would be turned upside down and that I might be disconnected from everyone I had ever known.

The process of becoming a woman before the actual sex change operation itself is a two- to a three-year process. I immediately began taking the hormones and during the first year my appearance began changing. My facial hair disappeared, my features softened, my hair texture was different, and my voice rose in pitch. I unconsciously adopted a somewhat effeminate way about me. I developed breasts but wore a tight band across my chest and shirts that disguised their existence. My emotions were scattered, and I often felt frail. I was still dressing like a man, but it was clear to everyone there were changes.

No information could have prepared me for the alienation I would feel. Every friend I had abandoned me.

～

My boss called me into the conference room without any witnesses. He told me, "I don't appreciate the way you look. You didn't look this way when we hired you two years ago, and we don't like your kind here." I was very nervous about my job, what with my children to support, and I knew I should consider that there was still time to reverse what I had started. Matter of fact, I had read that at this point, many men do decide it isn't worth it—that there is just too much at risk to self-express in this way. I could simply stop taking the hormones and forever abandon my desire to become a woman. I gave it serious thought and decided that in this job chances were good even if I aborted my plans for my life to please them—even if I would have disowned the part of me that was just beginning to give real breath to my life so they could have what they wanted—nothing would have changed. I would always be considered "undesirable" at this company. So I continued to do my best, and sure enough, a short time later, some trumped-up excuses were created for my discharge.

I elected not to pursue any litigation. I was still accepted as the father and single parent of my children at their school. My children certainly did not need any stress around this process that litigation might cause. I knew they would soon have plenty to face as I moved forward. As well, I had a strong skill set in information technology, so I knew I could find another job.

There is a requirement to meet with a qualified psychologist or psychiatrist for two years in order to be eligible to apply for sex change surgery with a qualified doctor. I also must apply for an official change of gender identification with the government. An additional requirement prior to the authorization of the reassignment surgery is to live out in public for at least six months as a woman. I had a long road ahead. I was in the process, but clearly only at the beginning.

When my colleagues met me at the next job, they probably thought I just had a rather effeminate way about me. They had not seen me before, so they did not know about the changes that had taken place. I was still safe for a while longer.

～

About this time, my father decided that my lifestyle was simply more than he could handle or that I should pursue. He thought my choices reflected poorly on him and my family and saw no value in my pursuing them. He told me, "I cannot stand to look at you." He gave me the ultimatum to change my course with this "thing you are doing" or be written out of his will and his life. He wanted very much to determine my destiny; he truly believed he knew what was best for me. I asked him to please consider his grandchildren in his actions, but that I was going to continue on my path. True to his word, he chose never to see any of us again nor bequeath to my children any of the nearly two million dollars in his estate. My father—a functioning alcoholic—continued to drink himself to death, a disappointed man.

My mother, although surprised and shocked, was always supportive. While we had our differences, I respected her ambition and her courage. Smart, capable, and outspoken, she had run a successful business for her lifetime—in a predominately male working world. I loved my mother as a person and as a good role model. My children were raised with her help and guidance as she shared her joyful and adventuresome spirit. While helping me with all the children likely wore her down, it filled her up in many ways, also.

~

It was a year later when I lost the second job. For a brief time, I nervously thought perhaps it was because of the continued physical changes and submitting the official paperwork at the company for the name and gender change. But the company was simply in financial trouble, and I was on the front end of the layoffs because the entire company folded a short while later.

By this time, I was now a woman in all ways except completing the reassignment surgery itself. I had changed my name from Daniel to Danielle, all the proper paperwork had been completed, I looked like a woman, and my children began calling me Danielle. Sometimes they still called me dad, but they adapted quickly. We purchased a home in a new neighborhood with good high schools. Most importantly, I began to feel like a woman. With two of my three daughters in high school and desiring to go to college, I wasn't sure financially when I would be able to get the surgery, but at least most of the outward public process was complete. I was living as a woman and as a mom.

~

Life has finally settled down in the last few years. No one at my job ever has discovered I was once a man; I still have two children in high school, and they do not need the disruption. I am finally beginning to enjoy the rhythm of a regular life as a woman with motherhood of young children behind me. All my children seem to have adjusted and are moving into their lives in their own way.

I continue to work out five days a week in skin-tight, black biker shorts, trying like any woman to keep the weight gain from happening. My testicles are non-existent from all the years of hormones, and I shower at home. I would not want anything to happen where the ladies would not be comfortable in going to the gym. The women are comfortable with me. I am one of them as much as I can be.

It is somewhat isolating at times, not yet having the surgery, but I am still thrilled with my life. And post-surgery, it will be different as I can openly be a woman in all ways. For now, I just need to be careful. I dare not risk meeting with others in "transition." Not everyone can "pass" as well as I can. Even so, as a tall woman, I wear only low heeled shoes and my face requires careful application of makeup to pull things off. All it would take is someone seeing me with a person in transition who doesn't quite fit for them to be curious about me as well. And I am not really comfortable with the complications that could come from meeting with other transsexuals as my process still isn't completed without the surgery.

Any "interest" on the part of a potential loved one could result in surprises that I still haven't had the sex change surgery. So, although I am a woman in many ways, I cannot respond to any advances either by another woman or a man. I live for now, and have for ten years, a celibate life.

I have a deep yearning to be a woman completely. I want to fully be a correct external manifestation of what is inside of me and has always been inside of me. If I'm lucky enough to fall in love, that would be wonderful. I know it will be with a very special person who can understand and love me for who I am. I know I will be extremely open and up front about my past, as whoever I am with will meet my children as well. I would never want my children to compromise themselves for me in any way. They have witnessed my journey to be anything but a compromise, and I want them to move forward in their lives with that same resolve for themselves and their lives. I acknowledge my choice hasn't been easy for them.

Even if I never fall in love with someone, I know one thing very clearly: I will have died loving myself and making choices for myself that I can respect. I continue taking each step, making each choice, each day moving a bit closer to my heart's desire of living my own life as a woman. Finally.

Stand With Your Truth

Each individual is responsible for making his or her own life work. All people are not the same. All have the same right to make their own choices and pursue their life in their own way, with no harm to others.

When we are truly compelled to move forward, we don't need anyone else to approve of or to be onboard with what we want. It isn't for us to manipulate others so they will be in our corner, just as we don't want others to manipulate us to feel obligated to be supportive of their choices. We want them to be able to call the shots for their own life just as we want to call the shots for ours.

Often, others won't be able to give us support, permission, or participation. They simply can't. They are made up of their own genetics, biases, life experiences, agendas, the loyalties they are serving, and the expectations they have—including the ones they have of us. Sometimes we may even become indignant when others don't give us the validation we are so wanting. In such cases, we may resort to manipulative tactics as we try to coerce them into being cheerleaders for our choices. Others are as entitled to their own opinions as we are to ours.

Fortunately, Danielle knew her father was just going to be who he was. Judging him for that wasn't going to make any difference in her decisions about how to move on with her life. While Danielle offered to make his grandchildren available to him, she did not try to manipulate him and misuse him to support her in her choices. She just moved forward with what she wanted for her own life. It is important to share the reality of these situations with our children as they will also have to make their own best decisions. Had Danielle's father lived longer, they might have chosen to have an adult relationship with their grandfather, had he been willing also.

We know what we value

Sometimes we move on from the friends we once had or find them moving on from us as we make new life choices. This is what happened with Danielle as she just stayed true to who she was and what she wanted. It is not possible to be authentic when we are hiding and fearful—focusing on pleasing others simply to keep them comfortable, or convincing ourselves to act or be a certain way even though it isn't what we want. We know what we value. In following rules that have no meaning for us—rules that simply don't fit for who and how we are—we may deny ourselves our own humanity. In living authentically in each moment, we honor it.

We don't need to give reasons, explanations, or stories for our choices. We don't need to know why something is compelling to us; it just is.
We may not cognitively know anyway, but we believe in our desires and in the pursuit of them.

Throw away the tally sheet

We are our own experts. Our true desires—our individual truth—belong to each one of us. Our senses alert us; our body informs us. Sometimes we try to use a tally sheet of pros and cons to assist us in making choices. We stare at the list, with its "logical" conclusion of more pros than cons, and we know—our body knows—that whatever it was we were assessing or considering, we don't want it at this time and maybe never will. All the "pros" won't make it so. Basing a decision on a tally sheet dismisses the innate accuracy and strength of our own authentic desires.

Daniel's journey to follow his truth to become Danielle was unlikely to be affirmed by any tally sheet. The same is true for decisions many of us are assessing; a list created by our head ("the king") won't necessarily reveal our strongest desires.

Often, once we begin to move in the direction of our truth, the formulas shift and change. This movement toward living a reality-based life is a game-changer, because what we don't see, what we don't listen to, and what we deny seeing can diminish and injure us. An important outcome of this shifting to a reality-based life is that, in no longer suffering at our own hands, our sense of personal fulfillment and happiness increases. We feel open to more possibilities. We may even eventually decide to go off in a completely new direction based on new information once we begin moving forward with our initial intention. We need not talk ourselves out of our truly desired choices by giving credence to pre-set notions, arbitrary speculations, or musings on some tally sheet—it is likely better to throw it away and just pay attention to the truth that resides within.

When we choose to stand with our truth, our better destinies unfold by those choices made from that truth.

11

Rashid's Story

Parenting Rumana

*I had never behaved this way before, and I had never wanted to be
that kind of parent. I was ashamed. I was just so convinced that she
had no idea what she was doing, that she was messing
with her destiny.*

We realized when our daughter Rumana was very young that she
was a prodigy.

Both her mother and I were biomedical scientists. It is not easy in
Bangladesh to earn the right or the money to travel out of our country,
to explore the world, but we did so by becoming experts in our fields.
Rumana demonstrated an interest in the biomedical field as a child, wanting to become a medical doctor, perhaps even a specialist. We provided
her every opportunity to get the education and exposure she needed to
become brilliant and accomplished in this field. We strongly felt it was
her destiny.

As her parents, we truly believed we knew what was best for Rumana,
and, given her potential and our country and culture, which choices could
offer her the best opportunities for her chosen career. We had spoken
at conferences around the world, and we wanted Rumana to have those
same experiences—and more. What parent wouldn't? We felt we were

doing everything right on her behalf so she would be able to access the freedom that could provide her a great life.

When Rumana was about fifteen, although already becoming accomplished in her burgeoning field and slated to begin university the following year in England with full scholarships to become a doctor, she began spending more and more time with what her mother and I called, "playing around on the computer." What had started as a tool for research was turning into more than just a break from her studies. The computer gaming industry was in its infancy, and Rumana seemed to live on the computer around the clock when she wasn't studying her sciences. It seemed like a total waste of time to her mother and me, as well as a major distraction from her goal.

Each time we tried to talk to her about her increasing obsession with computer playing, she claimed she was just exploring. But we sensed it was becoming something more. For us, that meant she could be throwing away her opportunities if she didn't get back on track and stick to the plan that she had laid out for herself. She had wanted it, and we assisted, but it was her plan. We couldn't understand what was happening.

～

It wasn't that we hadn't seen this same measure of passion in her before. Even at her age, Rumana had been an active volunteer in the medical field for several years. She had worked alongside some great doctors in a few remote villages the past two summers; and two days a week, when her classes were over, she volunteered, teaching villagers about food preparation, body movements, and monitoring their own health. She interpreted medical reports for them and enjoyed helping people learn what they could do to create new habits for healthier choices. The computer had made a world of difference in getting access to information to the people of our country, but the deciphering of that information was very problematic because of literacy rates as well as the entire idea of personal responsibility and choice. Our country has been experiencing escalating obesity rates, as well as other health issues that typically plague developing nations.

Rumana put her whole self into everything she did. Sitting on the computer, playing video games, and doing what she called "exploring the social content of the Internet" just did not seem the best route to a serious medical career in our opinion. Her mother and I had been given opportunities through our education and work that most could only dream of. We were very invested in making certain that Rumana took advantage of the opportunities presented to her and not waste them.

As deadlines closed in, we felt immense pressure from our families and those who had mentored and assisted Rumana in accessing her unique life experiences. We were encouraged to manipulate and cajole and punish Rumana for not following her pre-determined path. We were accused of aiding her in throwing her life away and creating a self-entitled and narcissistic child. We were repeatedly told that her wants and her desires did not matter, that she was our daughter and it was our responsibility to get her prepared for her life. We expressed our concerns to Rumana, strongly and sometimes contentiously pointing out what we believed was in her best interest, hoping to get her back on track. She resisted our pressure.

∽

In our culture, it is believed that parents know what is best for their children and "good" children are obedient, but Rumana had been reared to be her own self. Actually, we hadn't had much choice in the matter; it seemed she had always charged forth, and we were sort of pulled along. My wife and I had good friends, our own individual, vibrant lives, and we were happily married. We rarely bragged about our daughter to our friends; to have said much would have involved defending our way of rearing her. It was just easier that some things were not said outside our close-knit trio—we understood that each one of us was unique in our own way. I guess, somewhere in all of the pressure, I forgot about that.

My low point was when I got so angry and yelled at Rumana that she was wasting her life and bringing shame to our family with her damn computer games. It wasn't until she was crying and her computer was lying broken on the floor where I had thrown it in a fit of rage that I realized I was out of control. I had never behaved this way before, and I had never wanted to be that kind of parent. I was ashamed. I was just so convinced that she had no idea what she was doing, that she was messing with her destiny. But I was wrong, and on some level I knew it.

∽

Finally, we sat down as a family and talked. Her mother and I agreed to stay out of her choices and her process and give her every opportunity to explore her new passion without our watching and hovering. To do this, we almost had to put tape over our mouths and tie our bodies to chairs. We upset our well-intentioned families and others with our decision and finally had to make it a topic that was off-limits to them. This was not easy to do. Just the same, we took a leap of faith, albeit with reservations.

Rumana continued to pursue her new interest. Within six months, it was clear that her previous dream of becoming a medical specialist and doctor was not going to happen—at least not now. We waited. We held our breath—partly so we wouldn't speak and partly because that's just what is done when one is nervous. We were nervous. She began to create a new plan, but because of timing, she had to turn down the scholarship she had been offered from England in order to apply for a different program and scholarship in another field--a new field where she had no experience and no contacts for recommendations. She remained focused and aware as she put one foot in front of the other, taking steps to pursue her new direction.

∾

Rumana applied for and did receive a scholarship from the University of Cambridge and went there to study. The early programs in the now exploding field of Medical Informatics were just coming into being at that time. Through observation of the social content of the Internet, adverse events and predictions of trends in health are studied. Games and programs for cell phones that monitor and track healthy behaviors—creating a form of entertainment to those who want to be healthy—are now marketed.

Rumana was honored with an award from the Medical Research Council in Great Britain, which is the equivalent of the National Institutes of Health in America. She has already earned distinction in her field and travels internationally now, even as a graduate student. She is the happiest person we know. She has several job offers already and currently even does consulting work. We say nothing. The tape is still on our mouths. It should probably stay there because otherwise we might be seen with our mouths hanging open, gaping in amazement.

∾

It's always easy to look back, isn't it? But I will share something. When we aren't silently applauding for who she is as a person, we are patting ourselves on the back, grateful for the way we chose to parent her. From her infancy, we raised our daughter to follow her heart, as challenging as it was at times—often testing our self-restraint. Each time we thought about interfering in her life choices, somehow we came to know it wasn't okay to do that. Clearly, she has chosen something that brings her joy; and while we finally realized that even though it wasn't what we would have chosen for her, we are thankful that we reminded ourselves that her life is *her* life. Even if it hadn't turned out so well—even if it had cost her the opportunities we valued for her—we learned to trust that her journey is her own.

A Life Pursuit is Private—It is Out of Bounds

This life is ours to pursue whatever truly is our own desire.

It is the natural course of development of any organism to become self-reliant. We can see this even before we learn to walk or declare "no!" If the development of our self-reliance is encouraged and not suppressed or interrupted, nature takes its course as we move on to fulfill our innate nature's true desires through our actions. In doing so, our internal sense of authority is strengthened; we learn to trust ourselves. There is pleasure in taking on new and different experiences and in feeling productive or being effective in a way we desire. As we become more self-reliant, more and better options exist for us, and our choices are in harmony with the morphing organism of who and how we are.

Thinking we know what is best for our children, or anyone else, does them a great disservice. We risk acting as their life director; we may come to believe we can second-guess what is best for them.

How can we possibly even imagine what is best or "right" for another individual? What is right for others is what they feel is right, not what we may believe is right for them. How many times have we "helped" our children along their path, influencing and choosing? Age appropriate and safety interventions notwithstanding, how many doses of parental help are given before the unintended side effects dismantle a child's own autonomy, thus denying him or her the ability to live or develop as a healthy individual?

Children need to discover this ability to trust their own capabilities through untethered life experiences. We want to openly share our truth with our children when asked, but also remember never to upstage our children's truth. When they are guided by a smile or a frown or voices of approval or disapproval, they don't get to discover their own grounding. This can cause them to second-guess their own authentic reactions to their choices and make assessments based on those sideline cues, rather than relying on their own sense of themselves. They may even change their choices because of only that. This micro-management from the sidelines has the unintended consequence of creating interference and confusion that keeps our children from learning, growing, and developing—just trying to figure out who and how they are. It's no wonder then, when they have an experience that is injurious to them, they may have trouble handling it.

Shortcuts shortchange your child's development

Often we give our child the message that we want to offer him the benefit of our experience—even though at that same age, we can recall that we thought we could make the choice just fine without anyone's help. Why the disconnect? How is it that we don't seem able to recall our own childhood process of trial and error and how valuable it was? We know that if our child's choice doesn't work out for her, she'll need to self-correct. But often we cannot trust that she will prevail in the process. Perhaps we hope to give her a shortcut, but what we end up doing is shortchanging her development. We upstage her natural attempts at a full life.

If we want to assist our children to develop the skills of self-reliance, we want to surrender the child's authority to the child, not compete with her for it. When she is embarking on some other unfamiliar occurrence, like going for an interview or tackling a new project, we parents tend to want to advise her as to how best to accomplish something based on our own experiences. If our child wants to know what worked for us, that's fine; but that isn't necessarily what is going to work for her. She is unique. We *don't* know—we *can't* know—how it will work best for her, and if we do not let her develop this sense of internal authority, she will not be willing to take risks. For anything. Without sufficient development, she may choose non-action rather than action.

Do you trust that your child will figure it out?

There are many ways in which we risk robbing a child of the ability to discern—to recognize between or distinguish among possible options and pursue something desired. Perhaps we make, on her behalf, what we think are her "best choices." But caretaking doesn't mean having our nose in places it doesn't belong.

We all have potential, and it is ours to pursue in ways that compel us, should that be our desire.

We don't know what any child's destiny is, what her multiple destinies are. When we say, "Oh, she'll never be an 'A' student," how do we know what she'll ever be or never be? How do we know what her possible destinies are, based on the choices she will make? Her life belongs to her. If we are intrusively involved in her choice-making, then we are in danger of manipulating her life and, therefore, interfering with the development of her authentic self. In this way she may never be able to trust herself with her own choices. Is that love? We may say, "But I did what I thought was in her best interest; she has so much potential."

The notion that we should think in terms of our potential when pursuing what is desired can be a distraction. All kinds of potential and possibilities are available to us, and we are living them every minute of every day in the fulfillment of a life lived by moving from one wanted experience to another.

What do you believe about your child? Do you trust that she will figure it out? Does your *child* believe she can figure it out? Does your child trust her own capabilities to make choices, to self-correct if or when necessary? Have you, the parent, surrendered that authority to where it belongs? Have you respected that process?

Surrender your child's internal authority to its rightful owner—the child

Sometimes we just don't want to surrender our children's internal authority to them, often believing it is our job to guide, help, and advise. Frequently what happens instead, however, is that we misuse those intentions, and we attempt to mold, reconstruct, dictate, or imprint them. We may take our own conclusions—arrived at from *our* experiences and from observations of our child relative to *our* own life—and impose those on our children. Particularly if we still aren't convinced that we can make good decisions for ourselves as an individual and a parent, we may have difficulty appreciating the missteps and self-corrections our child may need to go through in learning to choose better.

All this disregards and disrespects the sense of autonomy and joy children experience when they are encouraged to make their own choices and arrive at their own conclusions. Doing so also denies children the feeling of personal reward that comes from making choices, however they may unfold.

Our children receive and achieve many benefits from their choices, whether the outcomes are favorable or unfavorable. This is part of the process of growing up that leads to self-reliance.

When we do not surrender to our children their own internal authority, we deny them the opportunity to develop their own life skills.

No claim to "ownership" of another's life

Rumana's parents faced a serious dilemma. Even after they came to their own clarity, they still had to fend off pressure from family and others who had acted as mentors and support people and therefore felt it was okay to foist upon Rumana what they believed was best for her. Even if an individual were to assist a child with access to pursue what he or she was interested in at the time, that does not give that individual—or anyone else—the right of "ownership" to any aspect of that child's life.

While we don't want our children walking all over us, we don't want to walk all over them either. The commonly-held notions that the parent is higher and children are lower, that the parent is king and children are subjects, that the parent is right and children are wrong, and that parents always know what is best for their children can inhibit them from growing up and figuring out their lives. There need be no hierarchy of status within a family, just mutual respect for all its members as simply people who are at different and varying levels of development. As parents, we always have the option to enlighten our children by exampling our own well-lived lives.

How can parents best guide their children in this process?

As we assist our children in building their skills for making choices, we want to remind them to honor their body's knowingness, to check in with themselves and to recognize what is resonating with them. We want to teach them that the cells of the body actually have intelligence and respond to ideas, and that this is to be valued. There is a natural evolution of access to information and choices as our children mature. It is our job as parents to invite this, in both dialogue and in our genuine response in the conversations and exchanges we have with them. Their interests or passions—their innate wants—are true for them.

Our job is not to find resolution for them, but to help them develop their skills to gain access and make informed choices so they can sort things out on their own and move toward what they want. How else do they learn to take the bus to get to soccer practice? How else do they learn to pack their own snacks and think ahead with awareness that their body will be hungry at some point while they are away from home? How else do they figure out how to earn the money for something they wish to purchase? We want to encourage them to find their own voice as we give regard to what they have to say. As they develop and mature, the sense of satisfaction they gain from making their own choices is of great value and should not be underestimated.

Within a small or sheltered environment, there is limited choice and, therefore, limited experiences for the responsibility of choice. A protected environment limits the privilege of choice in the real world. In a bigger playground or less protected environment, skills for assessment and discernment must be developed quickly to make determinations such as whether an individual is friend or foe. We want to be mindful to prepare them with exposure for practice for any environment they may find themselves in.

When given the opportunity, children will—just as adults do—choose things they want to attend to. They will seek out the path that satisfies their curiosity and pursue it and all that it may offer. We want them to. Yes—as safely as possible—we want them to learn to organize themselves and be able to move into better spaces for more and better access.

We can assist our children in learning that there are consequences in choice making. We can ask them to think of what might be some possibilities for a choice they are considering and then ask them to think about the consequences of those possibilities so they move forward with fuller knowledge. We can listen to them and then help them to consider their options. We can ask them if, given a choice, they believe they could handle the consequences—the outcomes—however they may play out. We can trust that as our children are pursuing their lives, there are no "mistakes"—just an evolutionary developmental process, a path chosen in any given moment, a choice they are making and we can communicate that trust to them. We can ask them what new options might be created if they went with a particular choice. In this way, the child learns to consider and anticipate her life choices beyond the moment. These are valuable skills that they can begin learning at a young age as we guide them to know themselves, what they want, and how they wish to choose and become more able with practice in choosing.

We each find our own harmony with reality

A child's life pursuit is private; it is out of bounds to others. We let society teach them, as they bump up against reality and find their own harmony with it. We may think we know what is best for them, but we can only make assumptions based on our own life experiences. Ours is ours; theirs is theirs. Our responsibility as parents is to create a safe environment for our children to become themselves.

Whether or not we believe our child is equipped to choose well, at some point we will want to surrender responsibility for her own life choices to her. If we deny our child the opportunity to take on that responsibility, we may be in a sense, "patterning" her for a life of dependency. Under these disabling circumstances, she may not function independently in life and act on her own behalf. If we want optimal developmental opportunities for her, then we will want to welcome and encourage her in taking responsibility for her own age-appropriate choices, beginning at an early age. While we may not agree with what she chooses, it is enough for a parent to simply encourage her to take responsibility for her own choices as she discovers what appeals to her.

Our children are entitled to use their lives for their own fulfillment and pleasure—not with the objective of reaching goals and attaining a set list of pre-determined accomplishments set by others. Each individual can find her own path that aligns easily with her nature. We certainly saw Rumana do just that.

12

Integrity Owns Its Own Authority

Many young people in this new generation are self-declaring, hoping against hope they will find a self they can love. We want them to. Isn't that what many of us still deeply desire for ourselves?

Integrity is primal. It owns its own authority—at nine months or ninety-nine years. When we are whole, integrated—living on the outside as we are within—we live a harmonious, open-hearted life. We take on actions or commitments that are in accord with our basic nature. We try to choose correctly for ourselves and to self-assess, self-correct, and figure things out as we go for what we want, realizing that our desires can change. It is simple; it isn't in our head. It is in our gut and our heart and our whole being. We notice there is an ease in our life when we move forward with that which compels us.

Contrast that to when we operate from a list of things we *should* or *should not* or *ought* or *ought not* do. We find we create stories, excuses, and rationalizations based on those listed items. We compromise and pretzel ourselves around, and we don't live our better destiny. We present a false image to others. We con ourselves; it is possible for us to become so accomplished at this and do it so automatically that we don't even know we are doing it or where the lie ends and our reality begins. In doing so, we become vulnerable to being misused, overused, or abused. Others may manipulate us with everything from guilt to tactics of reward and punishment, judgments of right and wrong and good and bad, and insistence on adherence to social proprieties that may not express our values. Some of us, in response to those attempts, will become adept at being the victim and the martyr. It can start to feel normal and comfortable to relinquish responsibility for living the life we want. And once we resign ourselves to playing those roles, it can become the way we identify ourselves.

When we seek to become conscious of living our own life, we can take on experiences that are in accord with our nature, with our heart's desire. This, however, may make others around us uncomfortable—particularly those who have known us as our more malleable selves.

Welcoming free and open expression as part of healthy development

Many parents and grandparents stress about the way their grown children or young people are openly and freely expressing themselves these days. When they experience children acting in a manner that is outside their approval and their comfort zone, these parental authorities may take it personally; they might find it offensive or embarrassing, and sometimes feelings are hurt by the directness. They may prefer to have children and youth mind their manners and not express themselves so openly and truthfully. They may prefer not to know. They may prefer that others cover up their artistic body wear and clean up their language.

Yes, many individuals (youth included) are self-expressing. They are saying, *"This is who I am!"* Still, some parents persist in creating stories to tell their friends in attempts to make their children look a certain way so that they, the parents, can look good. It can become more an act of image management than parenting. Parents and grandparents are sometimes willing to let the charade continue so their ego can be fed. This focus on image can cripple a child's growth, even an adult child.

In the natural evolutionary developmental process of growing up, children figure out who and how they are, developing their character and becoming their own authentic selves. To do this, they begin to self-declare, take on experiences, make mistakes and learn from them, and develop as normal, healthy adults. They learn to follow their own path. We may find them being forthright and open about flaws and dysfunctions. These kids may be cursing; they may be sullen. Yes, often, they are dead-on honest, and many parents and grandparents are finding this stressful.

It isn't helpful to children's development when parents jump in and fix everything, cater to them, or pretend that things are a way that they truly are not. These intrusions do not serve a child's normal, healthy maturation. So why do some parents do this? It is possible some view their children's behaviors or actions as selfish because they had their own agendas for them, and the child's behaviors or choices are in conflict with those agendas. Some may feel it necessary to manage their personal or family image within their social spheres; and perhaps for others, it may be that they have become overly conscious of comparison thinking, evaluating their own parenting capability by comparing their children's behaviors, actions, and successes to those of others.

Some parents may wrap their own lives around their children's lives

Sometimes parents interfere in their children's development simply because they don't have their own lives. How many parents decided to make their life all about managing their kids' lives and continue to talk about their developing children's private lives because they haven't created a life of their own? Sometimes children's lives become coffee table conversation pieces with parents having no compunction about telling others the intimate details of those private lives, even though they are being sorted out hourly and daily as children grow up. But our children's stories are not ours to tell; their lives are not ours to live or broadcast or second-guess. Our children have one shot at this life just like we all do.

It is not okay to expropriate our children's lives. What they create belongs to them. It is important for a parent—or any individual—to create for his or her own self.

Caring for one's own needs and self-interests is self-care, not selfishness

Oftentimes, we will hear people say of the younger generations that they are self-serving, entitled, and narcissistic. That isn't necessarily true. They may be more truthful and transparent in stating what they want—more than any other generation—and this straightforward approach may not be convenient for some, or it may affront some who find it unfamiliar. But self-care and healthy autonomy and living one's truth are not selfish or narcissistic, and no one wants to be irresponsibly labeled as such. Labels have often been used as just another way to manipulate others not to pursue their truth, to do and be only who and how some may want them to be, and thereby deny them the experience of developing their own integrity and living it.

Confusion is generated by a limited societal view that lumps together two completely different concepts: self-care and healthy self-interest are often not clearly distinguished from the act of selfishly disregarding others.

By pursuing their own life and acting in their own self-interest and happiness, our youth are taking responsibility for their own involvement in daily choices that culminate in different outcomes and different experiences. In following their own paths, they are dealing in reality and not laying their lives on others; this approach is requiring them to be responsible for how their lives go. There is no blame, no *use* of another. When they act in integrity and healthy self-interest, they are not interested in having someone else pay the price for any of their life outcomes, and they are not claiming that anyone owes them something. They are not asking another to prop them up and make them look good. They are just living their own lives responsibly, following their own path and self-declaring.

People can recognize when someone is pursuing his own life and going after what he wants. People can observe when another is involved in his own healthy self-care, which is a positive and important part of his developmental journey. Those who live their lives this way are dealing with reality out of natural self-interest and may freely express that reality if they are encouraged to learn, fall, get back up, struggle, and mature as normal healthy individuals. Recognizing integrity, people know when youth—*or others*—are genuine in their pursuits, their choices, and their actions. They just might not like it.

Giving without an agenda

When we create for our own selves, we bring the full expression of who and how we are into every situation. We are genuine. We then can give without an agenda. Until then, how can any individual or parent be trusted with what they are giving or wanting to receive? One becomes a whole being by coming to one's truth—no agendas are involved. The more developed the parents—the more self-reliant, self-correcting, and self-respecting—the less attached they will be to any agendas that involve fulfilling their own needs at their child's expense. As parents, we want to be able to offer the gifts of friendship and love to our children free of any agenda.

People who have their own life share differently from people who don't. This is true for any and all relationships, including our precious relationship with our children. The best thing we parents can do for our children is to example a well-lived life.
Our own life.

13

Clara's Story

For No Good Reason
—A Change of Heart

A relationship is like two formulas coming together; it can only become what it becomes, and that cannot be dictated by commitment. If the quality of the relationship keeps transforming and improving, then it does. It's just as possible that it won't.

Clara was a good mother, a good wife, a good worker. Her life was orderly, and she had enjoyed it immensely for many years. Her two children were in high school, her husband was a loving man, and her job gave her a lot of satisfaction. She had no idea how it all came about. Nothing really precipitated it. There was nothing that "happened." She just knew, her body knew, that she no longer wanted to be married. There was no reason. It was, quite simply, time to leave. After Clara had the strong feeling that it was time to leave, she waited. She believed that everything would be much less complicated, easier, if she could wait until the children graduated. Her situation wasn't bad—it just wasn't the experience she wanted any longer. It would be so much more convenient in two years. Two years wasn't very long, was it? So she waited six months. And still, her body told her it was time to leave—even more strongly than before. Always an upbeat woman, she became unhappy and easily frustrated. She felt like she was dragging herself through her days and had trouble focusing both at work and at home. She knew staying was living a lie. They talked.

There were no problems to solve. Both respected each other's choices. Both acknowledged that if they were not in the institution of marriage, Clara simply would have told him she was moving on, worked out the details regarding any shared property, and discussed things with the children. The issue at hand was not the wonderful past they had shared, the good times they had had. They weren't interested in making any of that anything other than what it was. They were not interested in making anyone wrong or anyone right. Clara's husband knew his wife, his friend, his lover of many years, wanted something different than to stay married to him. Clara knew she would be conning herself and her husband to stay and exampling something to her children she knew was incorrect for her to do. She had no idea how everything would work out. She was just willing to move forward with what she wanted, beginning with the first step.

~

People often want to know how negative a relationship has to be in order to feel justified in leaving it. Nothing has to be labeled wrong or bad. If everything inside of you is calling for a different experience than the one you are in, then it is time to leave. It really is our own unique nature that decides. People's desires change. As we develop, we make new choices for our lives that result in freedom, in liberation, in joy. We may have gotten into a deal, a friendship, or a marriage thinking it would be forever, but when we look at our reality and recognize a false premise, it may be time to reevaluate how we choose to live. Staying in a marriage—or any relationship or situation—if it isn't where you want to be, is generally not in your better interests. Working out the timing and the manner of disengagement may be challenging, but you want to be honest and earnest in your truth, to be authentic and mobilize with self-authority for your own life.

Well-intended friends who want to know "why" don't need to know anything. During the time of shifts in relationships, it is not your job to make everybody else comfortable—nobody other than your children. It is enough that you get yourself together to be able to make the transition. If someone wants to leave a relationship of any kind, then as a partner, our love for that individual would have us say, "Go and blessings be with you; thank you for the treasured time we shared." And if it wasn't a good relationship for one or the other of you, then go and hope you can take the understanding you might have gained from the relationship. But try to stay clear of the stories and just move on.

≈

That is what happened with Clara. Her loving husband remained a loving individual. The quality of the well-developed character they each had when married did not change when they parted. And the quality relationship they had as individuals with each other and as parents with their children remained so without the marriage. Yes, their children did the back and forth thing that children sometimes do when living in two homes, but they also received something very special. They were able to witness the beautiful reality of who and how their mother was and who and how their father was as unmarried parents and as whole individuals. They were able to witness their mother's courage, which allowed her to follow her heart's desire; and they were able to witness their father's courage as he made the transition easy and graceful for everyone. As a working woman, Clara moved on with her life, taking responsibility for her finances and her new home—in her own way. Both children were able to experience two very strong, whole, and loving parents who acknowledged that sometimes things don't play out the way everyone thought they would. They learned that marriage can be a beautiful arrangement, if and only if both people want to be in that marriage.

Several years later, after working productively in one field, Clara's daughter decided to switch careers to a completely different type of work, an interest and a passion she'd had for many years. She did not know if she could get work in that field, even once she was trained for it. She did not know if the relationship she was in would remain intact if she left for two years to go to school in another town. She did not know how anything would unfold. But she knew who she was as a whole individual, and she knew what she wanted and moved toward it, taking action and trusting herself to figure it out. Leading with her well-developed sense of self—as had been exampled to her by her parents—made choosing well easier for her.

Well-Developed Character is Our Refinement

Marriage isn't a goal. If marriage were a goal, then the spouse would be a "what" and not a "who."

There are many wonderful reasons people want to be married, but when someone no longer wants to be married—such as it was with Clara—staying married doesn't change that. You can't manipulate yourself into believing something that isn't true for you. Truth is truth—how you feel is how you feel. If you truly love someone, is it possible that this is what you could want for him or her? Marriage isn't a goal. If marriage were a goal, then the spouse would be a "what" not a "who." Where is the humanity in how one regards a spouse when he or she becomes merely the tool for the accomplishment of one's goal? He or she is no longer a "who"—an individual with a life to be lived—because that individual has then become a "what," a means to an end, simply a way for one to reach a goal.

Leaving a marriage—or any relationship or job or situation—does not represent failure; it is just a personal choice like millions of other choices. Staying in a marriage—or any relationship or job or situation—does not represent success; it is just a personal choice like millions of other choices.

When you consider marriage a goal, then to leave the marriage implies you failed at your goal. The notion that staying in a marriage—for any reason other than because you want to be there—is noble or the right thing to do needs to be examined closely. People who find themselves in relationships that have ceased to satisfy generally find that acting with a true heart means leaving the relationship.

Perhaps you always thought committedness was a virtue. But now you are beginning to understand that well-developed character is our refinement. Honoring the accuracy of what our nature is expressing is our refinement. For you to develop yourself, you want to be true to your own self. Are you now compelled to change something in your life? When we choose from our truth—our authentic selves—our choices are better matched for who and how we are. We find them nurturing and rewarding.

People stay married for myriad reasons, such as comfort, security, companionship, love, or convenience. There is nothing wrong with any choice; just know what you are choosing and how it serves you to stay. If your priority is to have an intact family, and for that you are willing to make concessions for other desires that may never be expressed, then that is your truth. Just call it what it is and be true to your own choice. Be at peace with whatever way you go. Or if your spouse is nothing but a paycheck to you, why wait until you are frustrated and in an angry moment and blurt out something such as, "You are nothing but a paycheck."? Rather, let your spouse know that in a moment of kindness, and he or she can determine if the arrangement you have is still one your spouse desires. If the two of you decide you can enjoy your lives together under those circumstances, then so be it. And when things change—when one doesn't want to agree to the arrangement any longer—he or she is free to walk away. No matter what you choose, there is no obligation, just truth.

Burnt feet

Do we need permission to change all those absolute statements we made as who we were—at that time? Are we not free to change our minds and our directions and acknowledge that right for others as well? People evolve in different ways. Maybe something or someone never was a match, or maybe became unmatched. Regardless, if something has ceased to satisfy, then it has ceased to satisfy. It may be that it is more convenient for us to hold others to their commitment; we often want to hold people's feet to the fire. We say "but you said" or "but you promised" or "but you committed." We may still be able to persuade and manipulate others to keep the original agreement by holding their feet to the fire, but we will live with the stink of burnt feet.

Experiences are temporary

All relationships are terminal. They either end in separation or in death. That is the stark reality of a tangible, material existence. Experiences are temporary, and each day offers a new choosing. If it is a quality "match made in heaven" kind of relationship, then it may well last until someone dies—with daily joy and thanksgiving—and that is a splendid thing; any match made so nearly perfect is a marvelous thing. Relationships, as well as marriages, last as long as they last. There is value in making the most out of every experience; and when it ceases to satisfy, we move to another experience that we do desire.

In living our lives, we all try to pursue that which we desire. Something in the nature of an individual desires an experience. We take that experience and extract from it what is freely given. At some point, we may find that what wanted to be fulfilled within our nature has been fulfilled. With respect and responsibility, well-developed and whole people—people with integrity—then move from one satisfying experience pursued and freely offered to another.

Discerning a "similarity to natures"

Throughout our life, we try to develop our life skills for self-authority and self-reliance so that we can declare what we want and be prepared to go after that. In choosing our mates, we want to come to the relationship as a whole individual seeking another whole individual to share a life together. We want to develop ourselves so that we will be better able to choose, thus giving us the opportunity to have a better quality experience in our relationships. Ideally, we want to learn to recognize a "similarity to natures." When we recognize this, and choose someone similarly healthy and whole to us, then there is a possibility of sufficient blending of our natures. In being out and about living life then, when each individual brings the new and strange and different experiences back into the relationship, those can enhance the variety and freshness of the relationship, if both people have an interest in them.

Clara and her husband shared similar values, and the quality they gave each other they also gave to themselves. Their similar natures blended sufficiently that they enjoyed their lives together immensely. With a similarity in our value systems and character and interests, our natures often blend sufficiently, and there can be a lovely match. In this way, true and deep friendships are built.

The exchange between Clara and her husband was never about what each one *needed* from the other because they weren't able to create it in their own life. Rather, the exchange was unique to what each as a whole individual brought into it. The relationship could then—as Clara and her husband were able to do as individuals—continue to evolve. When Clara wanted to move on from the relationship, the integrity—the wholeness—that her character and the character of her husband brought to the relationship remained consistent.

The character whereby you live on the outside as you are within—being an individual of integrity—makes for easier and more harmonious life experiences.

Respect and dignity

A relationship is like two formulas coming together; it can only become what it becomes, and what it becomes cannot be dictated by commitment, by staying power. It cannot be forced, contrived, or manipulated. If the quality of the relationship keeps transforming and improving, then it does. It's just as possible that it won't.

Clara's marriage was composed of two whole people of character, and that made all the difference; they offered respect and dignity to each other in the ease of terminating their marriage and in being whole individuals as parents to their children. If Clara had not acted on her truth, she would have been conning herself and her family. She might have waited and hoped that something would be different or that a "really good reason" would come to light that would justify her desire to take action to leave the marriage, but she knew better than to do that; her body's wisdom let her know that it was time to leave, and she paid attention. She spoke what was true for her, and she acted on it.

Staying power

Most of us enjoy a good celebration, a shout out, a rousing "Hooray!" And we do so in a number of ways in our lives. For example, we tend to positively recognize and reward what might best be called "staying power." In marriages, years are marked by special anniversaries with names of great value like gold and silver. In work, future employers smile upon those whose résumés demonstrate it and gold watches are given to commemorate years of dependable service. Yes, it can be wonderful indeed to rejoice with others who are enjoying the life they have chosen, staying because that is their deepest desire.

We may want to remember, however, to celebrate with and acknowledge those courageous men, women, and children who choose another path based on their deepest desires, and that is *not* to stay. They choose to leave, to move on. These individuals walk away from what they no longer want and toward what they do want, responsibly and with no harm to others. Moment by moment, they bring their wholeness to each new exchange, trusting themselves to figure it out. Engaged, curious, innovative, adaptable, agile, creative, truthful. They are continually preparing themselves with the life skills necessary for the freedom to choose responsibly and in so doing, they offer dignity and respect to others.

Often, with their movements, these individuals are expected to provide a story, a justification so that there were good reasons for them to act as they did. If what we are seeking in all our experiences, including our relationships, are those qualities that blend sufficiently with our own nature, then we may want to rethink the questions we ask and the value we give to the truth of those answers. We may want to actively observe and assess. Where is the appreciation for those who dare to take risks on themselves? More importantly, if that individual is you, are you appreciating yourself?

It is better to assess your reality and speak truthfully and then make some choices. Few people want to get to the end of their life and realize that they never lived their *own* life, that they lived a lie for someone else. There is no conflict within when following your truth.

Well-developed character, rather than committedness, is our refinement. There will naturally be concerns about the genuine engagement in an experience when agreeing only to "show up" becomes *the life*. Let's make it easy for all of us as individuals, whether we leave or stay, to seek out the experiences that we believe provide us possibilities for enhancing our lives. In this way, dignity prevails.

Some would claim the only "staying power" worth celebrating
in a life, is staying true to one's own truth.
That's a life well-lived, a life to celebrate.

14

Loyalty's Story

Your Life Is Your Own —Take It Back

What happened to the good times? You can be sure no one ever leaves because of the good times. One leaves because the sum total of the experience is no longer desired.

We all know "what" they are: dark, thieving forces revealing themselves as addictions and other unwell and unwanted behavior patterns that show up in the nature of an individual. Neither is a who. A who has spirit, a resonance, a heart that beats with love. These forces are dark urgings, longings—black and insidious—hurled into space and landing on the doorstep of a weakened relationship with one's self. Her name is Clitoria Huntinpecker. His name is Dick Deboner.

They have one goal: to be mistress or master of the life, to steal the life, to extract and suck and f**k the life force out of you or someone you love. How do they do this? Upon graciously accepting the volunteered invitation into one's life, they enslave.

Clitoria Huntinpecker and Dick Deboner are very good at what they do. They have practiced their craft. They go where the craving is always strongest. Where the chi has no argument, it usually prevails over the less conscious. When the wanting is so strong, there is no stopping. Where the loss of money, integrity, health, self-respect, lovers, children, friends, and freedom cease to matter in exchange for enslavement by what is so desired, they flourish.

Yes, upon acceptance of your mate's invitation, they arrive. And however Clitoria Huntinpecker or Dick Deboner eventually appear, they are, at first, alluring and charming. They sweet talk, dazzle, glitter, and impress. They don't "do it" to your mate; they are not to blame. They simply exist as a possible experience to be chosen. Something in your mate desires them, invites them.

Your mate's new "lovers" offer excitement, titillation, and stimulation, making them feel more alive and powerful and satisfied and gratified than they feel with you or with anything else in their lives. You may be mistaken in that you have never noticed this before, but it was always there, waiting to reveal itself…this hunger existed in your mate's nature. Whether it's pussy, porn, poker, pay, pride, or power, something in your mate welcomes them into their lives—in whatever form—and they thrill or satisfy in the basest way.

Your mate's choices belong to your mate

Ah, sweet taste of the first drink of bourbon. Perhaps, upon coming home, you see him ever so slowly begin to undress her. You feel like a voyeur as your husband removes the purple velvet wrap from around her beautiful body. You watch as he removes the red wax from her lips that seal her wanting mouth. You hear the clanking of the ice cubes against the glass, the call to attention that he is home, that your husband is in charge now. He takes his first drink, which will be followed by too many more. His mistress…he drinks of her juices, smacking his lips, sighing contentedly. She caresses him gently as he removes his jacket and loosens his tie. His welcomed playmate seduces him, teasing him one sip at a time as he becomes mad with desire for more and will pay any price—his family, his health, his life.

Later, as he staggers into the bedroom and fumbles in his attempts to be romantic with you, you smell her on his breath. He tells you he loves you and passes out. As you remove his shoes and pull the covers over him, you can hear his mistress, Clitoria Huntinpecker, all dressed up as a bottle of fine bourbon, laughing gently—the kind of laugh only a mistress who has enslaved can laugh.

～

The lies, the deceit. Her note said she was at her friend's house. Maybe she was, maybe she wasn't. You don't need to ask. It's been three times this week already, and it's only Thursday. You find her yet again in the same place. Purple flowered carpet jumps out at you, chandeliers sparkle, and dance music seems to mock you as you enter the casino. There she is. With him. With Dick Deboner, her new lover. Her master now. Cuddled up to his cold, metallic body, pushing all his buttons with the empty, stoic face of utter concentration. You stand and observe her as she makes love with Dick Deboner, who, with bells and jingles, seduces her right back. Available to her 24 hours a day, he offers showboats, fabulous buffets, inexhaustible energy, and all the free drinks she wants.

Yes, you watch your wife place her loyalty card into him like a wedding band…maybe she gets a free shirt or a few free bonus games in exchange for her life. How many hours has she been here, making love to him? How much money has she lost today? Where are the children? Have they had dinner yet? What about their homework? She didn't answer the phone when you called at three o'clock. She's with her master now, Dick Deboner, all dressed up in bright colors with flashing lights and empty promises.

~

On her second bottle of tequila, she comes stumbling over to the neighborhood gathering. She brings some mix, her blender, and two limes strategically placed between her triple-E-sized breasts. She's definitely been partying before now. One fake eyelash has partially fallen into her vision, so she squints from that eye. Wearing her too-tight Marlene Dietrich look-alike dress, the neckline swooping off her bare shoulders, the heel of her left shoe partially broken, she bellows. It is the neighbor lady, drunk yet again, wanting to find a fellow partier—another drunk— to toy with, to seduce. At six feet and packing two hundred fifty pounds of entitlement attitude, the sixty-year-old "has been" is the type of woman who some men pay good money to watch mud wrestle. But for her brother's owning the apartment complex, she would be on the street. It will only be another hour until she begins dancing, wailing, and braying to the music, staggering as she rubs her ass up against any man within range.

Still, she arrives with the kisses to allure and awaken, ready and willing to be any man's latest infatuation or the night's romp. You notice your mate watching her with lusty wondering. Yes, she's in heat tonight. You can smell it. She is Clitoria Huntinpecker.

~

You sit in his room at the hospital. He's in the shower with the doctor, the nurse, and the occupational therapist, learning how to remove the bandages from his burns, which cover seventy percent of his body. Oh, and the prison guard, he's in the shower, too. They found your husband stuffed in a car, left to die after the meth lab where he worked blew up. It started out as just a job, cooking meth. He didn't use at first. That came later. He got busted before, went through rehab, but the first night out went looking for it. He's forty-eight. He has no teeth. Debts are mounting. Your two grandchildren who you were raising were taken away by social services. You're off work today—without pay—to be here with him. Sweet Jesus, what happened to him? Crazy with desire, crazy with need. The meth took him—his master now. This was never the life you imagined. What's happened to you?

Reality comes knocking

Can you live with what your mates draw to themselves? Do you want to participate in their life choices? You have been cheerleader, audience, attentive partner. You have coddled and tried to cure or save. Is it a match or isn't it? Is this the life you want? What about your children? Do you want to pretend to be in love with someone who has a mistress or master? Is that love? Is that what you always imagined—that your days and dreams would be filled with finding your lover enslaved in the arms of a mistress or master? Is this the experience you want?

These unwell and unwanted behaviors in your mates will express themselves. You see it in missed work or no work, the bills that don't get paid, the responsibilities that don't get tended to. You see it in the parents pickled from alcohol, in the adult children who rarely call and never visit, the siblings whose only contact is an annual holiday card. You see it in the phony posturing of friendships that have no basis. You hear it in the blaming game of it always being someone else's fault, in the declarations of victimhood. You see it in the audience that is required to make them feel okay about themselves. You feel it in the distancing, the remoteness, the denial. You see it in the twisted logic of using another's money. You see it in the misuse, overuse, or abuse of others—in the manipulation.

What do you do? You stay. You make excuses; you compromise and con yourself or live in contradiction. You listen to someone else's rules and the external authorities for your life. You repress and suppress and restrain your own nature, your own natural inclinations. You attempt to create an image; you try to "manage it." But at some point, you are worn out. The children are crazed. Your friends are weary from listening to the same tales. Your vitality is diminished. There is no energy for your pursuits, your loves, your life's work.

~

We do not know what others choose or will choose for their life. It is their life. At one time, your mate chose you, the job, the children, your mutual friends. Now, your mate chooses something else.

While Clitoria Huntinpecker and Dick Deboner may indeed have presented themselves as desirable, your mates wanted what they offered. They wanted the experience of them; yes, they were drawn to those experiences like moths to a flame. It was in their nature. They were sniffing, searching, peeking around corners—looking for the next high, the next allure.

They wanted a fuller life than with you. A different life than with you. Than with your children. Perhaps they wanted the audience, the charade, the applause, the grandeur, the power, the allure, the high…or maybe just the next experience. That was their path.

Truth prevails. He is who he is. She is who she is. A cheat, a liar, a drug addict, a lush, a womanizer, a man handler, a pirate, a gambler, a workaholic, a shopaholic, a fake, a slut, a cad, a self-indulgent user, a narcissist. The experience beckons to them. It must be had.

Some may plead "But there is no abuse. No one hits me." Doesn't he? Doesn't she? What is that feeling in your gut each time you sigh, each time you tighten, each time you aren't sure?

Notice…observe

Don't ask. Why not? You already know all you need to know. You know it doesn't feel good to feel this way. That is enough to know. If it is not the relationship that brings you feelings of joy, laughter, love, honesty, sharing of mutual interest, discovery, truth, and respect, it is time to leave.

What happened to the good times? You can be sure no one ever leaves because of the good times. One leaves because the sum total of the experience is no longer desired. It's that simple.

~

One day, a new sensation rises up from your body, and you know it is beginning to be enough. You observe that the joy you once felt no longer exists. Perhaps there is a slight shift, a slight animation, perhaps a thawing of the frozen numbness, an unsettling realization of your own conciliatory mannerisms and niceties. Or perhaps you experience a moment's respite from the chronic fuming, just enough to notice there was a tradeoff made some time ago from joy to contention. Sleeping parts of you are beginning to awaken.

You hear faintly a beat, a tempo emanating from within you.
In a brief moment, your heart unmuzzles itself long enough for you
to recognize it is your own life rhythm, your own life cycle
attempting to reclaim its expression.

Every cell in your body is telling you to pay attention, stay conscious, prepare for change and movement. Yes, sometimes we know, sometimes we don't know. But what we most often sense—even with frail and blocked instincts—is when it is time to leave.

Why do we con ourselves and stay? The *whys* don't matter. Stay out of your head. Make ready. Perhaps *this* day you don't question yourself about why you are staying. You simply listen to your body.

Hmm…You notice yourself guarding some secret, energetic feelings to create a space, an opening, a possibility, maybe even a probability that you will not stay. Perhaps you will even take a small step of action to mobilize…

Hmm…You can almost sense your body synthesizing the information and telling your mind to begin processing arrangements to protect yourself, the children, your assets. You are responsible. Your children will have solid care and solid arrangements for safe, continued relations with loved ones…

Hmm…Perhaps this time when you hear the whispers yet again of how much you are loved while inhaling the smell of alcohol, hands clumsily grabbing at you, you may find yourself recoiling and hear yourself ask, "What am I supposed to do with that?"…

~

Nothing came between you and your mate. There was no "phase" your mate was going through. The relationship ceased to satisfy.

What was, no longer exists. Remember, "who and how we are" is *always* there, waiting to be revealed. At any point, none of us can be other than that.

Your choices belong to you

For you now, the willingness to con yourself is over. Yes, enough is enough. You are sick and tired of being sick and tired. It is time.

Do not make them wrong so you can be right. Do not trash them. You want to give it a name so you have a reason. It doesn't matter.

Appreciate being open to making new choices. Today, make ready.

Gather your belongings, pack everything of yours that is of value that you can easily find; somehow you know you will not be returning.

Don't dawdle. Don't deal. Don't negotiate to accommodate the lies.

Don't ask. It does not matter. *Do not waste your breath. Do not waste your spit. Do not waste your life.* Just go. Trust yourself.

Walk, crawl, or drag yourself to a better experience with peace. Keep the money that is yours while there is some to keep. Keep the health that is yours while there is some to keep. Keep the life that is yours while a glimmer and a breath yet remains.

Move on. Take action. Find your own path. It awaits you.

Hightail it out of there and don't ever look back.

You will find your way. You will create a better life.

Walk away and find what nourishes you. You will be loyal to yourself again. You will dance again joyfully. Listen, listen to your body. Your very life depends on it.

Each is Free to Choose

Each individual finds his or her own way; no one's journey has anything to do with another. From the first breath on entering this life, no one is there taking it for another. The path belongs to one.

With this life comes choice, and when presented with options, people choose what they want. We assume that people will make a choice for the better, ourselves included. But our assumption is in error.

All too often we watch our loved ones choosing what we believe to be destructive situations, jobs, or relationships. We watch the life force, the chi, being diminished or drained from them. We watch as the consequences of their poor choices consume their lives. The addictions, the difficult jobs, the negative relationships are all easy to see as an outside observer. We watch as their symptoms attempt to inform them, and we watch as their life choices begin to reflect in their declining health, their declining joy. We watch them ignore the symptoms. While witnessing this destructive behavior, we may try to do everything in our power to inform, help, or even manipulate them into what we believe to be a correct choosing. We are desperate in our attempts to have our loved ones choose well—to choose what we believe would be better choices for their lives.

We can offer help, guidance, money, but it is not possible to bring someone to health without his or her participation; there is no lasting change when choices are forced or manipulated. We can say whatever we are moved to say to them, but *not* because it is our goal to move them from the spot they have chosen. Each individual will ultimately choose what he or she will. At any point, people are only as developed as they are.

We can try to help mitigate the consequences of their choices as best we can with what works for us. We can remind them that they are paying a price with their life, with their health, by their behavior, by their actions. We can remind them that there are repercussions with their behavior, and that they are not victims of this life—that they are choosing.

If our loved ones are making decisions we believe are destructive, we still have to decide to what degree we will participate in their choices and how we will choose to interact with them. Short of incarceration or death, we cannot make them stop hurting themselves or others by their own hands.

For those of us who come from a place of recognition of our own truth, all we can offer is to example a joyful and well-lived life. We can stay conscious and authentic in what we choose. We can, in the end, respect another's life to be lived as that individual wants it to be lived.

And we can make our own best choices for ourselves.

15

Focus Positively on You

Those of us who want quality will choose quality; otherwise, we will simply walk away. Responsibly. No angst, no stories. We walk away from that which we don't want and move into those experiences where we feel good about ourselves.

When you find yourself on a path of self-discovery, wanting to make better decisions for a more satisfying life, encourage yourself to welcome rather than deny reality.

As you think about or move toward improving your life, the first step is simply to recognize and observe reality. When people notice signs that they've been unhappy for a while, they may berate themselves about why they haven't done anything about it before; or they may wonder why they weren't successful in their previous attempts to make changes. It is least helpful to do that when you are in the thick of a challenging situation, making a significant change, or leaving a situation. You can get twisted up in stories and excuses and rationalizations.

Focus instead on the reality of your situation. You will find that the reality of your life is not about waiting for something to be different or for someone else to change. It is not about someone else doing it to you or for you; that is not what is making it so. Your choices are what make it so. And with further development, you will begin to welcome reality and begin to address, one by one, what needs to be addressed. All the way to freedom. All the way to a more joyful life.

Choosing better

Focusing positively on you as you make new choices and changes does not have to be difficult. The efforting is minimal when you begin moving toward what you want and away from what you don't want, listening to your body's knowingness. You want to stay conscious of your reality and pay attention. As you develop with each chosen experience, you will gain the ability for keener observation and awareness. It will be easier to discern among options, and choices will be easier to make. Naturally then, better experiences come to exist for you.

We all want to choose well. Often we think we did. However, sometimes—little by little—through active observation, just a bit more is revealed; and we may notice being surprised by these revelations. Maybe we didn't take the time needed to observe and assess sufficiently before we got so involved with—or even "committed to"—someone or something.

Our responsibility to ourselves is to observe sufficiently whether other experiences (individuals, jobs, situations) blend with our own nature. This "similarity to natures" can't be discerned merely from what someone tells us, but rather by who and how they are in front of us. Behaviors do not lie. We want to be on the same page regarding quality and standards for our lives. Remember, when similar natures exist, there is greater possibility for continuous, harmonious development for each individual, as the other brings new experiences into the relationship.

Movement stirs

If we don't know what we want—if all we know is that we just want something to be different and we want things to change—we can take some very small steps, small actions in any new direction. In this way, we are pursuing an action even if it is only for the desire of becoming less uncomfortable. If that is all we do, it is still movement, and *movement stirs something*. Even slight movements can stimulate reactions in the body and create openings. This stimulation is key to making changes. It is not necessary to create out of a sense of urgency because we feel something is lacking. Our timing is unique to each of us; a small step can be as easy as checking in with our body to find out what resonates with us.

It can be easier to recognize when others are behaving their truth when we are available to see that their actions do not lie. A healthy and ordinary response with another is to manage our *own* experiences to our satisfaction and joy by asking ourselves, "Is this the quality of experience I want?" and to pay attention to our body's reactions to the experience.

Those of us who want quality will choose quality; otherwise, we will simply walk away. Responsibly. We accept nothing else; we walk away from that which we don't want and move joyfully into those experiences that resonate with us and make us feel good about ourselves.

Everything that can improve our experiences and develop us also happens through action—creating, informing, experiencing. We want to allow our choices to carry us toward our heart's desires with our actions. The physics, the chi—the life force and movement of each cell—will animate us if the desire is true for us in that moment. Nature compels us to take action even to dismantle choices of incorrect choosing for ourselves.

Everything that occurs with us, does so through action, and so each experience brings us information to know more of who and how we are and are not at this time. When we move and act on our truth within, it compounds and we find ease in the continued flow of further authentic expression.

Reactions inform

In focusing positively on ourselves, we want to understand and appreciate the value of our reactions. We may have heard the mistaken notion that when we have a reaction that puts us in pain, we need to "change our reaction" so that we can pretend we don't feel the way we do. This is not sound advice because it ignores the immense benefits and importance of giving attention to a body's reaction to an individual or experience. Disregarding this valuable—actually critical—information from the body's reactions and messages seems to be an attempt to override and defy nature. Our reactions are real, and we dare not ignore them.

We take an action and then have a reaction to it. It is a momentary state; the reaction does not carry us forward; therefore, we do not want to get stuck in it. Our reaction is just the messenger of the moment; it is the body presenting information to us about an experience we just had. We use this "intelligence" to prepare us to move forward into new choices and subsequent actions that resonate with us and we want more of and away from those that we don't.

Those who are experienced in choosing well for themselves are able to get up, get out, and make different choices once they are informed of the reality of an experience and have found it not to their liking (even if that experience is an individual). They can do this because they have come to trust that their body knows what resonates for them, and they are able to acknowledge the reaction and move on with new choices and actions. They don't sign up to have the same experience in the future.

Those who aren't as experienced in choosing well will want to learn to recognize and identify the reaction, but not indulge in that emotional reaction. Learning to move past our reaction—not getting stuck in it—is best done by moving into action. Why stay feeling bad? If we can't sleep because our mind is replaying a scenario that makes us feel bad or injured, we want to get up, drink some water, eat some protein, feed the brain, and move our body. The body wants to be in motion. Remaining stagnant in an emotional reaction keeps us from living fully and keeps us suffering—stuck and immobilized—in that emotion. In that realm, our minds are churning, ruminating, and reliving that particular experience, worry, discomfort, or whatever it may be. This is not helpful to healing or feeling alive. Those toxic emotions wreak havoc on our health and well-being.

No stories—our guesswork is meaningless

When we try to attach an explanation, a rationale, or a story to someone's behavior in an experience we have had, we misdirect ourselves from our true reaction. It doesn't matter how it came to be that a mate, a friend, a neighbor, a boss or coworker, or anyone else behaved the way they did. Our guesswork regarding their motives is meaningless, not to mention convoluting. When we start creating stories, we re-interpret what our body's reaction is conveying to us. We want to trust that our true reaction has value; it is always accurate. And the only question of relevance to ask is this: "Is this the experience I want?"

Who decides that? You do. Just notice. Take it in: "Hmm, I notice they behave this way in this experience." Avoid the stories and rationalizations and excuses: "Oh, they are just that way because..." or "Well, it used to be so..." Just observe without judgment, but with discernment, and ask yourself basic questions: "Is this experience something I want more of or less of?" "Do I feel good about myself and my life with this experience?" It isn't necessary to dissect every little thing—every interaction that occurred between you and another—in an effort to determine how you feel about it. The truth is that you already know.

When you try to figure out the "whys," you contrive false connections and meanings; and this hinders your ability to take your next actions. Whatever another individual or situation provides, you make the choice whether you want to take the experience. The way you respond to another individual's behavior or to a situation is your choice.

Not quite yet able, willing, or ready to take action

Some have the clarity to know what they have gotten themselves into, and they have determined it is worth it for them to pretzel themselves around and live in the contradiction, forgoing the opportunity to make choices for a better life. Others may choose to ignore the knowingness of the body. When they don't hear the body's messages—that whisper in their ear or that tap on their shoulder—that they are "done" with an experience, they are able to convince themselves of something that isn't their reality, believing a situation is something it is not.

And then there are those who know the reality before them isn't the experience they really want, but they aren't yet ready, willing, or able to make a change. It could be that the experience is still fulfilling something in them. When this is the case, they simply are not done with the experience. Their nature still has a "wanting" that hasn't yet been fulfilled.

Saturation is our friend

When we no longer want an experience we are in but we are confused about how we might move toward something more satisfying, the body assists us through the process of saturation. Saturation happens when we have had a sufficient number of experiences—the same or similar thing over and over again—until we just become sick and tired of it and find ourselves finally finished with it. In some way, our nature's wanting has been fulfilled. Sometimes we can more easily move on when we are fulfilled, as it was for Henry with his job on the reservation, or Clara with her marriage. We just get to the point where the obvious has become undeniable: what was once satisfying isn't any longer. When this occurs, our body lets us know that, and we will not—cannot possibly—take an incorrect action regarding that. We are done with the exchange.

How many times do we need to live an experience before we recognize reality versus fantasy, declare our truth, and take some measure of action? As long as it takes. It can happen more quickly when we forego creating reasons and rationalizations to justify staying when we know there's no match between what we want and the experience we are involved in.

With saturation comes cognition, and then spontaneous action occurs

Even when you don't yet know where you may go or how you will do it, when you have saturated—when you know you are simply finished with an experience—the brain then kicks into gear to carry out the details of your body's decision. It occurs almost automatically, spontaneously, as though you couldn't possibly stop it.

It is easier to move on when you honor your honest reactions instead of considering external influences and authorities, instead of making rationalizations. When you remember that the mind is in second position—that is isn't capable to be in first position—then life changes can be simpler and easier; no angst, just one step after another.

Some of you may be saying, "I could never say that" or "I could never do that," and that's okay. Maybe you can't do everything, but maybe you can do some things. Dismantle and disassemble to your own rhythm, always checking in with yourself. What wasn't an option yesterday may be an option today. If not today, maybe tomorrow, maybe even years from now. Keep moving. Keep staying in reality.

Once you've made a change and are making your way on a new path, you can begin to focus positively on you in a new way. Take a breath. There is no point in feeling bad about your past; there is no point in beating yourself up for staying as long as you did. Every experience offers development, and it is helpful to just accept the reality of the way things have been and use that experience as an opportunity to assist you in your own self-development. That was who and how you were then. This is a new moment.

There is often a benefit in kindly asking yourself if you know what was going on for you—what was it about the exchange—that kept you from leaving? You may want to explore this so that you will not choose similarly in the future. When did you "know," when did your body try to communicate with you that those experiences had ceased to satisfy, that they no longer fit with what you wanted for your life or what you truly desired? Any ideas as to what it was that kept you from moving on sooner, moving on to a better life?

Ask yourself, after the fact, "When did you know that it took more energy to preserve your "story" than to live your life?"

Learn to interpret your body's messages—reality will percolate

You may not know at first. Don't make up stories or create reasons to satisfy curious onlookers into your life or even for yourself. If you feel you want to say something, just tell people you no longer wanted the experience or that it was no longer a match or that you simply felt it was time to move on.

Take your time with this developmental piece. Be gentle. In time, reality will percolate; small bubbles of truth will emerge, and if you give credence to the sensations you have at that memory—then you will be wiser. "Hmm…Oh yes, this happened…" and "Hmm…Oh yes, I observed that…." Did you push away gnawing sensations when you felt something wasn't satisfying or didn't resonate with you any longer?

Pay attention to your body as you take this time to remember in what ways you began to actively observe, assess, and determine that the individual or the situation was no longer a match for you. When did you observe sufficiently whether you were on the same page regarding your values and standards for the quality of life you wanted? Had you not taken responsibility to adequately do this before, or did things just slowly become more apparent as you actively observed? Perhaps you now find yourself saying, "You could have knocked me over with a feather…I was so surprised. I had no idea…" You may claim you asked your mate to tell you the truth. Often, asking for truth from others is simply a way one denies looking at the reality that is presenting. It's okay…just remember for the future that there is no reason to ask another what is going on. Your truth lies within you, not in another telling you what's true. If you don't like how you feel in an experience, *that* tells you all you need to know.

Was someone else calling the shots for your life when you made the choice to stay? Were you playing by someone else's rule book for relationships or jobs or any experiences other than what your body was telling you? Maybe you were just so worn down that you wanted to avoid addressing reality. Perhaps you thought if you acted or responded in a different way, it would all be okay. Or it could be just that you'd already tried so many times before to make a change, and you were reluctant to risk disappointing yourself with yet another unsuccessful attempt.

When you no longer resonated with an experience, perhaps you "worked yourself" into changing your reaction to what you observed because you didn't want to address your truth—that you didn't really want or like your reality. Maybe, just maybe, you didn't yet want to, you weren't quite ready to, or you weren't yet able to make a change. It's okay. You made the choice now and will be better informed for your next experience.

Waylaid by expectations

Sometimes we just expected that things would play out differently. We never dreamed that things would look as they came to look. These expectations can result in an unrealized or unfulfilled life. We forget that the journey of a life, of self-exploration, is just that—a journey—filled with aha! moments, with embarrassments, with shocking disbelief and agony, and with ecstatic experiences as well. What can become our misery is a life filled with expectations of wanting a different life and forgetting that we can choose anew in each moment.

Often we get stuck in the memory of how good the choice was at one time, and we want to keep that memory alive instead of looking at the reality in front of us and what needs to be faced square-on today. One of the challenges of even considering to leave a situation is that we often piecemeal our experiences and convince ourselves that we should stay in it because of some of the terrific times we remember, thus delaying us in taking a new action. So perhaps we allowed the mind to use a tally sheet with pros and cons. Often there are—or were—some good things in the mix, but we want to make choices like this while looking at the *sum total* of the experience. Is it the quality of experience we want for our lives?

Along for the ride

Maybe we had lost touch with our own desires and with making life choices on our own behalf and so we just "hitched our wagon to someone else's train" when we thought it was going somewhere we wanted to go. Then as life moved along, simply by default or habit, we stayed with that decision. We were just along for the ride. As our discontent and frustration grew, it was easier to assign the cause of our discontent or agitation to someone else, ignoring that it was the result of our own lack of self-accountability for having chosen to be someone else's tag-a-long. We knew—our body knew—this was not the journey we had hoped for, but we hesitated to take responsibility to make choices and take steps that would create a life of our own, a life that would satisfy us and bring us joy.

Perhaps we were clinging to the familiar; and we thought that with a partner, we would have more security, not realizing that such a possibility is only an illusion. Maybe we didn't want to be alone because we've never developed comfort with being in our own company, so an undesirable relationship was better than being by ourselves. We worried about our image and what it would look like to others or what people might think or say if we made the decision to leave. We had qualifiers around our choices; we wanted to choose this if…, or we wanted to choose that but….

Perhaps we worried that we might not have the ability to cope. We wondered what our future status would look like, and we feared the outcome. Maybe we had doubts about our own abilities regarding our own self-reliance and self-sufficiency.

It is possible—and most likely—that we did not want to accept responsibility for making new choices and the outcomes of them. So we chose to stay and remain immobilized, ostensibly safe from the responsibility of making any choice at all. We pretzeled ourselves around what we thought others wanted, oftentimes dishonestly, inevitably creating discord within ourselves. We conned ourselves with rationalizations and excuses that lead us to misuse others in the pursuit of our own comfort.

It really could have been easier to pay attention to our own truth and act based on what we really wanted. After all, when it is time to leave, it generally *is* time to leave.

Your precious life moments

There is no need to dwell on—or diminish yourself for—any of your prior actions. In your life journey, your choices are not mistakes; they are part of an evolutionary and developmental process. Comparing yourself and your choices to the way you think someone else might have handled things, assuming others would do it so much better, does not serve you. It does not serve you to waste your precious moments believing if you had done things differently, the experience you left would have matched your "fantasy." The experience offered what it offered and all participants were who they were. It could not be more than it was. Now, rather than spending your energy fixing whatever you believe or assume needs fixed in others, you are developing yourself by moving to quality experiences you find satisfying. You have moved on, focusing positively on you. It's a new day.

Be of character, integrity, and quality.
Everything else will take care of itself.

16

Full-Flavored
in Our Substance and Variety

*We can embrace every aspect of our humanity
with all the gusto we have.*

We all come to this earth full-flavored in our substance and variety.
We have a genetic makeup that is unique to each individual and which
provides a certain level of wellness. We call this our genetic predisposition
or genetic preparation.

Many of us have heard our friends speak with concern about a disease
their parents have or had or illnesses from which a parent died. However,
with this knowledge comes little or no clear understanding of how much
influence this could have on their own health and well-being, except to
know there are restrictions and limitations genetically that they might
face. People talk about genetic predispositions to diseases and the feeling
of "doom" that comes with that, as though there is nothing we can do
about it.

With the scientific developments in the past several decades, we now
know that this genetic predisposition is far more expansive than originally
thought. It includes all the information, all the stimuli, all the tendencies,
and all the experiences of our ancestry. Indeed, the way our parents and
their parents chose and the experiences they took are all combined into
the genetic makeup of who and how we are. And science shows we can use
this information to make a better life for ourselves.

How do *our* choices fit with this?

Consider this:

Every experience we take, and every experience each of our ancestor's in our genealogical line took, gets mixed and matched into the genetic pot—a "bucket"—and this mixture that is our genetic makeup gives us a predisposition to some things; it gives us our tendencies to move in one direction or another. We are not all created identical. We all receive our ancestral heritages in our genetic code, composed of specific genetic ranges—a continuum. So, we all have certain vulnerabilities or receptivities (these are neither good nor bad) that exist in us by way of our unique, individual genetic predisposition. Our genetic vulnerabilities and receptivities were influenced by how our ancestors chose and what they experienced in their lives.

This genetic predisposition then accommodates the possibilities for experiences yet to come for us in our lifetime and those of our children and on down our future lineage. How might that play out?

Let's just say a grandma, by way of her lifestyle choices, stressed certain of her vital organs, therefore creating a negative vulnerability, a weakness with those vital organs. Either resilience or weakness is developed by this grandma's choices—in this case, it was weakness. So, this grandma has a daughter and granddaughter. There may be a pattern of distress—a predisposition—that could manifest in the daughter or granddaughter, should they choose similar or connected life experiences to Grandma's. If so, this increases the probability that the predisposition may manifest. As the daughter and granddaughter learn what choices grandma made and what experiences she took, they can be observant and sensitive to how their own bodies are responding.

We can all develop ourselves if we so choose. With awareness, we can choose to become evolved and therefore not necessarily subject to the same limitations and restrictions in the unwanted patterns of our ancestors in both illness and behavior.

Every experience lived, seconds ago by us or generations ago by an ancestor in our lineage, accommodates an opening—a connectedness—for something else (vulnerabilities or receptivities) to be mixed and matched into our genetic pot (our genetic makeup, our "bucket"). These experiences encourage the illness or the better health. We so often focus on our ancestors' genetic diseases when the focus may well belong on how our ancestors chose and the experiences they took. Our choices for our experiences taken matter. These experiences can and do have an impact at every level of our being.

What we are equipped with is unlimited—the "bucket" is limitless

Our nature—our body knowingness—supports us in nourishing our development; it is our partner in creating our life. In the context of the universe, what we are equipped with is unlimited—the extent of which no one really knows. Who can say what treasures eighty generations up the line before us had in their back pockets, waiting now to express itself in us or in the birth of our next generation? We are talking about thousands of years, and we never know where or precisely how that continuum will find its expression. The bucket is limitless—these gems and jewels know no limits. There can exist qualities—behavioral traits and characteristics—that can manifest themselves as a result of any of the choices we make.

We want to use our genetic history as an enhancing factor—not a limiting factor—in our movement toward what we want. Any awareness we can gain—through observation or story—regarding how our parents and grandparents and ancestral lineage lived and the experiences they chose, can benefit us as we learn from that history and make better choices for ourselves—choices that enhance our life.

The way we choose is supported by our genes; we want to avoid characterizing ourselves based on limited information, therefore presuming we are restricted from accessing our genetic predisposition—our possibilities. We want to give value to living our own truth, authentically in every moment, and not judge or attempt to predetermine how we, or others, may *always be* or *never be*, thereby restricting our potential for whatever we desire.

Our own evolutionary process

In addition to our genetics, we, ourselves are involved in an evolutionary process of our own maturation—as determined by our life experiences and the way we assimilate our reactions to those experiences—that allows our bodies to incorporate new information. This develops our genetics to expand and manifest further. We gain new information as we move into each new experience. We hope that, as we develop, we will be able to access our fullest potential from within our gene context.

We want to be the most of whatever it is we desire to be. The more we can access that part of us—our gene context, our rich genetic heritage—the more possible it is that we can develop and reach our full potential, should we so desire. Five minutes from now, something we never dreamed of may come into play.

For those who are conscious…

With the focus on how our ancestral lineage lived and the experiences they took, we are not necessarily limited by our genetics. On the contrary. While it is true that by way of genetic predisposition, a part of a behavior or a tendency is enabled to express itself in our life—this is no different from the way a suckling tree is connected to its genetic heritage. So, of course, a continuum is happening with the mother tree.

> *But what is truly amazing is that the sheer vastness of what is passed—the inherent information and programming, even thought patterns—is such that those who are conscious need never hinder themselves by sitting in judgment of what they were born out of.*

As a species, the body wants to behave its truth…to thrive

When we live authentically from our truth, we are supported by our body with its unique gene context, its unique genetic heritage; there is no resistance. It gives us messages that assist us in recognizing our reality so that from that place of reality, we can declare what we want and take action for better experiences, those that resonate with us, that bring out the best in us. The body always has the true experience. We want to be conscious—to wake up to our truth, live it, and count on being supported by our body. That's our part in living.

We hope we can improve and influence our lives for the better and that our choosing abilities improve with each generation. The greatest gift we can give our children is a life well-lived—openly and authentically— where our children can best see exampled or hear stories about their true genetics so that they, too, need not be limited by their genetics; but rather through the vastness of what is passed on, evolve themselves through listening to their bodies to make better informed choices.

Gifts from our ancestors—gems and jewels—exist but many are yet to be revealed. Among others, these gifts can includes our behaviors, our stamina, intelligence, fortitude and the ability to improve upon those. They can include our deepest desires and the tools—the skills yet in the making—to access those desires. As we move toward each chosen experience, our awareness of who and how we are and what we next desire, expands and deepens. With each experience, more gifts from our ancestors are revealed. We can give thanks for those before us. And as each of our choices inform our next experience, we can welcome our destinies to unfold in unimaginable ways.

17

Rachel's Story

My Best Friend Hannah

Regardless of who cried "uncle" first, they are no longer together, nor should they ever have stayed together for your comfort.

It had been over a month since Hannah had called me from her parents' home where she was temporarily staying to tell me about her father's decision. She had just finished her schooling and was preparing to move across country to begin her first teaching job. Apparently, her dad had left one morning for work, telling his "sweethearts" goodbye, and by mid-morning, he had called her mom to announce he was leaving her and the marriage that day. He said he would be by in the evening to get some of his things. When he arrived, her mother, in a fit of rage, had screamed and thrown things at him while he quickly grabbed some clothes and bolted.

I had just arrived to spend the weekend with Hannah at her new apartment to celebrate her twenty-third birthday. We had been best friends for five years, and it had been a year since we had last seen each other. Her sister, Julia, was working on an overseas assignment, her boyfriend, Jason, was in another state; and Hannah was now alone—in a new town, a new apartment, and a new job. She confessed she felt as though she were falling apart. I had never seen Hannah ruffled about anything—never heard her swear, never seen her cry.

A weekend with a best friend whose heart was breaking was a very new experience for me. I did the only thing I knew to do—what my own loving parents had always done for me—I let her know how much she was loved, I focused her on reality, and I let her know that I trusted that she would figure it out.

∽

"It was so awful, Rachel. I didn't even get a chance to say goodbye. A few days later, I called him. He was out bike riding and having a great time, and I was at home dealing with my hysterical mother. He didn't act like he wanted to talk to me or cared about my feelings at all."

She reached for a tissue and blew her nose. I waited for her to continue.

"It's always been like that. He never seemed to care anything about Julia and me. It was just about him…or him and Mom. It's like we weren't even there. What were they thinking Rachel, after being married all those years? I'm falling apart because of their stupid behavior. I didn't even know they had any problems like this. There was always tension, but I just thought it was normal somehow. We always tiptoed around my mom to keep her from going off the deep end—we still do, as you know. I've always had to call her twice a day. Now more. Yeah, she treated my father like he was beneath her, putting him down; and he was always jumping around trying to please her and then playing the whipped puppy when that didn't work. But I never dreamed he would leave us. I'll never forgive him for this."

I gently told Hannah that her father had left her mother and the marriage. He was still her father. He hadn't left her.

"I know. I just hate his treating me like I don't even exist. Guaranteed, he won't be there for Julia when she gets back and Mom tells her. And the stuff my mom has told me…he's such a loser. She says he was screwing around with someone, that he'd done it before. He's telling me he met someone a few days after he left."

I asked Hannah which one she believed.

"Neither—not anymore Rachel. I've discovered I was spoon-fed a lot of half-truths and even outright lies. Great models they turned out to be. Mom talks out of both sides of her mouth. Dad's a coward, and cowards say anything. He tells me now that they both went to several different therapists over the years, individually and together, that they tried very hard to keep their marriage together. How come I never knew that? My mom and I drive all the way out here to my new place, and I have to listen to her claim he's ruined the perfect family life and she deserves an Oscar for staying. Then she had the gall to ask me if I wanted to speak with a therapist. I thought we were above all that, so I turned it down. God, Rachel, they had every self-help book ever written. Why couldn't I ever figure out that something wasn't working?

"I was stuck in the house with my mom for over two weeks. I got two phone calls and one lunch with my dad. Whoopee. Has he flown out here to see that I'm okay? No. Where is he when he should be comforting me? Oh yeah, out partying with his new girlfriend he claims he just met."

I mentioned to Hannah that sometimes parents quit pretending once the kids are grown up and gone and asked if she had any indications they might not stay married.

"I didn't question it because we never talked about such things. We never had an honest conversation. We could talk about visiting the best colleges, what career I should pursue, how the 'lowlifes' lived—including those who got divorced—what idiots everyone else was…but not about our *real* life. A few years ago, Julia and I were home for the holidays, and we all went to see *Lion King*. In the car afterward, my dad and Julia and I were talking about the show, and my mom snapped and yelled, 'Can't you just not talk about it to death?' Everyone just got quiet. That was the example he set. Tip toe. My dad has never stood up to, or stood for, anything except what would make him look good. Like not creating any fuss. But we didn't respect him. Hell, *he* had no *self*-respect. Maybe I noticed more that time since I had spent the first part of the break with Jason's family where it is so opposite of mine. A similar thing happened this summer while I was there. Maybe that's why Jason says he's not surprised Dad walked out."

~

Hannah sniffed and turned to gaze out the window. I wanted to hold her hand, console her, but I hesitated to interrupt her. She was on a roll.

"When we were little and my dad would read to us, Mom would start slamming doors. He always stopped reading. Why? Until now, after all these years, whenever I called home, he said just a few words to me and then handed the phone to her." *Hannah paused.* "But he never called me from his work. It suited him fine not to talk to me then, and still does. If he'd wanted things to be different all those years, he'd have done things differently. I have no idea who he is without her. But I'm learning slowly. It seems he is more interested in being with the "love of his life" than with me. Why should that surprise me?"

I reminded Hannah that she, in fact, did have ideas of their dynamic, and now she was getting a better idea of who her dad was without her mom—basically the same as he was when he was with her—unavailable to her and her sister and intent on meeting his own needs. I suggested to her that maybe life would now get better for them both and they would be happier just exploring their own individual lives.

"Maybe. Dad told me he'd been unhappy for years and often drank himself to sleep. It will be interesting to see if Mom can ever admit that she was unhappy, too; but then if she admitted that, she wouldn't be able to put so much blame on my dad for leaving."

I asked Hannah if she really thought there was a "best way" to walk away from a "bad" situation? I suggested that perhaps the cowardly lion had finally taken a stand for himself. I had gotten the idea that Hannah thought her dad should have stayed with her mom, so I asked her about that.

She was silent for a moment. "I suppose not…but he didn't have to spring it on us like he did. He should have talked to us about it, at least talked to my mom. And it just burns me that he's out messing around while I'm suffering."

～

Poor Hannah. While I dearly love my friend, sometimes I do think that she believes the world revolves around only her. I told her that any way he would have done it wouldn't have changed the fact that it wasn't going to be comfortable for anybody. Regardless of who called "uncle" first, they were no longer together, nor should they have stayed together for her comfort.

Throughout the weekend Hannah shared with me more information she had learned over the past month, including that her dad had been married before. Curious as to why they would have kept that from her, I asked.

"Image. He was messing around on his first wife with my mom. How could we be the 'perfect family' with that behind us? Yes, my perfect and proper mother was sleeping with a married man. She'd have a heart attack if she knew that I know that."

I bit my tongue so I wouldn't say what I was thinking.

"And that's just the tip of the iceberg. My dad is going to his college reunion, and I said something to him about taking his girlfriend to it when it was Mom who put him through grad school. Turns out the whole 'put Dad through graduate school' was just another big lie. She worked part-time and got her degree while he was in school. He also worked. He said whenever she tried to work, she made it so unpleasant for him that he finally told her to stay home and not work. No wonder she developed the attitude that everyone's an idiot; she's never had to deal with people—except, of course, us. Anyway, Mom wouldn't have gone to the reunion. She never went to anything unless it involved Julia or me and still doesn't. They have nothing in common. I don't think she likes him. But then, I never thought my grandma liked my grandfather either—my mom acts just like her, stomping around—but *they're* still married. Who the hell does he think he is anyway? Pulling something like this? He's a nobody. Just a philanderer who placated my mom and paid the bills—a cheat, a liar, and a coward."

I agreed that her dad didn't do her mom any favors, but I reminded Hannah that her mom played the game, too, and suggested that perhaps with no one around to prop her up and make her life comfortable, she'd have to do a little figuring out of what she wanted for herself and how to go after it.

"I suppose so. God, Rachel, I always thought that managing my mom was my dad's problem, and now I can't help but wonder if it will be mine. All this has just made everything so much more complicated for me."

~

Hannah knows how "open" my family is with our lives, challenges, and the decisions we made and are making. I know her parents had no friends and that they had rarely seen any relatives—even though they lived nearby— except for her mom's parents. Hannah had always claimed that her mother couldn't stand to have anyone but herself love her daughters, and it was an act of God that both Jason and I were in her life. I mentioned that at least she had one set of grandparents in her life also. I had met them at her graduation.

"Yes, but that whole thing is strange also. When I was little, we saw them; then for many years we didn't. My parents explained it away, saying that my grandparents didn't approve of the way they were raising us, but now I've learned that my mom, in one of her "searching states" went to some trendy therapist guy who convinced her she'd been molested by my grandfather. So until she got straight about all that, we didn't see them. Just another lie they co-created."

I mentioned to Hannah that it was too bad they couldn't have told her and her sister about that when they got older—there are many people out there with bad information, and anyone can get duped when they are in pain and looking for relief and clarity. As the weekend wore on, Hannah confessed, that even though she regarded herself as curious, she hadn't ever questioned much of anything having to do with family matters in general, her parent's relationship, or really even who they were as people. And certainly, nothing of the sort was ever discussed. The next morning, as soon as we packed up and headed for a walk on the beach, she admitted she had never seen her parents hold hands or kiss, nor could she remember any kind of real joy expressed between them. Looking back, she was beginning to think whatever was between them wasn't love.

"There's something else I haven't told you, Rachel. My dad didn't decide to leave on his own. When I was talking with him on the phone yesterday, he said I could ask him anything I wanted. I asked him how it came about that he and Mom married. He told me when they were dating, he tried to break up with her, and she started sobbing hysterically. He couldn't stand it, so they got married instead of going their own ways. When I asked him what prompted him to walk out now, he said he had been considering it for a long time and had met with his regular therapist that morning after he left the house. Apparently, the therapist suggested that he might consider getting out of their marriage since, after so many years of trying to make it work, it had only become more painful. I guess my dad finally got the "permission" that together they couldn't get. Geez, it seems he got married because he couldn't hold to his decision to break up with her, and he finally left after all these years because some expert gave him the thumbs up."

I told Hannah that, given who he was, the chances that he could have done it any other way were pretty much nil, and she reluctantly agreed. I asked if she thought it would be helpful if she asked her mom to be more straight with her.

"I don't know if Mom will ever come clean. She's so obsessed with image. She has to be perfect and brilliant and so do Julia and I because she 'owns' us. We are her life, her creation. She has never separated herself from either of us, even at our age. What with Julia returning out here and my grandparents living in the wine country, she'll be at our doorstep as soon as she can arrange it, I've no doubt. When I asked my dad how mom would support herself, he said she'd be getting money in the divorce. But now that I think about what he said, it just pisses me off. Why couldn't he say she was getting money *and* she could get work if she wanted to? She may be helpless on her own, but he made it easy for her to stay that way. He never has seen her as well-equipped to work. Who does he think he's kidding? He doesn't see women as anything but of service to him. I wonder what he really thinks of my abilities to fend for myself."

I was surprised by her comments. Hannah knew full well she was quite capable. I mentioned that while her mom probably had no idea what she was capable of, she was smart enough to figure that out. And as far as moving out here, lots of parents live near their children and do it well. I asked her how she wanted things to be with her parents now that they weren't together anymore.

"I don't know what a relationship with my dad would look like—I've never had one. On the trip out here, my mom told me he'd sit downstairs after she went to bed at night, working at his business, getting drunk, and watching porn. So when they weren't arguing, he was getting himself all worked up in another way. Disgusting. I know I don't want to be anywhere with him alone. Why would my mother stay with a man who watches porn?"

I reminded Hannah that while it might be hard to hear, there were two people in her parents' marriage. Her mom had stayed. Why hadn't she moved on if she was so opposed to how he was? He didn't hide his behavior. It seemed to me that everything that hadn't worked in their individual lives was the other person's fault. I told her that any sane person had to wonder what was wrong with them that they had stayed together when divorce isn't that big of a deal. I suggested she might want to get to know her parents as people…to have grown up conversations with them about what they want for their lives.

∼

The following morning we had Sunday brunch along the ocean. I was relieved to see her mood had definitely shifted toward the positive. She seemed more willing to accept that they just were who they were.

"Rachel, you are right; both of them stayed for a long time. I'm just being judgmental because the whole thing is so damn uncomfortable for me. And inconvenient. And surprising. Well, maybe not so surprising now that I'm really looking at it. After all, how could they get rid of the elephant in the room when they couldn't even openly acknowledge it was there and unwanted? And they aren't dead yet; I suppose they could both get a different life. I've got to stop looking for a reason to blame one or both of them. I'm acting just like them, God forbid."

We laughed at her honest assessment and agreed that behaviors certainly seem to get passed on! By the time I left, it was clear Hannah was seeing things more realistically and that helped her feel more peaceful. I told her I was sure, in time, she would get this handled in a way that worked for her life. She thought so, too.

There is Nothing to Forgive

When an individual cannot operate with healthy self-interest,
a price is paid by those in his or her life.

With the concept of forgiveness, we are given all kinds of advice so that the real or perceived "wrongs" done by one individual to another can be made bearable. We may hear or even find ourselves saying, "I will never forgive this person" or "I forgive that person." Unfortunately, bestowing forgiveness has been exalted to a "revered and desired state of being." We are told that it is truly lovely to forgive, that it is compassionate to forgive another. This concept has often caused continued pain for those already aggrieved as they try to move forward comfortably. For many, the anger and hurt remain with the inability to forgive. Others judge themselves as somehow "not enough" when they are unable to offer sufficient love and compassion to forgive. With either scenario, there is additional suffering as we are entrenched in an idealistic perspective of the actions of ourselves and others, often further complicated by commentary from still others on the concept of forgiveness.

Most all of us want to bring more peace to our lives and yet, after injury, the very notion of forgiveness can distract us from choosing our own "correct action" for ourselves as we try to do so. The reality is that another's behavior is not something to either "be forgiven" or "not forgiven." It just exists or existed. Nothing can make it something it wasn't. Nothing can make it okay if it wasn't okay. That is our truth. Even the pursuit of legal action, once done, may not yield satisfying results.

We live in an "at risk" world. Offensive acts occur every single moment of every day. Numbers of people cause harm, often believing in their acts. Occupying ourselves with notions of forgiveness won't change that.

Recognize an individual's true nature and care for yourself

To say that if we do not forgive we have no compassion is a view that skews our reality and holds us back from "correct action." Take an example of a rabid dog: One can have compassion for a rabid dog—even love. One can wish the dog would behave differently or be in a different condition. But a conscious and aware individual does not extend a hand to a rabid dog because he or she knows that it will behave according to its nature—it will bite. How then, can we come to peace if someone expresses their nature in a way that is injurious to us or those we love, however twisted and horrific that may be—in wartime or peacetime?

Consider this: Our responsibility—once recognition of another's true nature has occurred—is to try to keep ourselves and our loved ones safe from repeated injuries as we move on. There is nothing to forgive. People behave according to their nature. How can individuals be "more" or "other" than who and how they are at a given point in time? Knowing what we know, learning to manage our own experience is key. Attempting to manage others' experience is faulty. And continuing to feel injured and hurt only causes additional suffering. When we distract ourselves with the concept of forgiveness, we are less able to manage ourselves in our own experience, less able to move on naturally—to bring peace to the self.

How does this apply to a grievance from within our family?

In our story, Hannah is judging her parents and has gotten caught up in the notion of forgiveness. From her viewpoint, as parents, hers just don't measure up to her expectations. Many of us have had experiences with family that didn't play out the way we expected or wanted them to, and we carry injuries from those experiences. Some of us are in the middle of such situations now and are struggling to make sense of things. As is true for all of us, Hannah was dealt what she was dealt as her parents acted according to their natures. Each of them at times—as individuals—demonstrated an inability to take personal responsibility for their parts in the charade of their marriage and the relationship with each of their children. Even with the breakup, they were not able to recognize or be aware of Hannah's pain or address issues about the family life that could have been different. They only could see their own needs.

For any of us, when we refuse to discern our reality and call it what it is, we are less able to act responsibly. What can then occur in some families is the creation of a "family pattern" of denying responsibility for life choices. Individual family members have somehow benefitted from not stating the truth. Reality and truth obligate us to our life choices. When we learn to give voice to things as they are—finding it acceptable to simply do so—everyone benefits. Our authenticity sets us free and gives us a better chance at happiness.

Self-care within our families

Hannah was angry because she felt she had been conned and betrayed by both her mother and father. They exampled to their beautiful children that to stay in a contentious and loveless marriage that isn't wanted was just how life was done—that it was ordinary and acceptable. In order to move on in her life in a healthy fashion, Hannah, as with others in our stories, needed to look at reality and give honest regard to her reactions and subsequent actions, allowing herself to be informed by them but not indulge them by wallowing in self-pity or denial.

Hannah is just now beginning to recognize that she has two parents who appear to display self-indulgent tendencies. This can be a difficult but essential reality to recognize on a child's path to her own internal authority, whether at age five or ninety-five. Generally, if we can, we try to avoid people who have these tendencies—or we leave them if we've become entangled with them. Some relationships are not ours by choice, as with family; and there can be a natural inclination—a natural desire—to be close with our families. Hannah has this desire. She is beginning to understand, however, that she needs to be cautious. She is waking up.

Walking on eggshells

Parents with self-indulgent tendencies have an unrealized life of their own and, through unwitting acts of manipulation, make it the job of everyone around them—including the spouse and their children—to try to make them whole. Of course, that is not possible. This presents a unique challenge for these children because the parents feed on all those around them like parasites. From their perspective, there is no room on the planet for anyone but those who serve their insatiable needs. These individuals have not realized their own self-reliance, so they must live through someone else's life. Others "owe" them. In this way, they may be happy because someone is caring for them in the way they want—or they may lay blame and be angry when the actions of another do not suit their expectations. They have a limitless need to be validated, taking little or no responsibility for their own life satisfaction.

Growing up has its own inherent trials and tribulations, but for children who are dealing with their parents' self-indulgent tendencies, there is added confusion. These children learn to walk around on eggshells in their own home (and even in coming home for visits years later), trying to keep their parents happy, always mindful of the fall-out of choosing sides. One of the biggest challenges for children of these parents is to avoid letting themselves believe it is their duty to bring their parents comfort, as they will be made crazy with trying to please and appease such parents.

When both parents display an unhealthy amount of self-interest, taking turns with it in collusion, they exact a price from those in their lives. In this case, the burden is born by the two daughters, as well as each parent at the hand of the other. Both Hannah's parents have a long history of misusing, abusing, and overusing each other and their children. They blame the other for the years of unfulfilled lives; they lay their lives onto each other and their children—expecting someone else to do the parts of their lives they don't want to be responsible for. Hannah's father chose to have children but not to invest any time, energy, or interest in their daily care or development. He indulged himself in being absent and willingly sacrificed having any meaningful relationship with his daughters so he could get what "fed" him from his wife and other interests that personally gratified him.

As she was growing up, how could Hannah possibly have determined how genuine either of her parents were? Both were motivated by the applause and attention they required from others—and to such an extreme that neither could take responsibility to leave a marriage that wasn't working, that was destructive to them both. No integrity exists when this kind of neediness is so great. With their avoidance of discerning reality and calling things as they were, they took a "pass" on accepting personal responsibility to that reality, including their parenting.

Developing ourselves from our family experiences

We all have to figure out how to sufficiently manage our experience with our families and other "involuntary" relationships so it isn't distressing for us, given who and how we have observed them to be. How might children—even grown children—deal with these situations? With intelligence, love, and compassion while taking care to remain firmly rooted in reality. People are who they are, family included. Responsible self-care may necessitate that we modify the nature or degree of contact as we responsibly guard our own happiness.

In Hanna's case, she may visit less often or for less time or not at all. Perhaps she will call less frequently. Maybe she will arrange outings in public so she doesn't have to be an audience to her mother's therapy attempts or feel uncomfortably intimate with her father. Hannah will want to find experiences with them that are less stressful and allow for more joy as she learns to manage herself in her own experiences—choosing correct action for herself. She may desire to ask questions to help her learn to know more about them, but then she will want to accept that there may be information they may not wish to disclose.

Hannah has the longstanding "family behavior pattern" of avoidance and while her boyfriend Jason commented he was not surprised her dad had left, Hannah claimed she was. At the conclusion of our story, we could see the con that Hannah did to herself was beginning to shift as she came to see her reality, including that had she wanted to, she could have recognized her parents' mismatched relationship for what it was. She admitted she chose to live with blinders on to make her own life more comfortable. While many of us know that it is never okay to use or misuse another person to make our own life easier and more comfortable, for Hannah, that was an expression of her genetics as well as what was exampled to her. And so she chose to delude herself into thinking her parents owed her something in the act of staying together—that she was somehow entitled to have judgment about how their choices affected her.

Hannah was not given honest interactions from her parents—those "tools" that prepare children to recognize and address reality and act authentically and responsibly in light of such honesty. The tools that help them to call—to name—things as they are, to self-express and state their truth. A ten-year-old with different genetics or who was raised in a reality-based environment would not have been surprised that her parents had thrown in the towel and would not have had the reactions Hannah did.

Responsible parenting

Whose rules were Hannah's parents living by? They had been to a number of therapists over the years in the hope that it would help them cope with the basic "non-match" that they were as a couple. So why did they stay together?

Herein lies the problem with the "why question." People give all kinds of reasons and justifications, often claiming it is because of the children that they try to persevere, but really, people stay in situations that are not satisfying for either of them just because they do. Until one or the other of them "saturates" from the unsatisfying nature of the experience and calls it quits, they tend to stay.

Support that focuses on encouraging a couple to stay together—that attempts to serve the "unit" at the expense of the well-being of the individuals—is not helpful. This support skews reality and gives a false message to the children about relationships that will not serve them.

It is important and rewarding to progress toward what we believe is our best choice for ourselves. Others will then simply have to make their own decisions around that—even our loved ones. Always, however, during the time of shifts in relationships, an important job as a responsible parent is to help our children to be as comfortable as possible while not compromising our own integrity. We want to deal with our children in the most honest way possible—even if we begin this relationship of honesty years later than we wish we had. It is never too late.

It is liberating for our children of all ages to see their parents lead a fulfilled and joyful life—one of their own choosing. Healthy parents want their children to realize that the role of a parent is not to fulfill a false fantasy for a child of any age by maintaining an image and an institution. Indeed, lucky are those children who get that reality check before they enter into, and possibly stay in, unsatisfying relationships of their own.

18

Family and Truth Telling
—Gifts from Our Ancestors

It is because a parent would, that a child is free to not.

Often we hear children say they feel they were cheated with the parents they got. Even the children who don't want to claim to be victims still feel their parents are somehow "less" than what they would have wished. There is great well-being to be gained in looking closely at our parents' behavior in terms of the gifts they gave us.

As a life form—a species—the totality of a child's substance, upon conception, is from both parents. Parents are external representations of what will be a continuance of their substance in their children. Their children will continue to add to what was given to them genetically—that which genetics dictate is only the beginning.

Parents example to their children—in various scenarios in living their life—their behavior, attitudes, preferences, language, and choices. Children see their parents' genetics exampled in their life and are fully equipped genetically to develop the same. And for better or worse, many tend to repeat those examples in their own lives.

All species, all organisms will move toward their own evolution

What does it mean for all of us who come to this earth, each with our own unique genetics? All species, all organisms will move toward their own evolution. In order to survive and continue, the organism must develop itself in its evolution. When we see an exaggeration or extremism in attitudes or choices or behaviors, we witness mutations of a species. These extremisms are unwell and unwanted behavior patterns that are out of balance in the *amount* of a particular behavioral characteristic that the species is attempting to integrate for its own development. The species, in its efforts to secure its own survival, is trying to find the amount of that behavioral characteristic that is healthy.

The child of a parent exhibiting extreme behavior patterns has an opportunity to develop himself in a healthier way, because once this information is internalized and tempered by comprehension, the child has accessed his or her own ability to survive and further develop.

It begins with removing the blinders

Without comprehension, when what we observe seems so extreme, so exaggerated, we may declare, "I'm never going to be like that." We take a negative and judgmental view of those genetic exaggerations and lose the value of seeing them differently. How do we get this comprehension? To begin, we want to discern, to recognize reality. The blinders need to come off. To gain comprehension, we want to take *any* opportunity to actively observe and learn about the reality of an exaggerated behavior without shame, judgment, or blame, and simply use that information for our benefit—to develop ourselves. While in the moment it is difficult to call it a gift, this expression allows for us to squarely face the reality of a behavior and the destruction it brings.

This isn't about disrespecting your parents, friends, spouses, or strangers. On the contrary, when we live in reality and out of our truth, everyone benefits. We have the opportunity to choose our own behaviors only if we own up to these behaviors and then refine them. This is about us, once informed and aware, choosing to exhibit the *amount* of the behavioral characteristic we want. When we recognize the level of exaggeration that exists, we may notice if we also have that tendency, that predisposition. With this recognition and comprehension comes an opportunity to temper that behavior and develop ourselves personally to our own betterment, should we choose to incorporate this awareness.

No, we are not necessarily condemned to repeat the behavior patterns of our parents or others.

Everyone benefits when we live in reality—live out of our truth

We can garner this information when we observe parents, friends, spouses, or strangers in any situation who are exhibiting any extreme behavior, and we can then self-observe and self-correct. Yes, we can learn from strangers, from reality shows, from observations of any source. We ask ourselves, "Is this how I want to behave in the world?"

Sometimes we may find these extreme behaviors so unattractive that we may swing our viewpoints like a pendulum in the complete opposite direction. But every behavioral characteristic has two extreme ends to it, and within each of us exists the potential to behave one way or the other. Even something so benign-appearing, as the healthy behavior characteristic of generosity can have two extremes. On one end, we can see someone spending lavishly, and on the other end, someone stingy and miserly. The behavior characteristic of self-reliance would have a victim at one end and a bully at the other end, both master manipulators at getting things from others.

The balanced quantity—the amount—of *any* behavior characteristic, is what we strive for. And when we are able to see and comprehend reality, we can then discern which parts of any characteristic or experience are helpful and which interfere with our pursuit of our own selves, our own development. We can temper any behavioral characteristic with comprehension if we want to do so.

What parts serve who and how you want to be and what parts don't? We retain the parts we want as we find that quantity of each of all the behavioral characteristics that are healthy for each of us, that make us feel good about ourselves.

With saturation, more is revealed

Remember, sometimes saturation is brought about when we are simply sick and tired of the same old unwanted behavior and we choose to move on; we're "full up"—fulfilled. When generations are denied the benefit of hearing about, observing, or experiencing the exaggerated behavioral tendencies that create saturation, development of the species does not occur. With any unwanted behavior, once acknowledged or addressed or let out, saturation is possible. When that happens, there is an organic moving away from that exaggerated behavior. We are just done with it.

When parents are not authentic with their lives or what went on in their pasts—when they play "pretend" with their children's world and mask reality—these children can't see clearly. They may have inklings about what was or is going on, but with a big "hush-hush cover up, keep the skeletons in the closet," reality is not expressed or discussed. Children then lose the benefit of hearing or learning about their genetic heritage and how their parents and grandparents managed their experiences and made their choices—how they reacted to their reality around them. These children then lose access to examples of life choices that might relate to them, that they may later use for cognition and self-development. When these children don't get exposure to this valuable information about any extreme exaggerations, they are restricted in their development.

This is what happened with Hannah in Chapter 17, "Rachel's Story: My Best Friend Hannah." With Rachel's assistance, Hannah came to recognize that when her parents refused to discern reality and call the mismatched marriage what it was, they were unable to act accordingly—to take responsibility for their lives. They couldn't demonstrate to their children what a parental relationship built on friendship and love looked like—they couldn't have one together—but they couldn't address that. Without receiving the benefits of her parents passing truthful information along to her—thereby giving her an opportunity to broaden her recognition and comprehension—she was predisposed to be rather like them.

Contrast that to Rodney, the truck driver, in Chapter 7, "Rodney's Story: No Right Choice, No Wrong Choice." He fully recognized and comprehended the extreme behavior of his father. He didn't choose to pretend that the behavior of his father, as he physically mistreated the dog or Rodney, wasn't intense reactivity to a given experience. He got it. He understood that his father did not "own" his extreme reactions and subsequent behavior of physical abuse and, therefore, did not do what would be necessary for him to temper the predisposition he had. His father either didn't want to or he simply wasn't equipped to be able to do that.

Bring the skeletons out of the closet

With only mediocrity, there is stagnation, and the species terminates. Of course, the parent doesn't have to "play out" the extreme behavior; perhaps the parent has evolved but is aware that the behavior exists or was present in his or her parents or grandparents. But if the parent knows there is a predisposition to a dysfunctional behavior, then the parent may want to express or tell the children about that reality so that the children are made aware and can make better choices.

Every responsible parent wants a better life for their child than what the parent had. There is value in passing on the full family history—the good, the bad, and the ugly. Disguising the truth, denying the truth, withholding or deceiving, robs our children of the information they could use to create a better life for themselves. Parents may think they are doing their children a favor, but they are not.

When this awareness is denied or hidden or not expressed, the child remains unevolved, stagnant, and at unnecessary risk. The child then just accepts the parent's behavior and relationships as normal, as ordinary—not knowing the parent is denying or hiding or stifling or muzzling their true desires and extreme behaviors. The child stays uninformed and undeveloped in this regard. This is what happened to Hannah until her father saturated from an experience that was not what he wanted and took bold steps to move himself out of it.

It is because a parent would, that a child is free to not

Honor and enjoy your lovely times with your children by co-creating conversations, memories, traditions, and quiet moments. Bring the skeletons out of the closet! Have a laugh, a cry, a fascinating conversation. Learn about your history, the challenges facing those who came before you who dared to expose or address them, however it looked; after all, this is part of your genetics, a part of you. Even in looking at the level of exaggerations—the extreme behaviors—that existed allows us to be mindful of those genetics and behavior patterns as we make our own choices. We can embrace every aspect of our humanity with all the gusto we have.

Help your children learn to self-assess, self-correct, and become self-reliant. Their way. Remind them to listen to their own bodies when making choices for their own lives. Give your children your very best—example the character, integrity, quality, and love you want to be, even as you are developing yourself.

Let their very essence—their very being—resonate within you. It is possible that your children may become your best friends.

19

Vicki's Story

Out of the Mouths of Babes

*Black wasn't going to be white and white wasn't going to be black,
and I couldn't make it so. I couldn't construct another reality
to make it work.*

Stuart showed up for our first date together with every piece of information I would ever need to know—a six pack of beer to put in my refrigerator for himself after our creek-side bike ride and nothing for me.

I wasn't noticing then, and instead I fell head over heels in love with him, his charismatic style, and his charming wit. He was educated, tall, blond, and handsome. He had the "gift of gab" and could fill a room with his very presence. I loved being part of it all.

We married, and as the years went by, we both had decent jobs and enjoyed adventurous times together. At some point, I started to notice that Stuart had certain lifestyle patterns that couldn't be questioned. The first beer immediately after work was not optional; it was a requirement. There was a lack of spontaneity to our lives once this time of day rolled around. Regardless of the reality observed, over the next several years we had three children. Eventually, Stuart's drinking transitioned from a few beers after work to a beer in hand until bedtime.

As they grew in this environment, our children reacted differently; my eldest began to develop anger issues; the middle one, anxiety; and the youngest one, sickness. As for me, I had incredible feelings of exhaustion and weakness, with either the flu or a cold or some acute symptom every week. Eventually, I began to understand, and I began to refuse to be manipulated, but clarity still has to follow understanding.

Stuck-ness ensued…dragged out separations followed.

On one occasion not long after Stuart and I had geographically separated for what would prove to be the final time, he was visiting us in Council Bluffs at the little house we had bought years before. He had rented an apartment in Lincoln, where he had taken a new job. He came up on a Saturday for the day, and we were all getting ready to go out for something to eat late in the afternoon.

We were trying to decide where to go and opened it up for discussion among us. Stuart wanted us to go to a neighborhood Mexican restaurant that was close by. Todd, the middle child of our three, didn't like the choice; he didn't like the food there, and he was hungry.

Stuart was annoyed by the inconvenience of this stumbling block to the plan, and he became obnoxious in his behavior toward Todd. Stuart had no patience for Todd's opinions because this was occurring at the "bewitching hour," the time of day when Stuart generally began his drinking. Stuart was hungry, in need of a drink, and he was eager to get the show on the road. The Mexican restaurant was within walking distance, and this would allow Stuart to indulge himself without having to take any driving responsibility—so he was very invested in this locale for dinner. Irritable and caustic, Stuart told our eight-year-old son, "If you can't cooperate and come along with us, then you can just stay home." Todd looked his dad straight in the eye and said, "Okay, I will. I don't want to be around you the way you act anyway, Dad."

Not one of us had ever reacted quite so accurately in the moment and confronted Stuart with the truth like this—directly and plainly. This was a first.

Stuart turned to me and gave me a disparaging look that said: "What are you going to do about this?" He knew where he could wound me most, and that was in admonishing me for not rearing perfectly behaved children who responded obligingly to their father. I could see that he had been exposed and he was angry. There wasn't anyone covering for his behavior or making excuses for it; no one softened the blow. We were entering new territory. Stuart was acting like a petulant child, and he was desperate to deflect the blame onto Todd or to have someone rescue him in some overt or subtle way. It didn't happen.

With a few more comments, Stuart continued his attempt to create the pretense that Todd was the one who was acting unreasonably. I said nothing.

Then he just stopped. A heavy silence hung in the air.

Nobody made any attempt to smooth things over. No more pretending. Just silence.

Then I said, "I'll stay here with Todd." That was all. That was that, and in those few minutes, the pact of protectionism was broken. I was no longer a mom who would be manipulated, nor would I allow for the manipulation of my children—not from me or anyone else.

Dumbstruck, Stuart ushered the other two kids out the door to walk to the restaurant. Todd and I made hot dogs and then went out for ice cream cones. I told him I was glad he had spoken what was real for him—that it was important, but I realized he understood that without my saying it. I think he was as tired of my behavior as he was of his father's—my always smoothing things over and diffusing the discomfort and awkwardness. Todd was light years ahead of me. He was clear.

Our family dynamic was forever changed. The course of our lives took a new direction.

～

The following year, we invited Stuart to Thanksgiving dinner. As Stuart freely imbibed himself in the one contribution he had brought for the dinner—his booze—reality was made clear yet again out of the mouths of babes. At one point during the dinner, I looked around and noticed that my three children and I were staring at Stuart with glazed-over looks. You know the kind of look you get when you've invited your uncle or your neighbor to dinner and he becomes drunk and you just want him to shut up and go home. In this case, there was no drunken uncle or neighbor. This man was their father. Stuart was the only one talking, rambling on and on, and had been for a good twenty minutes. Not one sentence came out of the man's mouth that wasn't a story about something related to him. It was like a fishing expedition where he posed a question to one of the children, but only to invite an opportunity that would bring all the attention back to him, his opinions, and his stories.

This day, this time, I did nothing to "manage" his image with the children. I allowed them to take in the reality of the experience and make their own assessments. I said nothing to divert them; they were free to take in the experience for what it was. There was no conversation for the children with their father. He never inquired about them and their lives, and they were aware of that. Black wasn't going to be white, and white wasn't going to be black, and I couldn't make it so. I couldn't construct another reality to make it work.

During cleanup in the kitchen afterwards, I commented to my ten-year-old daughter, Nicole, about her father's behavior. "Oh, you know he's just that way when he's drinking." I remember her lifting the garbage sack out of the trash bin, preparing to take it out, pausing, standing tall for her years, looking up at me directly and stating firmly, "No, mom, wake up. You've got it backwards. The drinking doesn't *make* Dad act that way. Dad drinks because that's just the way he is." Plain and simple. The truth.

∼

Gradually, the contact lessened to none at all. That was Stuart's choice. Within a matter of months, a letter arrived announcing the expiration of our insurance due to termination of Stuart's latest employment. For a few years, there were some rambling, drunken voice messages to me on the answering machine, but they never included even a mention of our children. It's been several years now. I suspect he lives in a half-way house somewhere, but I'm not sure.

Everybody's Growing Up

In an honest relationship with our children, we invite honest expression.
We deeply desire to know who they are and how and what they think.

There were a number of pivotal moments in Vicki's journey to understand alcoholic behavior and the grip it had on her life and the way her children and she were intricately tied into it through her husband, Stuart. Much of her eventual understanding came through an unspoken body knowingness, informing her that her energy and life force were being drained from her as she sensed the effects on her and her children. The rest of her clarity came through the unfiltered sensibilities of her children themselves when they periodically cleared the air with a reality-based statement or act: a statement of fact, a declaration of truth, an accurate observation. Out of the mouths of babes.

Example a healthy relationship

One of the most important things we can do when raising our children is to help them learn to choose and develop healthy relationships. We want them exposed to behaviors that support this in both male and female. In essence, we want them to learn how to identify what is healthy and what is unhealthy—to identify friend or foe sooner rather than later. That is what will help them discern among the many options available, how they want to move forward in their lives in both work and play. This discernment is important as they choose who they want to be with. Many adults have a need to learn this, as well, in their caretaking of themselves and their children.

In an honest relationship with our children, we invite honest expression. We deeply desire to know who our children are and how and what they think. We want to nourish them in making their own best decisions, even if they choose something other than what we might choose for them. Many people and families have not yet developed the ability to engage in healthy dialogue around different ideas and viewpoints. Taking a genuine interest requires actually listening to what is going on with them.

If you want your kids to develop the life skills to make good decisions, you'll want to begin to deal with reality with your children from a very young age. Life energy is squandered trying to convince, cajole, or manipulate a response other than what is real. Lives are lived wanting something to happen other than what is being expressed in reality. If you don't want to know, and you don't want to hear, your reality is that you don't want to participate in your child's life. If you prefer not to engage in nourishing, respectful, and beneficial dialogue with your children that may give them the information they need to begin to form their values and their opinions (based on how you got to yours), then don't. Just be real and say that. But don't carry on in a way that distorts their truth or make them wrong for being who they are. Don't make up stories that aren't true so you can look good. Just give it a rest, give it a break, and if they've already learned self-destructive behaviors, then get them some professional help if you can.

Both mothers and fathers can play very important roles in the lives of their children. However, the statistics used to promote the benefits of a two-parent family are misleading. What is necessary is not whether there exists a two-parent home, not whether there is some involvement from both parents, but whether there is a parent who is responsible and as such, cares for his or her child by focusing on developing a genuine and interested relationship with that child. It could be life changing if there were at least one parent who filled that role.

Recognizing, choosing, and developing healthy relationships

There is a lot of information out there about how important it is for a child who only has a father to have a mother for a role model, or for a child who only has a mother to have a father for a role model. We are unduly influenced to take unnatural steps to try to be the best parent possible by getting our child this needed role model. We are told that if our children do not have these appropriate role models, they will do less well in school, participate in unhealthy activities, be more likely to be involved "in criminal activity and more likely to be involved in premarital sexual activity." Not to mention more involvement in drugs and alcohol, gangs, and the list goes on.

Children will see—will sense—from their parent or parents, standards or issues that that parent or those parents set upon the child. This is in no way connected to whether the parent raising them is male or female; it has to do with the parent's behavior that the child witnesses. For example, if any child senses that any parent—male or female—does not manage his or her own sexuality in a healthy way, then this child is taught to misuse his or her sexuality. The same is true for standards of any behavior—from eating disorders or drug use to allowing others to manipulate or treat him or her poorly.

A better way to teach our child about recognizing, choosing, and developing healthy relationships is to have a healthy relationship with him or her. It is necessary to deconstruct the myth that, as parents, we need to find role models for our children. The term "role models" has been given importance in a skewed way. Our children need to observe, to see, to know different examples of different behaviors and different characteristics. That is what is important. It isn't necessary that they become attached to a single role model, but rather have exposure to many people who offer examples of various character traits.

Certainly, men and women are different, and both can example character to your child. Most individuals to one degree or another have traits of nurturing, gentleness, a comforting and protective presence, emotional responsiveness, intellectual inquisitiveness, curiosity, and playfulness. Your children will find both men and women who have varying degrees of these characteristics and others. Whether they run across business people, neighbors, coaches, employees, co-workers, classmates, or teachers—they will find them.

Go shopping

If you teach your children about healthy relationships and *you* example healthy interactions in your relationships, your children will be just fine. Children are usually clear until, over time, we confuse them by rearranging the truth, creating stories, and denying the reality of a situation. In our story, Todd and Nicole were clear and, in fact, were giving their mother clues—tipping her off to the fact that she was muddying the waters for them by justifying and smoothing over their father's behavior. Vicki did eventually get clarity and took courageous action. Sometimes we are guilty of participating in the manipulation because we simply don't have a fuller perspective. Maybe it had to do with the environment we were reared in, and our genetics were limited. Maybe we did not have the concepts and ideas and perspectives to look at things differently.

Perhaps we even followed someone else's rules, those of societal standards or mores that state: "Your child needs a father/mother or he'll end up on crack cocaine. Keep the one you've got or go get him one. *Go shopping.*" The mistaken notion that it is the job of a responsible parent to find appropriate role models for his or her children by getting a replacement parent for them smacks of a misuse of another individual as well as being a distorted viewpoint of role models.

If a single parent does not make a hasty decision to "get them a mom" or "get them a dad" with the purpose of misusing another individual for the "sake of the children," this parent is exampling character to his or her children—not a parent who is willing to manipulate another individual for his or her own comfort. Ownership of others is bred into our culture—in religious prevailings, government interventions, and in creating citizenry. It is a tendency we have, to "own" another individual, found in our repetitive choices, in our value systems, in our surrendering to authorities outside of ourselves. This investment in concepts of institutions creates an illusion of security with a two-parent family that is not necessarily true. It weakens and attempts to displace our internal authority for our individuality and capacity to be self-reliant.

If you believe your child needs another parental image besides yourself, you are saying, "I'm not willing to take on the responsibility of self-assessment and consciousness to be an example to my child as the parent. I'd rather pick someone else. Thereby, I am shirking my responsibility." If you want the best for your child and you are the only parent, you need to sit down and interact with your child and do the best things you can with your child. If for some reason you can't—or aren't willing—to do that, then act responsibly in light of your own condition. If this is the case, you may find it helpful to seek professional assistance and avoid misusing another individual to simply fill a role.

We sometimes hear this from parents who want a divorce: "But if I divorce him, the kids won't have a father figure." Or, "But if I divorce her, the kids won't have a mother figure." The father is still the father; the mother is still the mother; whether or not you are together in the home does not change that. How much involvement there may be and what that looks like—how much propping up is ever done on the part of either parent—is the lie you create on behalf of "image management."

You may do this propping up because you think your children will benefit in some way if they grow up in an intact family picture. They won't—not under these circumstances. This maneuvering dismantles our children's ability to address reality and to eventually become good parents themselves.

No interference

The irony is that it is simple nature. The truth can only get fleshed out; things can only become clear for our children if no one is interfering with and complicating their perception. Our children will find examples of varying characters just by living their lives. All along throughout life, they will learn to recognize people of character, particularly if you have exampled a quality relationship with them. They will recognize these people from a place of health—energetically and vibrationally. This can only happen when their perceptions haven't been manipulated and twisted by an external authority—when they are allowed to see reality with their own parent or parents as it presents itself. For example, there can be no double standards. If we, as parents, have exhibited poor quality behavior and our child calls us on it, it is imperative that we don't deny it or excuse it or rationalize it away. No "I did this but I had a good reason…" There is just the truth: "I did this."

If you have not behaved in a way that examples the "who and how of you" that you want to model to your children, then own up to it; otherwise, you are messing with your children's sensibilities; you are creating confusion for them. It is normal that we are not perfect. Just as it is not a loving act to excuse and mask the reality of a partner parent's behavior, it is not a loving act to be disrespectful toward the other parent because they don't behave in a certain way.

What happens when one parent does not live up to the expectations that the other parent had of him or her and the parent communicates that to the children? The children are then taught that there are (subjective) expectations of how both a mother and father should be. When they then don't see that expected behavior exhibited in their parent, they become unhappy, frustrated, and disappointed. Does any parent want their children to be unhappy and frustrated and disappointed?

Loving your child includes helping him to address reality and what it is he wants for his life. Each parent is who and how he or she is. To put expectations of disappointment or non-reality in your child's head when another individual is just behaving as who he or she is does not serve your child. It's better to just call things as they are, matter-of-factly.

Parents do not need to present a unified front to their children; each parent can be unique in his or her perspectives and opinions. Your child can learn the acceptance of another individual—in this case, the other parent—simply for who he or she is and comprehend that it has nothing to do with the child. This prepares a child to be able to seek out and pursue the experiences he wants with those who can exhibit the care and involvement he desires.

We imprint our children

Often, even when parents mistreat their own children, they nonetheless become indignant when they witness others doing so. We imprint our children with the way we treat them, and that—along with what they learn to accept—creates a vibration of acceptability for the way the world can treat them. Sometimes our children see their parents accepting ill or disharmonious behavior from others, including their spouses. Again, this muddles and disorders their sensibilities and creates confusion for them. How could it not? Responsible parents call things as they are so their children can learn self-care and begin choosing those experiences that make them feel good about themselves. Choosing quality.

It is helpful to assist our children to not accept ill or disharmonious behavior from others, even from a parent or an adult. We want to support our children in standing up for themselves just as Vicki did in this story because how we treat our children is how we are telling the world to treat them.

If we teach or example to our child the acceptance of ill or disharmonious behavior from others or ourselves through rationalizations and excuses, he will be drawn to those experiences. He will desire more of those because he got into the habit of accepting this behavior pattern; people will figure out they can treat him a certain way and so some will. He may develop an indignant attitude or an identity of victimhood. He simply doesn't know how else to be. We want our child to honor his reactions and become responsible with action for himself. When it feels undesirable or uncomfortable for him to be with certain people—when he finds other people's behavior not to be the quality of character he wants in his life—he will then navigate to new people and new experiences. With practice, eventually he will desire to be with those people who bring out the best in him. He will naturally and easily choose and gravitate toward that which supports and nourishes his own well-being. Life is far easier and more fulfilling that way, and we want that for him—for all our beloved children. We want that for all people.

In our story, Todd and his father both basically said, "Thanks but no thanks for now." His father walked away, allowing both of them the dignity and humanity of choice: his father, to booze it up and behave how he wanted in his own environment, and Todd to not be around it. Fortunately, Vicki was able to realize what was happening with her children and allowed the relationship they had with their father to be a relationship among them; she was clear that it was not hers to manipulate. Of course, by accepting this reality and not conning herself about it, she had to accept the sole responsibility for her life choice to care and provide for their three children on her own.

Assist your children in seeing reality

This child, Todd, knew that someone else's dad came to his child's ballgames, that someone else's dad had inclusive conversations with his kids at the dinner table. This child knew that his dad didn't. Yes, this was his dad, but he was not interested in Todd's activities or life the way some other fathers were. Todd had observed other fathers—of all natures. He understood who and how his own father was, and who and how he was not. His was a father who was not involved and who appeared to prefer drinking to spending time with his children.

Todd's perceptions might have been twisted if someone had manipulated reality and attempted to impose on him a false and untrue image of his father as someone other than who he was. In this case, it would have been an image of a father who was a "propped up guy," being presented as a perfect father figure. This would have gone against every instinct and natural observation in Todd's body that told him otherwise. If you are the parent doing this to your child, you will want to be aware that, in so doing, you interfere and disrupt his own ability to claim reality, to develop healthy discernment, both which are important components of a self-reliant life. A life of his own choosing.

If this is not what you want for your child, let reality reign. Yes, facing reality can sometimes mean facing disappointment. With responsible parenting, you are helping your children to build their own character, distinguish fantasy from reality, and find experiences that bring them genuine joy.

When you manipulate their reality, your children quit checking in with themselves. If you engage in this type of manipulation with them, they will clearly recognize who and how you are, too: a reality manipulator and not a parent who can be trusted to let them develop their own truth. Now you, the one individual who could have been in their court—helping them develop themselves through life—just sold them out to an image, to lies, to myths, to unreality.

We want to encourage our children to call things as they see them and support their attempts to assess truth and reality—to discover and recognize—even when it may cause us some discomfort initially. By example and through our support, we can guide them away from any tendency to cast aspersions or become judgmental when their expectations are not met.

People are who they are. Situations are what they are. Jobs are what they are. Parents are who and how they are. Adjust to it. Knowing what you know, knowing the reality as it appears to you, make your best choice. Assist your children in discerning reality so they can develop themselves to make their own best informed choices.

It's one of the jobs of a responsible parent and can set the stage for an easy, trusting, and loving relationship with your child…this beautiful child of yours, who may have only one individual in his whole world who he can fully count on to love him enough to do this.

You.

20

Mona's Story

The Gift of Choosing Responsibly

My mother remained positive. She also continued the life of a determined smoker. Even when she was on morphine, I would find her smoking near the trashcans with some of the staff on break, having wheeled herself out of the hospital.

Our parents can influence us, even in their dying. I loved my mother. She came to live in the same neighborhood as my daughter and me when Elizabeth was in high school. We had wonderful times together. I had a successful business, great friendships, and the love of my daughter and my mother. I was on top of the world. I had always considered that I had a very blessed life, a juicy life. I was born happy; I knew that and appreciated it. When my daughter left for college, I never had an empty nest moment. Life was fabulous, and my mother became my new best friend.

All the same, I knew it was just a matter of time. My mother had smoked for sixty years. Even after the diagnosis of cancer and the prognosis of only months to live, she asked me while puffing on yet another cigarette, "Honey, what do you think...will I die from this?" Some of you may ask, "What part of the health risks from smoking for sixty years didn't she get?" Yet Mom fully understood the risks, and she was willing to live out her life as she wished even with those risks. I, on the other hand, had been annoyed and even upset at times with her all my life for her choosing to smoke when she "knew better."

I look back now at those last six months and marvel at how I even survived. My business almost fell apart as my assistant struggled with her own health issues and I did the work of two people. With each worsening month of my mom's condition, new care, new arrangements, and new decisions had to be made. There was no blueprint to follow. The availability of yesterday's services weren't the same as today's services. New medicines, reactions to medicines, new treatments, home health care, Meals on Wheels, and trips to and from the doctors filled our lives. Every day, I felt like I was reinventing the wheel. Something would happen in the middle of the night, and my entire schedule for the next day had to be re-arranged. The bathing, the help, the food, and the pain management all took on a life of their own. There was no one source to get all the information or assistance needed; so I was running ragged, chasing down what Mom needed. We fortunately had a little money to get some hired help, but even that took interviews and time and my mother's capabilities one month were not the same the following month as her condition worsened.

My mother remained positive. She also continued the life of a determined smoker. Even when she was on morphine, I would find her smoking near the trashcans with some of the staff on break, having wheeled herself out of the hospital.

By our next Christmas, it was over. She was gone.

∼

In the months that followed my mother's death, I slowly went through all her boxes I had moved into my home when emptying out her apartment. There was no schedule to complete this task. One evening after work, I'd get through half a box; other times it would take a week to do even less. It largely depended on how much time I spent crying. My daughter had moved back into town to finish up school and had an apartment with friends. I wanted to be careful not to burden her with so much grief since it was her time to enjoy her senior year of college. But it was awful. I was in more pain than I had ever experienced before. My doctor offered a prescription, but I refused, choosing to express my grief naturally. I continued to carry on, believing that it would get easier. At least I hoped it would because I was in a serious funk.

My weight, my longtime nemesis, began to really get out of control with the extra responsibilities on my time and the comfort eating I had resorted to. Already heavy for years, I was at least fifty pounds overweight by the time the last box of Mom's stuff had been dealt with. Although still athletic, I knew if I continued overeating the way I was, I would continue to gain even more. I wasn't kidding myself about my weight. Not only did I know my health was at risk, but I felt exasperated by how I saw myself. Close to another year passed, three sets of friends moved away, and I felt even lonelier. My daughter had moved on to new experiences, which was normal and as it should be in her life. I could sense that my season of grieving was waning. I craved the joy I once knew, I desired to get my weight under control, and I desired to get a life again.

One day I came across some previously overlooked paperwork—Mom's final credit card bill. The last item she had charged was a carton of cigarettes. Unlike my mom, whose choice made her happy—regardless of any health implications or what others thought—my own choice of overeating and overeating the wrong foods wasn't bringing me any joy. That was my real problem.

I began to wonder why I was hesitant to look at the reality of being so overweight. I wasn't in denial. I knew full well each and every day I was carrying around the weight and how it made me feel. As an aggressive downhill skier, I'd always had strong body awareness. I knew how much I was exerting. At one time I considered myself an attractive woman, and I knew I no longer felt that way. I had lost interest in selecting clothes; and when I did purchase clothes, I made sure they were huge on me to attempt to disguise my weight. I hadn't even had a good belly laugh in two years and I wanted that again.

I knew that choices held a cumulative effect for me. I knew that joining an organization might not yield great friendships after the first meeting; but in time, places and people become familiar and pleasant, and friendships get formed. And I knew that forming new habits worked the same way for me. It seemed to me, upon reflection, that I'd just over the years, slipped into some habits of unconscious eating and no movement. I wondered when it was I had started skipping breakfast or grabbing a pastry or bagel? When had I begun to cut out the last mile loop when walking my dog? It didn't matter. I took a breath, patted myself on the back, and set forth to try for the life I wanted…a life that gave me pleasure, one where I felt good about myself.

∽

I did some volunteering to get out more than just my work, and began changing my eating regimen, beginning with a protein rich breakfast. I became more conscious about the foods I ate, the amount I ate, and my patterns of eating. I tried out various movement programs that I really enjoyed and rarely missed. Nothing was difficult or over the top, I took it slow but very steady. At first even *moments* of cardio about did me in, but eventually, my daily routine just became my new habit. Eventually my new patterns became even more fun as I tried out recipes, restaurants, dance classes and of course, shopped for new clothes. I was feeling better about myself and my body began responding with some weight loss and better endurance.

I remember sorting through clothes that were now too big and holding up a pair of pants I had worn twenty-five pounds before. I began sobbing hysterically with shame that I had ever let myself get so large. My god, these were Jackie Gleason pants. Had they really ever been on me? I recalled how many times I had gone back for second and third servings. Now, I could no longer even remember that "stuffed feeling" that I used to have every time I ate. *Always* stuffed. Overly full from the wrong food and too much of it.

It took well over a year, but gradually I arrived at a good weight for me. The deadly five to ten pounds a year weight gain stopped. There was no diet. A lifestyle change is what it took, a simple change of habits. One step at a time, I changed the way I purchased, consumed, cooked, and regarded food and movement in my life.

Nothing gets in my way now of enjoying being actively engaged, out and about in the world. It is key to who I am. I feel restored to even better than I was before. The confidence that I've always had with work now transcends how I dress and how I look. I weigh myself every day, even though I understand weight fluctuates. I also try on a pair of "perfect fit" pants every morning to make sure that I stay within comfort. If they ever feel even somewhat tight, I am reminded to pay attention to what I'm eating. I know what it is like to bend over in a pair of pants and have that terribly uncomfortable feeling, to have my thighs rub together. Not anymore.

And no, I don't wear super smart missionary shoes, I don't sport a visor, and I don't do elastic waist bands on my pants. I have no pantsuits and no white Adidas tennis shoes. I don't mean to make fun of those who do, but I have discovered my own style now and I like it. These past five years are the first years of my life I haven't had to consider my weight when shopping.

~

What a liberating gift of life my mother gave me. It may sound strange, but in choosing to openly enjoy smoking cigarettes her whole life, I saw that my mother did what she wanted, lived the life she wanted. She knew the statistics, and she still chose to live her life as a smoker. It was an ugly death, yes, but she lived her life her way and did so responsibly. She didn't ask anyone else to pay for her cigarettes or to smoke with her or go in the poor house when she died. She never tried to quit that I know of. My mother chose a life that gave her pleasure; she liked and accepted herself, she was a blast to be around, and that is how I remember her.

For me, when I began to make the choices I wanted for my life that gave me pleasure, everything else seemed to shift. I started moving with ease on a whole new roll—vacations, dinner events, travel, new friends, outings, a zesty four-month relationship with no regrets when it ended, and the list goes on. It was really about finding the "new normal" for me. My former muted-grey life transformed to full, living color, and I wish that for anyone with what they choose. And I'm belly-laughing now.

> *Habit is habit. It is not to be flung out of the window by anyone, but coaxed downstairs a step at a time.*
>
> *—Mark Twain*

Respect Another's Choice

The life we choose is always reflected in our health.
May our choices bring us joy.

If each individual chooses and is happy, it is a happy life. Who are we to judge? So many times we think someone should want something that we think they should want. It is a disservice to another's life force to think that. It is a judgment that the psychology world puts on them. "If he could just have a better life…" Who is to say the life should be any different or what a better life is for any organism? The self is doing the choosing; the self is finding the best life one can make. Everyone makes his or her own best choices about that. Mona's mom lived the life she wanted. She lived her choice for her own life, regardless of how long or short it might have been. When another makes decisions for his or her own life and it is the life desired, we want to wish them well.

Each organism has internal intelligence for its best. Every organism is compelled in its own evolutionary process, regardless of how that might appear to others.

Mona's mother was not in denial; she knew the risks of smoking and did it anyway because she enjoyed it.

Mona witnessed her mother living the life of her own choosing, which led her to consider what Mona wanted for her own life and her expression in it. There are drawbacks to being overweight. Were her choices of over-eating the wrong foods bringing her joy or did she want to make changes in her life? Mona decided she wanted something different and she became aware of what it would take to feel good about herself. Then she started taking action. It worked.

What a helpful gift Mona's mother had given to her. Many of our ancestors before us have given us special experiences we can draw strength and wisdom from. In knowing this, we have the option—if we want, if we can—to choose better. Mona got to see how her mom did it, and through that example, to make a more conscious choice for herself. Each individual comes to his or her own reality. It is best to stay out of the ugly space of judgment. Life is easier for all of us if we can respect another's choice and, regardless of their life lived, just appreciate the outward and open demonstration of responsible choosing.

Mona's story does not advocate that smoking is either for you or not for you, or that extra weight is either for you or not for you. It is an example of an individual making and living her personal choice. How do we want to experience our life? Mona wanted her body to move, her weight to be comfortable, and to enjoy looking good in her own estimation. She wanted to accomplish that by adopting a different lifestyle—changing some old habits and living with more consciousness of her desires.

With choice, people can have their own life. We may not agree with other people's choices, but we can't deny the beauty of an individual exampling choice and knowing a life of joy because it was a life of their own choosing. It can be liberating to do what we want to do, accepting responsibility for the outcome, taking a stand and declaring how we want to live our life—authentically living our truth.

Yes, Mona's mother knew she was going to die, but in Mona's mother's case, who is to say a death by another disease would not have been as difficult or might have happened even if she hadn't smoked? She was willing to accept the responsibility that her choice to smoke—which gave her joy—might have consequences. She made the decision she wanted. May our choices bring us what we desire.

I'd rather be my own fool than someone else's genius.
—Howard T. Monroe

21

Susan's Story

Whose Rules am I Living By?

*I was so intent on preserving the marriage that it never occurred
to me to ask myself what I really wanted and then
to move in that direction.*

Smart, sassy, daring, and bold, I was both tough and tender. I'd
hitchhiked, ridden across the country on a motorcycle, had several jobs,
and thought I knew what I was doing. Yes, at twenty-one, I was doubly
sure I was my own person because I hadn't lived long enough to know
I wasn't.

It was the summer of 1971 when John and I met at a repair shop
while waiting to get our respective Volkswagen Beetles serviced. A long-
haired, dope-smoking, bright guy, he had a quick wit and turned out
to be fun to be around. From the day I met him, John was very clear
with me about who he was, what he believed in, and how he wanted to
live. There were no mysteries with this man. He was his authentic self
in every moment. Right from the beginning, he told me that he would
smoke pot until the day he died. Now, who, at twenty-one years old,
would believe such a tale? I thought he would change his mind and
grow up. Isn't that what we all were supposed to do as we got older? As I

look back, I am baffled about what part of his honest declaration wasn't crystal clear to me. What was I thinking? I must have been thinking that smoking pot was just a phase that some young people go through and it would pass. After all, I didn't know any grown-ups who smoked pot; but then again, I didn't really know any grown-ups except some of my friends' parents. None of them smoked pot. I undoubtedly thought that he would eventually change in the way I wanted him to. Of course, the truth is I wasn't thinking clearly. My thinkin' was stinkin' as I like to say.

It never occurred to me that John was just being his real self. In hindsight, what was truly remarkable about this man was that not only had he said what's what with him, he lived it. One-hundred percent. Yes, John was the real deal. But who he was and the lifestyle he offered were not what I wanted. Based on what was in front of me, I should have said, "Thank you, but no thanks" and walked away. But no, I married him instead. As the saying goes, "she married him to change him." After all, I'd seen many women doing just that, including my mother and grandmother. Not that they had been successful. But, growing up, I had been privy to the years rolling by of the same frustration, the same disappointments. Even my own mother had claimed she knew early on that my father wasn't who she really wanted for a father for her children, and then she had four more kids with him. It wasn't long before I started to recognize what I had done. John went right on living his life exactly the way he said he would. He didn't change his mind or his ways.

≈

Financially supporting his habit of smoking pot—in spite of job layoffs—was a constant source of concern for John. Being the enterprising, bright young man that he was, he figured it out. He began dealing marijuana. Only to friends initially, but soon the clientele became friends of friends. Then my industrious husband decided he would try his luck at farming; this way he could control the quality of his product. Now I'm not talking about acres here, just the conversion of an open area in the house we rented. The space was built out with a door; the walls and ceiling were lined with insulation. Black garbage bags were stapled up for maximum heat retention and light absorption. Grow lights were hung in an orderly fashion at varying heights. His greenhouse was up and running.

A percentage of each unemployment check went toward purchasing special bulbs for the light fixtures that hastened the growth of the marijuana plants. Installed with electric heaters for warmth in the cold New England climate, the room became known as "The Plantation."

Word was getting around that my husband had "The Plantation," and people would stop by to have a look. It was like showing off a new baby, a new piano, or the home addition you were proud of building. The beautifully cultivated marijuana plants created conversation. Information was shared and exchanged; for me, this experience was becoming more like being on the fringes of a cult. I simply didn't share the interest. This was in the era of the Chicago 7, the Kent State Massacre, and when folks were singing the "Prison Song" from Graham Nash's *Wild Tales* album in protest of differing states' laws for smoking grass. People would bring their guitars to our home; we'd put up a big pot of clam chowder and sing songs into the night. Groovy. No one seriously entertained the idea of getting busted.

Our relationship began to degenerate; no big arguments really, it was sort of just a sad distancing on my part as I grew weary. This wasn't the joyful marriage I had anticipated. I don't know how I could have realistically expected it to be anything other than it was, but in my experience married people had jobs and a house and kids and grand-kids and friends with varied interests; they had some sort of life where they "lived happily ever after." I guess I hadn't really thought about it much when I said "I do." Our only friends were pot smokers, and while good people, I craved a blend of friendships and a warm and light and inviting home with an open door policy to neighbors who might stop by. Our house was always dark with heavy curtains pulled closed at the windows, shrouded in secrecy.

Soon it was deemed that the greenhouse could provide additional utility if John could also grow magic mushrooms. At this point, my entrepreneurial husband brought in a partner who was experienced with this science to go over the plans for the extension and diversification of the business. That's when I ceased to exist. It was as though I disappeared—even to me it seemed that way; I had lost touch with myself.

It is said one never leaves for the good times, and there were many good times in this life we lived. I loved the get-togethers with many of our friends, playing board games, gardening, canning chickens, baking bread from scratch, making fruit cake from a treasured 150-year-old Norwegian recipe. John was intelligent and kind. But I was weary and tired, afraid and isolated, and I began questioning my future with him. No one knew how unhappy I was, maybe not even me.

⁓

I came up with all kinds of reasons that were, in reality, just poor excuses for not leaving when I no longer wanted to be married. I guess I had these rules I was living by; I have no idea where they all came from but I bought into them hook, line, and sinker. Somehow in my mind, I thought that getting divorced meant personal failure. It meant low life. It meant I hadn't tried hard enough. It meant that I didn't respect the vows of marriage and what it meant to build a life with another person. It meant breaking my word.

It never occurred to me that it wasn't the marriage itself that I needed to respect, but that I needed to honor and respect myself. I needed to listen to my own desires and ask myself what exactly I did and did not want from my life, from myself. I was ignoring that nagging voice inside my body that every day was telling me to leave. So, instead of figuring out how I could get out of the experience and start a new life, I put my efforts into figuring out a way to live with the situation—to "make my marriage work"—and be happy.

I separated a few times, one time distracting myself by becoming involved in a church that was active in its recruiting efforts. I was looking for relief and purpose and took to heart the job of preaching to others so that they wouldn't go to hell and burn forever. My husband, true to his nature, didn't see any need to change me; but he didn't want me to try to convince him of anything either. Eventually abandoning my proselytizing days and coming to open-hearted beliefs that held meaning for me was key to me becoming happier.

I had imposed other rules on myself also–the arbitrary rules of the religious influence on the institution of marriage, dictating that you stay even when everything in your body tells you to go. And then, of course, there was that rule that says never leave one thing without a well-established plan for where you are going next, as though you wouldn't *possibly* be able to figure it out once you walked out the door.

John had been honest, and I simply hadn't wanted to acknowledge that it wasn't a fit for me. I became more and more sad, crying all the time—at home, at work, on the way to work. I felt stuck; I knew I had chosen poorly for who I was. Even at that young age, I knew that it's never someone else's fault when a person is unhappy. If there was one thing I had learned from my seeing how my grandmother and mom were, it was that. Both of them not only felt their unhappiness was their spouses' fault, they spent untold amounts of energy trying to convince everyone else how right they were. My feeling was that no one did it to them and no one was doing it to me; of that I was sure. It was just a mismatch. It was me who was being a fraud. I had a decent job and wasn't afraid of being on my own, but I had these "rules" that came from who-knows-where, such as "Marriage is forever, till death do you part; you promised before God." Perhaps I was simply invested in the preservation of an institution comprised of two people from an origin that predates recorded history.

～

In time, I became "full up" from a situation that wasn't a fit for me—I had been like a sponge sitting under the slow and steady drip of a leaky faucet until it became soaked. One of the big drips occurred one Saturday when my mother—who lived just a few hours away—came to have lunch. For some reason the door to "The Plantation" room was unlocked that day, and my mom went inside. When she came downstairs, she asked me, "What are all those trees up there? They aren't going to grow in the dark." The timers had been set to allow for just so much light and so much darkness. How do you tell your mother that your husband grows and deals drugs, not for profit, but for a social venue to provide him with a way to support his habit of indulgence in always being high? Tough moment, but with a straight face I told her the truth. Expressing concern about the legal risks, she said to my husband, "Do you know what could happen? Not just you would go to jail, but my daughter would go, too."

She quietly declined dessert and coffee and left shortly thereafter. My poor mother. I wasn't sure if she was just relieved that I was no longer proselytizing, or if she just couldn't comprehend and grapple with the choices I was making in general. My lifestyle was just too much for her to take in. I guess she was probably hoping that I would just grow up so that her life could be less worrisome. Not much else was ever said—she seemed to know that I would sort it out.

～

It took me some time to finally decide this wasn't the life I wanted and that what I did want was to leave and make a new life for myself. I began imagining a different life and figuring out ways to expand my job and living options. While I had sometimes shared my discontent with my husband, neither of us was mature or healthy enough to know where to begin. Of course, it came down to what I wanted to do, and I had trouble making that decision. In truth, I preferred avoiding the responsibility of taking new actions; maybe it was that simple.

Chances are if I had just dated him and not married him, we would have enjoyed each other for a while and then broken up when it was clear we weren't a match. I wouldn't have had any expectations. We would have just been two people who might have moved through each other's lives at a time in our history without a lot of "to do" and no "I do."

Eventually I came to understand that my husband had the right to his own choices and that I needed to respect them and figure out what I wanted. While he wanted to get high and be married to me, in that order of preference—those were his choices, the way he wanted to live his life. I had not considered what I wanted for my own life—my own desires and choices—until that day came when I just knew it was time to leave. To the core of my very being, I knew. Yes, that sponge was soaked to its limit. And with no elaborate plan, I borrowed a bit of money from friends, John and I divided our debts, kissed each other good-bye, and I left.

～

I am so thankful that after four years, I did not waste another moment of this beautiful life I was given in thinking "any moment now, any day now, any year now, he will change and things will be different." I have friends who are still waiting for their spouses to change—four months or forty years later. They have lived their choices, and I wish them well. But for me, the wedding vow of "till death do us part" was a prison. Staying with anything should come from a sincere desire to be there.

Expectations Lead to Misery

To determine another individual's destiny—to place rules on another's life, even our own—is to steal one's humanity. We want to choose, to ask ourselves, "Do I want to live a compromised life in deference to old promises that have become destructive for me?"

As we go about our lives, we may delude ourselves into believing that we are our own life director, fooling ourselves into thinking we're not listening to anyone else tell us how to live our life. We believe that we are living by our own rules, making our own decisions—choosing freely. It may not have been our intent to follow any particular dogma or societal mores—perhaps it just happens gradually over time and we are simply unaware—but somehow it seems that we have. One morning we wake up, unhappy with our lives, questioning our decisions as this realization catches us off guard. We may wonder why we didn't recognize the conditioning or the multitudes of clichés we had bought into to that became ingrained into our psyche, some of which we seem to have embraced as gospel. This serves no purpose. On any given day, we make hundreds of decisions, but how often do we ask ourselves, in full consciousness, "Whose rules am I living by?" and whether we are making our decisions without paying attention to the messages from our body?

More than we may realize, we can be profoundly influenced by parents, religious doctrines, clichés, friends, "should" and "ought to," and many other external sources. We can find ourselves bombarded with advertising, marketing efforts, and mass media in their attempts to condition and direct us. We can hold to images and ideas without questioning where they came from or whether we agree with them or want them ruling our lives. We get an idea in our head that, if sufficiently reinforced, can become dogma before we've even questioned whether that thought or idea or cliché has any genuine meaning in our life. That idea might simply be something we just latched onto, something we repeated many times until it became familiar and seemingly normal—for us. We may not realize that we impose these rules on others' lives as well as on our own. In so doing, we diminish our own humanity and the humanity of others. Sometimes we do this openly, knowing full well those rules aren't now—or never were—our truth; and sometimes we aren't aware that this has occurred.

Many of us grapple with the challenge of making sense from broken bits of wisdom. Perhaps these "nuggets of truth" might have served us at one point and in certain contexts, but they no longer feel genuine; they simply don't support us in our new thinking. Some of it may just be plain bad advice. But we can get caught up in it all—unaware—and we may base our choices and actions on those old premises, even when they conflict with our very being. What once seemed to hold meaning for us may cease to do so at any time. Even when we are aware of this, we may be hesitant to cast those "nuggets" to the wind. With Susan, as with many other characters in our stories, it can take some time to come to terms with mistaken notions, even once they are identified.

As we begin to stretch and grow in new directions, some people in our lives may find it uncomfortable and perhaps even unnerving as they sense that change is in the air. Yes, something is shifting, and things won't stay as they were. Just take a breath, take your time. Even in the midst of others' unrest, you can stay true to yourself and follow your own path. Try on your new life, one moment at a time.

Absolutes

As we could see in Susan's story, she was living from an expectation; she wasn't going to fail at her marriage the way she perceived that her parents had failed. She had all sorts of misperceptions about what it meant to fail in the context of marriage. She wanted her "word" to have value, a self-imposed rule that was holding her captive. Like many people who—with the best of intentions—give an absolute statement of commitment, Susan wanted to uphold her vows. She had given a promise to her husband with God as her witness, but her conviction was based on an arbitrary rule rather than on her truth and, therefore, became destructive to her life.

Most of us want our word—once given with good intentions—to have value. We are aligned with it when it is true for us in that moment we give it. However, the absolute nature of the concepts of "commitment" and "promise" can become problematic because, in reality, there are no absolutes in a human life. It is a contradiction to the finite life we live—in a material existence—to think there can be an absolute. Every micro-second of every day is new.

When we feel we need to make a change to a promise, we may feel "less" as an individual. It can be painful. But to do otherwise—to live the lie—means we are no longer committed to our own life; the inability to be forthcoming about changing what was once a promise can devolve our own life. Staying in a mismatched experience that is no longer correct for us may give us an illusion of virtue, but there is no virtue in suffering; it is self-destructive to remain—feeling trapped—staying when we want to leave. The reality is that the promise we made just doesn't apply anymore relative to this moment. Expectations based on an absolute statement made in reference to a nebulous and unknown future is a fantasy that may lead to misery. It is as unnecessary as it is unrealistic.

In the workplace "at will" contracts are evidence that, even in business, statements of commitments and promises are not always realistic, and not permanent. Similarly, couples more often now write their own wedding vows to design a marriage based on their truth at any point throughout the marriage. In these ceremonies, gone are the notions that a partner is one's "other half," "complement," or an "until death do us part" partner. After all, how can anyone promise their life into the future—even with the best of intentions and desires? These enlightened and more realistic vows honor the individuals in the marriage who do not want to limit themselves or their partners' lives, but who would rather join in agreement to nourish, respect, and participate in their evolving lives as partners in love and truth for as long as it is just that— their truth. More of this will improve and make natural the beauty of marriages.

What individual—who loves one's own self and another—would want to watch the devolving and the destruction of a life? What individual—who loves one's own self and another—would want to restrict or deny the option for change, to characterize that either partner would be acting deceitfully if he or she desired to change what was once promised? We all want to be cautious of the true nature of absolute statements and speak our truth as it is for us in the moment.

Changing course

It would be great if we all could see the reality that lies on the path ahead before getting ourselves between a rock and a hard place, in the middle of a partnership or a job that isn't a fit for us. But if reality hits us after the fact, so be it. Susan's desires for who and how she wanted to be were morphing, as they can with all of us, and her active observations of her reality showed it not to be what she wanted. There is no deadline for when we can self-correct or change course. It can happen that forty minutes, forty days, or forty years transpire from the time we realize the experience has ceased to satisfy to before we take action.

Even if Susan had been able to finesse the rules she was living by, her expectations had become obstacles that were bringing her misery. She wasn't conning herself into believing her situation was something it wasn't, but still, she knew the experience wasn't what she wanted as she found herself pretzeling herself around and ignoring her body's wisdom in order to live in the contradiction.

If we pay attention to our body and to our honest reactions rather than deferring to external influences and authorities, rationalizations, or someone else's rules, eventually our body will let us know when we are finished with an experience. However, we can also learn to be more careful about making absolute statements, even as we acknowledge that the experience before us is one that we no longer want. When we are ready to move on from the experience, we will know that others will either accept it or they will not. We can move through relationships and experiences, being responsible only for our own life, rather than dancing to someone else's reactions. When a promise or commitment can no longer apply in truth—relative to this moment—then there is no promise. There is just a lie.

There is risk in all choice

There is risk inherent in all choice. In Susan's case, choosing to avoid the very real possibility of consequences of engaging in illegal activities was a choice. Her decision to stay in her marriage and in her situation was a choice. For others, choices with inherent risk may be evidenced in financial loss, loss of friendships, lessened status, poor health, or other injury to the body. We may realize the risks before making the choice, or we may only learn of them many years later. We want to be mindful that the responsibility for ownership of our choices and the consequences that arise from those choices are ours. This includes ownership and responsibility for what occurs when we avoid making a choice or taking action – when we *do not* make a choice. Avoiding the responsibility of choosing does not absolve us of responsibility, and it does not protect us from risk. We are equally responsible for the consequences of that avoidance as for any choice we would make, such as is exampled in Susan's initially not choosing to leave. As her mother had pointed out, Susan and John could both have gone to jail if they had been arrested.

Acting from her truth

Susan put rules on her own life and in doing so she participated in disallowing the true expression of her own humanity. She was able to finally free herself from living a compromised life in deference to old promises, a life that had become destructive for her. She came to realize the reality was there were no "rules," there were just other people's ideas about rules and a whole bunch of made up stories. She may have been in a marriage; but with her truth of not wanting to be there, she was no longer able to bring wholehearted love, friendship, or intimacy to it. Her act of courage to leave the marriage was one that was respectful to her *and* to her husband.

22

Caroline's Story

"Get Real!"

*I was living the same split I had felt as a child when my body told me
one thing, which was completely opposite from those who claimed to
know what was true, and I couldn't reconcile the two.*

Always, I have wanted a peaceful, loving, fun, interesting, and happy
life, a life that's a fit for me. I don't suppose I'm much different that way
than many others.

My grandfather died when I was eight years old. No one liked my
grandfather, and people openly spoke about how he had beat his son, my
uncle; even at the funeral several people said that they were glad he was
dead. My mother had always disparaged him as well. However, shortly
after his death, I heard my mother begin to say what a wonderful person
he was. When I told my mother that she was not telling the truth, she told
me that it was not God's will to speak ill of the dead. I asked her, "Why
not, if it is the truth?" I was told I was heartless.

This was not the first time my mother and I had had words about
God and the truth. Even as a very young child, I was always questioning what I was told. My brain seemed to be more logical and factual
than my immediate environment allowed for. My mother believed in
a religious dogma as doctrine, and my daddy was "his own man" so to

speak. In other words, he didn't believe. At age five, I told my mother that I did not believe in a punishing God, and she switched me on my bare legs with tree branches tied with white rags for saying so. It hurt like hell, but I would only scream and cry inside. I was not going to let her see me cry for saying what I believed. It seems as though that has been my path for much of my life—seeking what was true for me and not letting anyone make me cry for asking the hard questions and attempting to express myself.

~

For many years I mostly tried to hide from any belief system; I ceased to be a seeker. I read no more about the Bible, theological philosophies, anything agreeing with or contrary to commonly accepted dogma, or anything requiring deep, contemplative thought. Off and on over the years, the evolution of my beliefs would take off once again, and I'd find various philosophies I resonated with, mostly having to do with holding our humanity sacred. It was always a wonderful feeling to celebrate with like-minded friends on such things.

After an out-of-state move, a new friend invited me to join her at a new thought event for visualization. The philosophies were certainly far afield from what I had known, but I was willing to check it out. It seemed to me there was a lot of focus on getting wealthy, but I just figured maybe the current gurus threw that stuff in there for marketing purposes. Perhaps they thought that more people would pay attention to the good messages if money was in the mix. There seemed to be a lot of emphasis on the idea that through a process of visualization you could get anything and everything you could possibly want to manifest in your life.

I hadn't been dissatisfied in my life prior to this, but more joy and an exciting job and a loving husband all sounded good. However, the more I began to follow the program's format, the more I found myself feeling the limitations of my life. There was very little attention paid to living in the present, which was my attitude prior to looking at this visualization stuff; everything seemed to be future focused. I was told there was a format to be followed, and always a good student, I was eager to learn these "visualization process techniques."

I was told that my subconscious mind could not differentiate between what was vividly imagined and what was true, and so through this suggested process I would manifest what I wanted in my life by believing it was already achieved. It largely seemed that all you needed to do was to visualize correctly by stating affirmations in the present tense, convincing yourself that you were already the person you wanted to be and had the things you wanted to have. By doing so, you would begin to manifest those things into your life. I was told the brain could close the gap between my current reality and my goals.

Always an active person, I wanted to think I was doing something; after all there was a lot of "doing" going on in my mind. So, I convinced myself I was taking action by visualizing, but in truth I was sitting on the sofa, having experiences in my mind. Nothing could have been farther from real action or reality.

Still, I continued to practice visualizing as I was taught, and I would put all my statements in the present tense as though those events had happened. Not "I will," but rather "I have…" or "I am…". In doing so, my body began to scream at me "Like hell you have that!" or "Like hell you are that! Get real!"

Clearly, something was telling me just to live and I would figure it all out. I felt a sense of "resistance" inside—clues from my body that told me I would recognize what wanted to be recognized when I saw it, and there was no way to see it without experiencing it. In real life. But I was a good student, and so I ignored those hints.

It was suggested to me that I needed to feel it, see it, smell it, taste it as if I was there, as if it was real so I could have success with my goals. I was "corrected" and "belittled" by others telling me I was doing it wrong or I would have had success. I began to feel like I was losing myself to the whole process. I was becoming more and more out of touch with the changing way I believe we are naturally, as I repeated old affirmations out of habit. I felt like a child all over again when I had sworn to myself that I would always hold to what I believed to be true for me. And yet, here I was, in this struggle, feeling more and more confused.

Instead of looking at reality and the beautiful messages it can bring, I ignored the clues over a period of several years. Everything was a lot of effort, a lot of disowning a part of me—largely my body's persistent messages. I found myself always lacking, always seeking. I was beginning to feel like a follower of Moses who had wandered in the wilderness for many years, trying to find something, but I didn't know what.

〜

Then one day, it happened. There I was visualizing, and in my dreams I was working at the most interesting job in a new field with great people and we were laughing and I felt accepted and comfortable. In another dream, this beautiful man came up behind me, and my body felt warm. I felt loved and romantic. When I left the class that day, of course I thought, "This really is going to happen—this is working!" I went back to my life as it had been, expecting that any day the job of the dreams and the man of my dreams were going to appear.

My life consisted of going to work to pay for the courses I attended to get a different life, a future life. I can't recall what had happened to my innate curiosity and exploring nature—not to mention my sense of humor—in those years. But my willingness to purchase the intriguing and peaceful life I was seeking took precedence and cost didn't matter. I just didn't know at the time that the real cost was to embrace a pretend life in a pretend world by conning myself into believing something that I knew wasn't really true for me. Nor did I yet understand, that aligning myself in all ways with what was true for me—not fighting against it—is to experience peace.

~

My problem also was that once something *did* appear, I became so attached to what I believed I had manifested that I couldn't seem to see beyond my fantasy version. Twice this happened.

Within days of beginning my "perfect job" without adequate discernment, the destructive environment became visible, and with it, the con I began to do to myself. Red flags were popping up at every turn and the discrepancies I uncovered were mind-boggling. Bold-faced lies surfaced. Continued promises to the customer that were impossible to be kept rolled off the lips of the silver-tongued leadership. Energy was spent fabricating cover-ups for what couldn't be delivered. Staff who could clearly see what was going on quit, and the workload increased for those of us foolish enough to stay. Payments to contractors were delayed for weeks and longer. "The post office lost the checks" became another fabrication. Balls dropped, fingers got pointed in every direction—usually at whoever stated the truth, because the leadership took every pronouncement of reality as though being told their baby was ugly. My visualizations turned into nightmares and I couldn't sleep. Still, I continued to put in horrendous hours, becoming exhausted from living the contradiction. The tasks I was required to do didn't harmonize with me, but convinced that what I had manifested must be correct—my visualization result couldn't be wrong—I ignored my sensibilities, and convinced myself that things would get better.

A similar experience happened to me when I believed I had manifested the perfect mate into my life and moved forward again without adequate discernment. As our time together progressed, I began noticing that I was not particularly enjoying spending evenings with him watching B-rated movies or listening to him wax poetic about himself while he drank. But once again, with my attachment to having manifested this perfect man into my life, my abilities at observation were obscured and everything else I didn't want to see, I rationalized away. I hadn't wanted to notice how dissimilar some of our values were. Warm and deep relationships were important to me, but he had neither close personal relationships nor much contact with family and friends. Although he had "reasons" why his relationships were so, I knew—my body knew—that we have the relationships we want; otherwise we pursue something else. He began to express interests in lifestyle choices that held no interest for me and I found myself pulling away. The acquaintances he was drawing into his life were not my people. I was finding myself becoming less and less interesting, even to myself, and noticed how alive and engaged I felt when I was just by myself or with my friends, pursuing what held genuine interest for me. But believing I had manifested my perfect mate, instead of walking away, I began reading books, listening to CDs and attending workshops about how I could better live with my "not a match for me" mate. My "studies" focused on questionable notions that ranged from accepting the planetary limitations that came with me being from Venus—and the consequent "work arounds"—to understanding the four stages of my unique mate and how I could lovingly manipulate him in each of those stages in order to get what I wanted.

In both cases, I was hell-bent on ignoring my body screaming at me to quit being an idiot and get real. Every time I tried to affirm and visualize, my body tensed and my neck cramped, and afterwards I'd get a headache. I was living the same split that I had felt as a child when my body told me one thing, which was completely opposite from those who claimed to know what was true, and I couldn't reconcile the two. I had simply forgotten to ask myself if where I was, was where I wanted to be. Oh, the folly.

～

Eventually, with all that disconnecting, I began to recognize how I wasn't trusting myself. I thought about those two friends of mine who claimed to have such success with their visualizing. They didn't just sit around and visualize. They were courageous, outgoing, energetic, and happy people who lived full lives. They had lives in action—always had. They made tons of choices, took on new experiences and friendship, even new business ventures. In their lifetimes they had made many mistakes, fallen down, gotten up, changed directions, and carried on. They laughed with life, cried and laughed at mistakes, and didn't kid themselves. They were both actually good at making choices because they had made so many in their real lives.

And so, one day it just hit me full in the face. People who claimed success at visualizing were attributing their success to the visualization process and not to their own efforts and lives of action. They were learning, growing, developing, and doing what they loved. Wait a minute! *Correlation does not equal causation.* Who said their wonderful lives had anything to do with visualizing? That works for selling a program and they may even believe it, but for me…EUREKA!

I stopped doing what I knew wasn't true for me. I stopped living the lie. It was enough already. I started laughing! All this psychobabble pop psychology stuff may be for others, but it wasn't for me. It wasn't my true path.

And so, those many years ago, in that moment of fully seeing what was really happening and admitting I wanted something else, I began new steps of action and have never stopped since. Now, at seventy-six years old, still working part-time because I enjoy it, travelling, and loving the richness of my life, my advice to my children and their children and all my loved ones? "Try not to wait well over half a century to learn to trust yourselves; don't lay your precious life on others. The one to trust is yourself and your own choices. Your truth will set you free. Always." And then of course, given what seems to be in my DNA, I add, "Amen."

Visualization is Not Personal Development

How can there be such a thing as, "speak the truth as though it is your reality"? When your truth is your reality—when they are the same—there is a mesh, a synchronicity. When speaking the truth "as though" it is your reality, it is a con.

A twelve-year old child remarks to himself as he is looking out the windows from his sixth grade classroom, "When I get out of school today, I can't wait to jump in the pool." He sits there in class, imagining the experience. He "feels" the sun warming his body, the cool water splashing around him. He hears his own laughter. He is not actively attempting to visualize; he is letting his desires surface in a thought. Both children and adults daydream; they yearn, they can taste the experience, they get in touch with their heart's desire.

There is nothing wrong with daydreaming about one's desires; it is perfectly wonderful to have a vision. You envision yourself walking through the experience you are planning to have. The body is preparing, you are organizing, synchronizing for when that experience occurs.

But some have taken this natural and ordinary pattern of day-dreaming—these beautiful desires expressed in one's daydreams—and misconstrued it. They've created a philosophy that rests on the premise that what we *visualize* as real *determines* what is real. To change our reality, we don't have to take action; all we need do is visualize reality as we want it to be. "Visualize and you'll get what you want" seems to be its ultimate take-away. If you take this advice literally, as Caroline did, it has the potential to strip away your choices yet to be made, your beautiful experiences yet to come, and most unfortunately, your life yet to be lived.

You cannot fool "Mother Nature"

People visualize because they are lacking something in their life, and visualization technique programs have been promoted and sold as a "practice," "method," and "technique" of attempting to artificially create a life experience. We are told to take that natural yearning that has motion and life to it, (like in sixth grade when we felt the sun and the water while sitting in the chair daydreaming), do it in your mind, and "it will come." We are told this process will create connections, but we are faulty in what we imagine. Marketers have misrepresented the way our brain wave pattern functions when we are daydreaming. It is true that thoughts can trigger the release of a chemical formula from the glandular system. Happy thoughts make us feel happy, and the body likes that. Sad or angry thoughts harm the body. But visualization technique programs that promote the mistaken notion that we cannot differentiate between what is vividly imagined and what is reality create misinformation that encourages us to convince ourselves to believe we already possess something, already are something, and have already achieved something when—in reality—that is not true. Do we really want to spend our precious moments attempting to fool the mind instead of taking action for our lives? Such fanciful ideas can lead an individual to surrender to non-reality from the comfort of a sofa.

Numerous self-help programs promote the notion that there are immutable laws of success, wealth attraction, partner manifestation, and so on. They package, promote, and sell a fantasy that "the good life" is out there somewhere, and all that is required to attain it is to visualize it in just the right way—conceive, believe, and act like we already have everything—with enough intent to magically manifest it. In reality, there are no such laws. Our humanity cannot be so easily dismissed. These programs promote an unrealized life, a life that is not actually experienced in the flesh.

There is no whispered "secret" within the body

Positive thoughts naturally make us feel great, and we all enjoy hearing stories of happiness. But true inspiration cannot be created artificially by techniques and manipulation, image building, or fantasy. These false and limited practices can only offer us a course in daydreaming because actualizing requires action on our part. If we want a genuine relationship with ourselves, with our own life—if we want to find the people, the work, and situations that resonate with us (in which we feel in accordance)—we simply take actions and experiences in real life that guide us to know ourselves.

If we are sincere, speak the truth as we know it to be for us, and actively pursue what we desire, others can then choose whether they want an experience with us. The outcome emerges naturally, and we will move with it. If we are in sync with something or someone—the frequencies are a mesh—things will move one way; if we are not in sync with something or someone—the frequencies are not a mesh—things will move another way. The body will not be fooled; it knows when something is naturally and organically meshing. There is no whispered "secret" with the body. The body intelligence—that knowingness—yells *loudly and clearly* when we live an awake and conscious life. We have only to choose to act, and as we step into each experience, pay attention to whether that experience truly resonates with who and how we are.

Consider this: *Look, pursue, figure it out, and go get it!*

Instead of sitting back and doing the passive "ask, believe, and receive" thing, we instead "look, pursue, figure it out, and go get it!" If you like your life and you are living your truth, you can trust it will unfold to your liking. Instead of "believing will create it," you can begin to get acquainted with yourself, become aware of yourself, and begin to believe in yourself—knowing your body so well that you will hear any message it conveys with open ears and heart. You will know if an individual or situation is the best choice for you in that moment, these real people and real experiences with their inherent rich complexities and unique characteristics. You will be living authentically with that information, and you will make your own best choices from there as you move forward. That's what coming to believe in yourself can accomplish.

When we are invested in visualizing or living out of fantasy as a means of attaining, we stop listening to our bodies, to ourselves. Reality is our friend, and in manipulating our reality, we choose not to pay attention to what may possibly inform or injure us. We cannot listen to the truth that wants to be heard if we are deluding ourselves with fantasy that distorts our truth and attempts to "fool" our bodies. Scamming ourselves with manipulation deafens us.

When you are living consciously, you can learn to trust yourself. But if you are busy engaging in techniques that would have you shutting down your body's reactions to reality and mentally fabricating a belief that something you want is already in your life, how can you possibly trust your sensibilities?

In the universe, there is a free and available exchange

Sometimes we hear people who are delighted with an outcome say, "Oh, look what the universe sent me." While a sweet cliché of gratitude, it is important to be conscious of what we think about that. Can the universe actually "give" us anything just because we want it?

Consider this: We design and create our own lives by choice and action. In reality, you do something; you make a choice and take an action and move your whole being toward an experience you want. That experience is in harmony with your unique heart desires; it is not based on someone else's idea of what you should choose, or should want, but what you truly want. And when that movement occurs by your action and deed, the wholeness of you and the universe together orchestrate in the direction of your heart's desires, and you feel a connection—you feel that things make sense. When acting from your truth, there is wholeness—there is integrity. What could be more natural than that?

Our harmony with the universe is interactive—there is always a free and available exchange—based on our active participation. If we can come to know our truth—that truth that resides within—and choose and act from it, more pathways will naturally change and emerge. The key to connecting to the universe in an interactive way is to participate with harmony in action. This cannot be manipulated or fabricated. This can only occur when you are acting out of true desires—living an authentic life.

Each daily decision shows up as a cumulative effect, taking us down one path or another. If we end up, by our choices, irresponsibly taking on a path that is disconnected to what we deeply desire, it is irrational to think we are moving ourselves closer toward what we desire. Caroline's participation in her fantasy kept her from walking away with minimal effort from what had revealed itself to be what she no longer wanted.

A skewing of reality

How did it happen that people have fallen prey to these techniques?

How could a lovely pastime like daydreaming and envisioning get conscripted for this kind of convolution and distortion? How did it happen that a whole industry has been built around a basic premise of a child's daydream? Perhaps it is because this appears to be a consequence-free, passive path. Action, on the other hand, obligates us to the responsibility for the action. Easy fixes tend to entice and sell. Visualization techniques, while time consuming, give the illusion of action. Remember that Caroline felt she was taking action even as she was just sitting on the sofa. Action requires energy; it produces outcomes and offers experiences that can be used for access, for information, and for development if desired—none of which can possibly occur merely in thoughts and wishful dreams.

Some people, when they find themselves in personal or work relationships or jobs that are not satisfying, have been instructed to use visualization techniques to convince themselves in present tense that everything is beautiful or loving or satisfying. We begin to accommodate the information instead of seeing it for what it is. For Caroline, taking any action, such as quitting her job or breaking off her relationship with the man she was dating, would have required that she be responsible for that action. She didn't want to do that. She preferred fabricated feelings, which kept her safely distanced from her reality. With her mate, she believed she needed to try to understand how she could learn to live with and compensate for "why" her mate wasn't a match, rather than act on that reality. In both cases, she realized she hadn't discerned a "similarity to natures,"— she was becoming aware that was true—but she thought things would "straighten out" because after all, she had manifested it.

There is nothing wrong with fantasizing about a great job and the people there or true love with someone wonderful. We daydream all the time. But when something or someone stands before us in full and living color, we need to get real—stand grounded in our reality—and dispense with the fantasies, allowing others to reveal their truth in their behaviors. We observe their actions and their interactions with others. People reveal their authentic selves through their behavior, regardless of what they say. Their truth may not be immediately apparent; but it is in their nature, and eventually it will be revealed. Observe and listen. How do they live their life? How do they make choices? How do they run their businesses and treat their people? Who and what do they seem to attract into their life or surround themselves with? Notice the choices they make. We want to ask ourselves, "Is any of it of interest to me?

If the actuality of what we are observing in another is not a match for us, that is the reality to accept. It is best to avoid rationalizing or imposing attributes from our wishes or visualizations that don't exist.

Welcoming reality

If you aren't happy, maybe you are missing the chance to practice living, practice loving, and practice discernment up close and personal in your real life—not in your imagination. Ask yourself, "Am I being someone who could have a life like that or a relationship with that type of individual I like and respect?" Then begin to take steps to develop yourself.

We've often heard the adage, "practice makes perfect"; and yet, many people have chosen to sit idly by for years, vividly imagining another life and not engaging in *this* life, *this* reality. The healthier we become in our development, the less likely we are to engage in a process designed to shield us from reality or in instruction designed to distract us from being our own expert at determining if what is before us, is really what we want at this time. What was going on for Caroline when her body screamed, "Get real!" as she experienced neck aches and headaches while participating in a process that was out of accord with her? Visualization techniques may create a skewing of reality, a muting of reality in favor of non-reality. As we develop ourselves further, however, we may become unwilling to settle for anything less than reality. In Caroline's case, her body demanded it.

Getting real with ourselves and our lives

Do we really need to bend, twist, turn, manipulate, trick, or fool?

We do not need—nor is it possible—to use the manipulation of our thoughts and feelings to connect with the universe so we can have the life we want. To bend our destinies to our will by simply claiming something to be so is not possible. Relax. Put down the heavy weights. Just take action. Participate in life. Seek out an experience and if it is agreeable, life may get better. If you like the way your life is unfolding, life circumstances don't affect you in the way they do when you don't like the way your life is unfolding. It need not be an alienating and lonely experience to lose a friend or lose a job when we view all our pursuits and interests with openness. Life itself is like an open library. With each action step of choosing, ask yourself: "Am I moving toward better experiences?" If your body tells you that you are not, choose something different and try something new that makes you feel as though you are moving toward better experiences. You do this fully conscious, one hundred percent in reality with one hundred percent participation in a real action.

We can't foretell a destiny; our destiny is not a "goal" to achieve

People will sometimes say, "Oh, this is perfect for me—I will be in this or do this forever!" It may sound nice, but we can't know those things. We have today, what is known today. We cannot foretell the future of a situation or relationship or anything else. It is not something to be decided; these things can only be experienced and known. We can support it to be the best it can be, but the quality of the experience may or may not keep improving. It's best to simply pay attention and recognize the reality that is presenting and not succumb to trying to force reality to conform to some beautiful fantasy. That way, each day we can look anew at what is in our present lives without any blinders on.

Compelling dreams—feeling compelled—that's what will drive action. We want to keep the focus on the actual life. It is necessary for us to put our own life in accordance with what we want to live today and in this specific moment. Our desires are created and influenced by our experiences, which means that our desires will be continually changing as we take on new experiences. Our lives evolve. We choose today, do today, accomplish today; and with each new day that is lived, desires change. Desires rarely have the chance to change and grow when our life consists of reciting yesterday's visualizations.

What if instead of encouraging our friends, our children, and our loved ones to visualize the life they want, we encourage them to daydream and fantasize to their heart's content, then look, pursue, figure it out, and go after it. We let them know that we trust they can do it. We tell that to ourselves as well. Then we are all discovering what satisfies us and moving toward getting ourselves some of that goodness. We call this living.

And wherever any of us end up in any given moment, by our choices and actions, that it our destiny in that moment.

23

Our Symptoms Are the Expression of Our Body Speaking to Itself

Nature offers the "gifts of health"—awaiting expression. These gifts of health are our true desires. If we suppress them, repress them, or ignore them, we may subject ourselves to symptoms, and if those are ignored, to compromised well-being.

We have previously noted that the effects of unhappiness and stress can be monumental to our overall sense of well-being. We all know people who just don't ever seem happy. They don't anticipate with joy what will be next. They may fixate; they may depend on, blame, and expect from others; they may "get in someone else's life" but they don't ever wake up and love their life, their day. Often they either aren't able or aren't willing or just don't know how to begin to take responsibility for their own lives and to make choices and take actions that could bring them joy. So they remain unhappy and unfulfilled. This unhappiness can be a byproduct of the sum total of a life lived in conflict with one's authentic desires.

Our bodies are organisms. As such, we recognize that the ordinary daily life stresses (without extreme discord and living mostly in harmony) cause wear-and-tear on them, which is reflected in different systems in the body, including its vital organs. Our bodies can easily use their regenerative capacity to restore wholeness and balance in these circumstances, such as having a hard day once in a while, hearing an unkind word, or simply facing life's daily challenges. These experiences have a minimal effect on our bodies. But when the stresses become more aggressive or more consistent relative to other factors, a different scenario begins to develop. When the amount of stress becomes more severe, as when the contradictions we live— and no longer want to live—become more apparent, and therefore more aggravating, we can see the effects in the misuse and overuse and abuse of our bodies. Is it likely any of us would suggest that unhappiness and stress don't somehow affect our sense of well-being?

In every experience we take, we pay for the choices we have made. Our choices can be our undoing, our rebuilding, or our creating. If we are not living our truth, we may want to ask ourselves, "Am I compromising my well-being by living in conflict with myself? By staying unhappy, worried, stressed, fatigued, living the con or contradiction?" Our wellness and our compromised health may be byproducts of whether or not we choose our truth; we can tax our well-being when choosing compromises.

Symptom alerts

Our body may signal us with what might be described as symptoms or alerts as necessary through gut instincts, knots in our stomach, gagging reflexes, inklings, nagging thoughts, and other sensations and clues more directly related to our health. We may feel confused, jittery, unhappy, exhausted, hazy, unsure, listless, or overwhelmed. We may be plagued by more obvious health issues such as frequent diarrhea, colds, flus, and headaches. There are many reasons we choose to not hear our bodies' cries for acknowledgment or choose to ignore those signals. Maybe because we are busy. Maybe because discerning what is causing these symptoms would make us uncomfortable. Maybe because we know we need to make some changes and we aren't ready to or don't want to. We may simply pretend not to see, not to know.

We may try to change our reactions to people or situations in order to deflect our symptoms, and if so, find that the signals from our bodies may increase in intensity and volume. Sometimes this may result in more serious attacks to the body as our symptoms try to warn us of danger. When we do not pay attention to our body's messages—adjusting and responding accordingly—the resulting possibility of compromised well-being may even cause disease to develop.

When living out prolonged experiences that do not resonate with us, there is exhaustion and depletion—diminished energy and diminished motivation. Our life force is negatively affected. On the other hand, experiences that do resonate with us will energize us; we may even feel intense motivation because our life force is positively affected.

Acute symptoms may be an expression of life happening

Consider this as you explore how you want to think about and view your own individual health: Continuously, the body performs functions of repair and functions of rebuilding and exchange. The body uses proteins and good fats as the materials to repair and facilitate the exchange of old cells for new cells. To avoid a chronic disease, you may want to allow the acute symptomology (referred to medically as acute disease) such as colds, flu, inflammation, upset stomach, etc., to express itself. These symptoms are "triggers to cure"; the body invites infection to help you get better. It may be that nothing is "wrong." These primary symptoms such as colds, flus, and allergies—these acute diseases—may be attempting to dismantle the predisposition to chronic diseases. Through the expression of acute disease symptoms, we benefit as nature assists us to get well. These symptoms give us information. When symptoms are supported—not stopped or denied—they offer a way for the acute not to become chronic. They are the body's way of showing us there is a problem.

Symptoms are the manifestation of the body attempting to ward off disease. They are the body's expression, speaking to itself in its movement to homeostasis—in its efforts to regulate and keep its internal health stable and functional—to return and maintain balance in the body. These symptoms are an expression of life happening, of an active immune system, one that is necessary to achieve and maintain better health.

How do we mobilize?

If we injure ourselves by making life choices that bring us into distressing life experiences, we are burdening our health by causing stress to our body. By these choices that bring us emotions expressed as stress, we may be cultivating disease. We stress the body systems and vital organs and functions. Stressful experiences or expressions that are not connected to our innermost desires may result in feelings of exhaustion, like a run-down battery, an empty life. The life lived by these choices will then support us in our offending, suppressing emotions—in our disease.

Any choice relating to a toxic emotion is not our best choice. Notice the emotion, the momentary reaction to an occurrence, or situation, or an individual; it often just lasts for a few seconds and helps us recognize what we like and don't like. This reaction is a tool for confirmation about that experience. If it isn't to our liking, we may want to take a different action. We may find value in welcoming our truth and listening to our body. When we trigger unhealthy emotions, the resulting body chemistry destroys healthy tissues. If we can take cues from our body and notice any toxic emotions from choices we have made, then we know those choices are not the best ones for us. Those who have been indulging toxic emotions for years often find that a slight addiction has been created. Without healthy development, these people may be drawn to repeat similar experiences that may not be in their better interests.

We can choose experiences that are less difficult or more difficult. If our desires are in harmony with our actions, more ease exists and less efforting is required. And those choices of quality are reflected in better health as we mobilize into our destinies through our actions made by choice.

Nature offers the "gifts of health"; they are awaiting expression. These "gifts of health" are our true desires. But if we suppress, repress, or ignore these true desires and wishes—if we are not receptive to better choices, and if we ignore our body's messages, our symptoms—we may become susceptible to disease. It is our life choices that either encourage our wellness or compromise our well-being.

We want greater exposure of our truth

When we are experiencing discomfort, rather than taking action to ameliorate it, we may come up with lots of excuses to avoid addressing the discomfort head on. Some common expressions are "oh, well…" and "you know how so and so is…" and "whatcha gonna do?" There is also the shrug of the shoulders, and of course, the far more insidious management techniques that can cause abuse to or misuse of ourselves or others. Maybe we don't want to validate that the discomfort has purpose, so we just try to manage and accommodate it or pacify ourselves.

Contrast that to those who are willing to take notice of the body's messages and confront their discomfort with action. Sometimes even the smallest steps of action can create immense movement toward a more satisfying life. The body will be healthier than the mind will allow. These new experiences actually shift the other experiences of discomfort, and in this way, we begin to maximize the expression of our full being. Greater exposure of our truth—our true desires—then becomes more possible. This happens because the body—as our partner in creating our life—will go toward the experiences we want. Any physical movement propels some opening, so going toward the experiences we desire stimulates reactions in the body. When we trust that the body knows and we align ourselves with its messages, we may come to enjoy more peace and harmony in our lives.

Nature supports the development of every organism

Movements boost energy; they enhance our sense of comfort and self-esteem. They stimulate healthier sleep and better ability to deal with stress. If our mind is distressed, disturbed, chaotic, or agitated, we want to get centered and move that old, interfering, imploding energy out of our body with movement. Often, the mind is able to reorder itself in this way. We move, trot, walk, or pace; we breathe. The breaths are palliative, restorative. These actions help to bring order and quiet, ease and thought; these movements stimulate fresh perspectives and free us from where we might have gotten stuck. We feel calm, centered, and harmonious. There is no argument. We simply know and we do.

There is an exchange chosen in moving to more optimal wellness and vitality and that is in making different choices.
Choices made from our truth.

When we stay conscious, it is easy to engage this natural process; after all, we feel it when our life is working and we feel it when it is not. If we have desires that are clear to us, then we can begin to take actions that engage and satisfy them. If what is right in front of us is not what we want, a simple "no, thank you" will do. We want to either shake hands and walk away or begin the steps that will allow us to do that.

When we make life choices that nurture, encourage, and support more joyful life experiences, nourishing ourselves with joyful emotions, we are then encouraging and supporting the development of health. We enhance rather than stress the body systems and vital organs and functions. That life so lived will then encourage us in our positive and nourishing emotions, in our healing and wellness. Satisfying experiences or self-expressions that reflect our truth result in creating a more energetic and harmonious life, one with a greater sense of wellness.

If a plant cannot live according to its nature, it dies. So a man.
—Henry David Thoreau

24

Ben's Story

Self-Declaring

When an individual "self-declares," it often doesn't happen all at once, but it can. In one moment or through a series of moments, in choices possibly even made with small steps, he or she chooses to become full-bodied, whole, and exist in his or her own light.

*C*haracters: *Mom (Elizabeth), Dad (Bill, who lives in another state), Ben (their 9 year-old son)*
Setting: *Soccer season*

The phone rings.

Mom: Hello.
Dad: Hi, Elizabeth, is Ben home?
Mom: Hi, Bill, yes, one minute, I'll put him on.
Ben: Hi, Dad.

Conversation ensues, laughter, fun, connection. Ben has just finished telling his father about the good times he is having playing soccer. The conversation continues:

Dad: Now, Ben, I think that's great that you enjoy soccer, but I want you to go out for baseball as well. You know, I played baseball, and so did your Uncle Bob and Uncle Jim and even Grandpa. It's a great sport. You enjoyed it last season. Remember when you were here and we went to the Giants game? Wasn't that fun?

Ben: Yeah, Dad, that was really fun. But I don't want to play baseball anymore. I like playing soccer. I won't be signing up for baseball, Dad.

Dad: Soccer's great, but you can like baseball, too. I want you to sign up for that and give it another go.

Over the next few weeks, the same conversation is repeated over and over. Sometimes Dad cajoles; sometimes he tries to make Ben feel guilty about breaking the family tradition. Finally, at the end of one conversation:

Dad: Why don't you put your mother on the phone?

Ben: Mom, Dad wants to talk to you.

Mom: Hello, Bill.

Dad: Hey, Elizabeth, great talking with Ben today. He sounds really happy.

Mom: Oh yes, he's doing well. He's so excited about his summer.

Dad: So, Ben said he's not going out for baseball this year. He had mentioned that a few weeks ago, and he and I had spoken that you were going to get him signed up for it. Why didn't that happen?

Mom: Well, Bill, it seems Ben really likes soccer and doesn't care to go out for baseball again this year. He told me that he told you his preferences. Soccer seems to provide him a lot of movement and teamwork and a lot of fun. Are you familiar with soccer? I know I never played it.

Dad: No, not really, but our whole family played baseball, and I recall you played softball. I'm sure you can remember how much fun you had.

Mom: Yes, I recall. Those were some good times.

Dad: Then we can agree that you'll get Ben signed up for baseball.

Mom: No, I won't agree to that because it isn't what he wants and he's made that clear to us.

Dad: Well, get him signed up for baseball. He can do both.

Enroute home, after winning the county championship soccer game.

Mom: Wow, that was such a great game, son!

Ben: Yeah, we really played together as a great team! Did you see when I stole the ball and kicked it over to Alex? Awesome!

An hour later at home.

Mom: Would you like to call your Dad and tell him about your fabulous
victory? (This had become a ritual since the beginning of the season.)
Ben: No. Not really.
Mom: *(Inquiring kindly)* Care to share what's going on for you?
Ben: Mom, Dad doesn't really want to hear about my soccer game. He just
wants to hear me say that I'm going to play baseball.
Mom: I understand, Ben. It's important to hold to what you want and like
for your own life. I'm so glad you had a good time.

Becoming Our Own Life Director

"All of us, when given the opportunity, choose the things we
want to attend to. We want to live on the outside as we are
within. This is harmony. This is integrity."

– Karen Sontag

We've read about a number of characters in our stories who were able
to self-declare their truth about what they wanted—what they believed
would bring them a more satisfying life—and how they began to take
actions toward those desires by developing themselves along the way.
This is possible for anyone who so chooses. It may come piecemeal. It
may come years after the initial thoughts; but eventually, in order to be
your own life director and to have the options you want for a life of your
choosing, it needs to happen.

The life belongs to the individual and no one else

At nine years old, Ben knew what he wanted and understood the
resistance or lack of support that was presenting itself from outside forces.
Even though that resistance was from a loved one, Ben fended off the
pressure to change what he wanted. It wasn't the first time, nor was it
to be the last, that Ben would face the difficult decision of whether to
follow his own inclinations and desires or default to pleasing others.
A parent's inability to fully participate in his or her child's true desires
and encourage him to go with his own innate knowingness can have a
severe negative impact on that child's ability to develop his own internal

authority. Children often know when they are being manipulated. Ben knew. Ben was learning the life skill of discernment.

When time gaps exist between the conversations you have with your children, it may seem to you as though their desires are moving targets—ever-changing. Naturally they are. All people move in and out through experiences and interests, and our children are no different. Do we presume to hold our children to an interest they once had but no longer have? Each individual owns his or her own well-being and is meant to pursue his or her own opportunities in life.

Allowing a child to self-express may cause conflict between parents when one manipulates the child, and both the child and the other parent are aware of it. As the parent who knows what is happening, you risk betraying both yourself and your child if you do not openly acknowledge your child's truth.

Any relationship is about an accumulated past. Two experiences are involved in any relationship, and both are likely viewed differently as each participant brings his own unique perspective to it. Therefore, each experiences the interactions in a completely different way from the other. Sometimes a contradiction may be going on because one individual cannot recognize the complexities of the co-created relationship from the other's perspective. The other individual may be trying in every way he knows how to make himself heard, but he feels that he simply can't get through.

This is often particularly true when someone is convinced that he knows what is best for the other, or when he believes the other individual has "potential" to be or do something, and he persists in this pursuit regardless of a clearly stated lack of interest from that other individual. In Ben's case, it was his father who believed it was in Ben's best interest that he play baseball, even though Ben repeatedly stated that wasn't his interest or intent. Perhaps his father had been successful in his efforts to convince Ben of something in the past, but the relationship was developing and changing; Ben was maturing, his perspective was shifting, and his autonomy was developing. He was not living for approval for his own choices; he was living for the experience—his *own* life experience. Ben was becoming his own life director.

Seeking a level of comfort with making choices

Choosing to act is a risk, and if our children or anyone hasn't been allowed to refine the skill of making choices of risk and to develop their own sense of internal authority, they don't know how—and will not have a level of comfort—to choose action; they won't know themselves. How can they feel good about vying for their own experience—their own life—if they don't have their own life? We want to be careful not to steal it from another. Not from our children *or* from anyone else.

If ever any child or adult falls prey to that or consciously chooses to go along with that and doesn't exercise their freedom to choose their own life, then they will live someone else's version of their life.

Ben's father was not familiar with soccer, he himself had never "accessed" soccer, and he wanted Ben to remain with a prior choice of baseball because it was familiar and known to his father. All of us are at different stages in our lives, and at any given time, our lives will be lived (if lived genuinely) in a way no one else could possibly predict. There is an evolutionary aspect to each individual's journey. New information comes in, new experiences occur or are chosen, and new paths are followed. Things change. We will encounter new people and new ideas at different stages of our lives and may never even encounter or consider an idea someone else may have on our behalf.

Our character is built on the experiences we choose

Most parents desire to provide shelter, education, and financial support, and they try to be available emotionally for their children. But some parents seem to find it difficult to trust a child's natural developmental process. Sometimes parents want access that a child doesn't want to give or ownership that a child refuses to hand over. Through manipulation and coercion, parents may attempt to get their child to live and do as they wish, as they believe is best for the child. As our children get older, they become aware of what is going on. As they become young adults, they naturally claim ownership for their own well-being and their own opportunities in life. They call dibs on those. Parents do not have any right to live through their children.

Can it be that our priorities as parents have gotten completely twisted around? Our children can have all the opportunities in the world, but without character development, it won't matter. Our children are best served—best parented—when they have been supported and guided in this development. A priority of any parent is that their child figure out for himself or herself whether they are an individual of character and integrity. That is what will sustain our children through their future. They can't do this when someone else is making the decisions for their lives.

Our responsibility as parents is to raise our children in support of their developing sense of internal authority and not simply "train" them to seek out and rely on external sources for direction and validation in every choice they make. When children receive signals and comments that their behavior is acceptable or not, they learn to seek praise and to please. They take the cues to do whatever it takes to get the good reactions from those who they believe hold the authority to determine if they should feel good about themselves or bad about themselves. They have assigned their own authority to someone else. Many, even as adults, still find themselves living for approval rather than just taking the experiences they truly want. However, we know that all of us, when we are welcomed to make our own choices, become happier and more fulfilled.

Access is key to connecting to our innermost desires

Our truth awakens our access

Sometimes when we are out in the world, living our truth and living our own individual lives through actively taking on different experiences—BAM!—a connection is made that is exactly what we needed at the time for what we were pursuing. Yes, when we are out in the world, guided by our true desires, we are far more available to notice—to recognize—when we cross paths with pertinent information or the correct individual or situation. This collective data—this input—can come in the form of any experience: grocery shopping, walking, meeting new people—in essence while just doing life. This access is a tool for our developmental evolution. When this occurs, we may choose to take on new opportunities to act on something. We want to trust ourselves. This information, these people, these experiences exist around us all the time, but when we are not living our own lives—following our own truth and pursuing our deepest desires—we are not available to them; our senses are dulled to this recognition.

When we have access to broader fields and sources of information and communication, we are not so locked into what we might have once believed works or doesn't work. Many of us are consciously choosing a path of self-discovery from a diverse variety of sources, moving forward and trusting our own senses. We step into experiences, we are informed by them, and we use that information to take new steps. Sometimes what we choose may be uncomfortable or unfamiliar. We may feel anxious—but alive. Without developing our skills for dialogue, we may feel frustrated and ineffective. So we practice expressing; we engage. It won't always be a process of continuous forward motion. It is an iterative process. Sometimes we will step forward, backwards, or even side-to-side. Sometimes there will be missteps. But with practice, we improve and life becomes easier.

Multiple points of data are tools to awaken access

When we receive information from only one source—one data point—we likely will acquire insufficient input and make incorrect inferences or draw incorrect conclusions. Our logic may be faulty and inadequate because it isn't formed from a broad-based sampling of experiences. The Internet, for example, provides multiple data points— reviews, reality television, news articles, anecdotes, and blogs. This access provides us with a more broad and varied range of viewpoints than we've ever had before. And so it is with jobs, coffee shop conversations, playing basketball with a friend, or any experience or activity. Having access to varied sources of information allows us to break up arguments, dispel fallacies, and wrestle with deductions that we might have once made with limited information.

Multiple points of data—access to wide and varied sources of information—are tools to awaken access in our evolution, and when we cross paths with the correct information or the correct individual or situation as it is presenting itself, we may choose to act on an opportunity.

The ability to be controlled rests in the ability to be contained

When one participates in creating his or her own access to whatever is desired, dignity prevails. People have varying degrees of abilities in this regard. As well, access is not available equally to everyone. A country, a government, an organization or company, a parent, a spouse, or a family may prefer not to allow access. Why would this be? If someone is given access, the barriers that restrict people are removed. When access is available, then choice in the world is available. Options may present themselves that, if chosen, would necessitate a change, perhaps affecting others. Some do not want to suffer the impact of this change created by others' choices. They are not willing to make adjustments. They like things as they are and find their investment in preserving the status quo to be at risk when others exercise their choices.

The ability to be controlled by others rests in the ability to be contained. This may sometimes be presented under the guise—the agenda—of "protection." But if control is what is wanted, if lack of knowledge is what is wanted, if suppression and manipulation are what is wanted, then restricting access is an effective way to accomplish these. We are all aware that sometimes making the choice we believe is correct for ourselves is not viewed as acceptable. In such an environment, we may be labeled as "selfish" or "anarchistic" when others discover they can manipulate and use us with such labels.

Satisfying a level of information it is seeking

It is helpful to be involved in creating your own access to whatever holds your interest, your desire. Perhaps what once held your interest no longer applies, and you may feel frustrated or unhappy—you may feel blocked. Any movement propels; any movement creates an opening. So, in exploring what may be of interest, we take on experiences, which inform our next choices. When the body has sufficient information gained from these experiences and they resonate with you, then you may be compelled to move forward. If the desire is alive in you, stimulating reactions will occur within the body, an enlivening—a waking up. On the other hand, if the body has sufficient information gained from these experiences and they do *not* or no longer resonate with you, you may not feel compelled to move forward; it feels lifeless.

Remember Elaine in Chapter 8, who for many years wanted the theater experience in New York City. Step-by-step, we watched how Elaine, through movement, created her own access to her desires. She took experiences that awakened her, stimulated her reactions, and propelled her forward. And when her body had sufficient information, she simply was compelled to take on the next experience. Wild horses couldn't have stopped her. It didn't matter that she was in her fifties, whether anyone else went along with her, or if she had to leave a job of many years, or whether she had everything figured out. She was compelled to pursue the experience that had been in her wanting for many years and was still alive. Her desire was breathing new life within her.

We are our nature and our nature wants to satisfy a level of information it is seeking; we call that "pursuing our desires." Each individual has a unique nature that is compelled to take parts of an experience to complete itself by going toward a *chosen* experience. We, as an organism, are compelled to extract from our chosen experience, that which is freely given in order for our nature to fulfill itself naturally—to complete itself. Once fulfilled or satisfied or saturated from an experience, we begin to get "messages" from our body—our nature—to move on.

If we are fortunate enough or developed enough to self-declare and seek out a life whereby we are able to choose that which we want to attend to, it can be liberating to find the path that satisfies our curiosity. It can make for an easier and more rewarding life.

25

Experiences Just Exist
—They are Offerings

Every moment of every day there are new experiences available to choose. It feels good to indulge our desires while being responsible. Which ones will we walk toward? And, equally important, which ones will we walk away from should they cease to satisfy?

Have you ever found yourself making choices that were immensely satisfying, that gave you pleasure? There is nothing wrong with indulging your desires when you are doing so responsibly. People, places, and things are offered as experiences, and we go for them.

Life is a continuum of experiences that come about by the choices we make. Our time, our money, and our life energy are all bartering tools in exchange for what interests us. We wonder what experience we want to access and often focus our consideration on whether we will both like and then stick with the outcome of our choice. But a fundamental question you may want to ask yourself is this: "Am I prepared to take action for the experiences I want and own the responsibility for those choices, however they play out?" After all, as we make choices, we are constantly aware that things change—even our desires. At any time we may enjoy trying or tasting something new and different as we strive to be at peace with whatever we choose.

Experiences—offerings—just exist. It may be an individual, a place, an event, a situation, or a thing. Our own body—our nature—moves toward what we want. While we may wish that something is compelling to us because others or society thinks it should be, because our parents want it to be, or because the exchange of our time, energy, or money is beneficial to us in some way, we know—we really do know—if something is what we want or not. Our organism knows.

An experience does not beckon to us. It does not compel us to access it. It's just an offering. Nothing outside of us can compel us. We—as the directors of our own lives—pursue that which we truly desire.

Every moment of every day provides new experiences that are available to us, millions of them. While marketing and advertising efforts will attempt to make some offerings appeal to as many people as they can by making them more affordable, more tempting, more available—or even free; nonetheless, offers just exist. As we well know, not everyone chooses them, even those who could. Some offerings simply hold no interest to some of us. Marketers attempt to stimulate recognition of the allure of what that experience might offer, but they don't make the decisions for us. We may claim we were influenced; but if we want to be influenced, we will look for that—we will look for someone to talk us into what we want anyway. But nothing and no one is "doing it" to us, forcing us. Even in such instances, we are still the ones who make the choice to pursue something, should our nature be compelled to do so.

People will often tell you "it's free" or "it's available" as though that will determine whether you take it. It may or may not make any difference at all. When something is free or available, it still comes with responsibilities—perhaps to house it, maintain it, water it, care for it, store it, play with it, pay taxes on it, and so on. Responsibility of one kind or another accompanies every choice.

Immensely satisfying choices made responsibly

If we can, we all choose what we want. Maybe it's pretty packages of electronics—the biggest, the newest, the best on the block. Or the new boat or motorcycle or sports car – the one with the most horsepower, gleaming in reds and blacks and chrome. Perhaps it is the fabulous Mediterranean home with the nearly Olympic size swimming pool or the volunteer work you find immensely rewarding. It could be the "envy of all your friends" dream job with all its status or the luxury of organizing and participating in fun family gatherings. Maybe it's working at a job that provides a good retirement package so you can enjoy more of your life down the road. It could be working in your garden or spending time with the exciting new lover or the exotic vacations where all your friends gather to celebrate life. All these are possibilities for your life, and they may enhance your life, if they are your true desires.

Decisions

Every moment of every day unlimited opportunities for new experiences present themselves. Yes, it can be a wonderful feeling to indulge our desires while being responsible. We choose and take action for an experience—out of the millions available to us—extracting from it what is freely offered that serves us and meets our desires. But not every offered experience appeals to our better instincts and healthy desires. When we're not living our truth and recognizing our reality, we may make choices that we know are not leading us to toward a better life. Our bodies know when our choice is not correct, and the only question is whether we will listen and act. For some of us, any self-assessment and self-correction may require more than we are sometimes willing or able to do for ourselves.

Millions of offerings are available for us to choose. Will we make the exchange with our time, our money, our interest, or our life energy to take on an experience, to move toward it? Perhaps even more importantly, once in an experience, will we give our full regard to our body's reaction to it, and take action accordingly? Will we, should it cease to satisfy, walk away from it, whether this is immediately after choosing it or many years later?

The Gold Digger

An Offering: A Palm Beach Darling

"Tonight I come draped in furs, impeccably stylish clothes, beautiful leather heels, gorgeous hat, and lace push up bra with just a peek-a-boo look for a titillating tease. My skin is bronzed, my long, flaming red hair flows in ringlets down my back. I smell like the ocean and the name of every alluring perfume every woman ever wanted to be able to afford to splash all over her body. Whatever any woman had before with her lover, darling, it is over from the moment I decide he is mine. I have needs, and I will stop at nothing to get them met. I am feral, and anyone who expects me to mind my manners or play by any rules will be sorely surprised. I cheat, I lie, I steal. I smoke, I drink, I f*ck, I live my life exactly how I want and take exactly what I want when I want it and how I want it. I have one thing in mind, and that is meeting my needs. And when I've had enough or I'm bored, I move on to my next prey. I'm really not so unlike anyone else, am I? Kiss, kiss, darling."

⁓

"Where did the three years go? Swirling by in a mix and maze of parties, fine alcohol, fabulous cocaine, high fashion, and beautiful people. More than anything, I want to stay here in Palm Beach. It is the perfect party playground for me, wouldn't you agree? The freedom, the pretty things, the modern conveniences. I really was born for this life of luxury—beaches, sun, fine food, and wealthy people. That is what I want—to stay here. In style. Javier's money is almost gone. Damn divorce lawyer, I should have had twice that amount; after all, the man had it to give me. And Pierre before him. Assholes, both of them. And this damned economy. Three years now, and they want to deport me. My ticket to stay here—my sweet little shop—has failed to produce a living or provide me the wealthy male contacts I deserve. I honestly don't see what any similar shop on Worth Avenue has that mine can't compete with, but I haven't netted a dime. Such harsh rules here in America for us foreigners.

"Where are the wealthy men when you need them? The stark reality is I'm broke and getting deported unless I marry money…I mean, marry a man with money, quickly. Jesus! How can I only meet gay men? Sorry, darling, you are wonderful. And of course, darling, it was sweet of Jonathan to offer to marry me so I can stay, but it doesn't solve the problem of me being broke—who would pay my ongoing bills? I need to think about my future, wouldn't you agree? I've got apartment rent to pay, and I'm currently ten months behind on my rent to the Preisners for my shop. Damn! I had such a good deal, but now with their daughter taking over managing the building, the rent will be due and soon. Why couldn't she keep her nose out of it, the bitch? I wasn't taking advantage of her parents; no one would have rented it anyway with this economy. Britta says I should put more hours in at my little shop, particularly she thinks I should work both weekend days when people are available to shop, but it's so terribly boring there with no customers coming in. And what does she know about work anyway? And besides, darling, when would I party? That sale I made two years ago at Christina's fabulous event? Why, if I hadn't been there, that wouldn't have happened. That carried me for a few months without needing my reserves. And everyone should have time off, wouldn't you agree? Oh, all this is history. *C'est la vie.*

"One little drink with me, darling, to get me going, because tonight is the night that I go hunting for the quick kill: a husband with cash. How hard can it be? After all, I've done this before, and I can do it again. Now, don't be so unkind, darling. You and I both know there are no victims, only volunteers. Now, I wonder who wants to volunteer to be my next husband. Kiss, kiss, darling."

~

"Oh my yes, darling, I do have someone in mind. He's close by and, as a matter of fact, I've been toying with him for quite some time. He is so transparent; he almost drools openly. A shame he is so boring, a shame he is so short. And no, he has no status and most unfortunately, only a million. He's newly retired, looking for some thrills he's been missing from his past, but perfectly capable of continuing to work. If he doesn't return to work? Then I'll make do while I have to and prepare for what's next. Yes, darling, I should have sobered up and handled things sooner, but there was just too much fun to be had. Now I must act quickly to avoid the deportation proceedings. He'll do for now. I'll join the yacht club with his money; Alicia told me there's good fishing there for my future.

"Yes, darling, no worries, this one wants to be naughty. I see it. I know his type. He's dying for some real attention, for some big applause, for some contention and strife. He wants to be adored and loved and told how g**damn good and smart he is. He wants to argue and f*ck and smoke and snort, dizzy with sensation, with desire. I'll give him the fight, the parties, the audience he's begging for. I can do all that. Of course, darling, I'll take photos of him with my beautiful girlfriends—everyone will see the Don Juan he craves to be. Ah yes, easy. Whatever he wants—great cocaine; a three-way; hell, he can have my ass. Oh, I suspect he'd love a romp with Rodriquez, as well. Yes, something tells me he'd like that very much. And Rodriquez would be very generous with me for sharing my new lover's sweet virgin ass—he's got the finest collection of scotch. I was born for this, wouldn't you agree?

"Yes, tonight he'll be mine. My next prey. I will make him feel alive like he has never felt before. I will render him unconscious, *just the way he desires to be.*

"No, darling, not a catch like the others; hell, this cowboy doesn't even know what an opera is. Of course he's pleasant enough; but if my life were a movie, this fellow would be buried in the credits as something like "Second Errand Runner." But he'll do. Come to think of it, he will be quite perfect at errands…Oh I do hope his groveling won't get on my nerves too badly. But, I so miss my Highland Park 30, and I can't remember the last pack of Nat Sherman's I bought. And the Rolls needs some major repairs, and it has been weeks since I've had a massage. It's just not fair that I should be running out of money.

"Tonight, at show time, I will own him, and he won't look back. Won't be able to look back. I've heard him say something about wanting to buy new experiences. Well, he can buy me and buy me my lifestyle. Hmm, I hope he doesn't remember me mentioning how poorly my business is doing. Oh well, darling, before I'm finished with this cowboy, he will choose not to remember anything except how g**damn good he feels. He'll break his neck to give me whatever I desire, what I deserve."

≈

"What, you say not enough of a challenge for me? F*ck you, darling. Give me a month, and he'll be my new husband. How's that for a challenge? Duped, dazed, and delirious all the way to the dotted line—with his tongue hanging out. Oh, I must show him the 1.5 carat Cartier I still have from Javier; I'm certain he'll find it necessary to best that. He's just the type. No wedding at The Breakers with this one, but a good springboard, I think, for my future. Did I mention how very good I am? Just one more little drink, darling, before show time. We drank the bottle? Then open another; we must toast my next victory. *To me!* Kiss kiss, darling."

Charles Takes the Experience

From the first, you observed and "knew" things about her that could bring trouble. She did not overtly mask her behaviors and circumstances. Setting aside and denying this information, you were determined to pursue what you wanted and your soon-to-be wife certainly piqued your interest. Your last "little romance" had just moved on, the nights spent alone in your bed could almost be counted on two hands; you were lonely and ready for company. Appearing to be a charming, successful, and flamboyant business woman, this dynamo came on to you like a Mack truck. Your new, attentive devotee made you feel like a brilliant sage as she sat at your feet, drinking up your words of wisdom and all your most expensive scotch. In your first month together, you could hardly catch your breath, what with all the glitz, glamour, drinking, drugs, and parties. That woman paraded you in front of everyone, hanging on you like a flashy ornament on a Christmas tree. Your life had never been adventuresome in this way; there had been no glitzy parties with seemingly artistic and cultured people from all over the world. You'd never had such devotion, great sex from both men and women, and so much attention.

In Texas you had run a small firm of oil and gas engineers; your whole business world had been dealing mostly with men, and your work life had been dotting i's and crossing t's with some golf and a little pussy on the side. Your former wives had been sensible women who wore cultured pearls and flat shoes. This woman brought you a new "crowd," a new audience that was providing the attention you'd only ever dreamed about.

When you married that gal, you transformed from a boring, retired engineer and businessman—who wore a ten-gallon cowboy hat to look taller—into a knight in shining armor, saving the damsel in distress from being deported. It was about the most exciting thing you'd ever done; you were on top of the world, and applause and envy abounded. A real crowd pleaser you were, a real winner.

Although it was all extremely titillating at first, active and sober observations eventually allow you to notice more about your new wife. She is the consummate party girl, and that's exactly what attracted you, but now you have concerns. With her spending habits, the bills are mounting, and she clearly believes these are your responsibility. Her weekend bar bills alone could buy groceries for a month. You worked hard all your life to be able to live comfortably in your retirement and did not plan to work again. But she is clearly a fiscal liability. She doesn't have a job that earns money; she has an expensive hobby, working half-heartedly at a little shop selling items she collected over the years—purchased with money from her inheritance and former husbands. This business was her "front" to stay in America; she owes a year's back rent, and you notice she doesn't belong to any business organizations.

Your wife *is* generous, that would be true—with your money—as she has none nor does she appear to be concerned about that fact. She had been spending both of her former husbands' money the past several years, but that is gone now. You don't want to look cheap to her "crowd," but those folks party through an oil well in a week. When you try to talk to her about it, she just pouts and points to what she wants next. You've gotten to the place where you just shrug, say nothing, and buy her whatever she wants; it does no good to argue with her. And now, among everything else, you worry about your liability when she drives drunk. So you've become her sole support, her errand boy, and her taxi driver, all in one.

It was such fun at first. She seemed so kind then, so loving. But now, not so much. Sometimes, when she looks at you as though you're "less," you feel like you've been hit in the stomach. Lately, when you drive her home—passed out and snoring in the seat next to you—you notice a slight sighing in your body. You have frequent headaches, and you are short-tempered and forgetful. You've become prone to outbursts. You want a drink earlier in the day now and find yourself shaky when you don't have one. You get wasted most nights and worry incessantly about money. You thought that you had found love and intimacy and friendship—but you find yourself having doubts about all of that.

The Outcome

Charles' body tries to communicate to him that this might not be the experience he had hoped for, but he doesn't want to listen. The unravelling has begun—reality has reared its head and it isn't pretty—but Charles chooses to ignore nature's whisper in his ear and tap on his shoulder. With each month's credit card bills coming in, his worries increase. He is becoming desperate in his attempts to justify—to himself and others—the choices he made, and confusion abounds as he sorts and weaves through the fantasies and rationalizations and excuses he creates.

As he re-evaluates his choice, he wonders to himself, *"When she proposed the idea that we get married, it just made sense. She could stay in Palm Beach and also have work options if she wanted to close her shop at some point. Why not? I was crazy about the gal, having a blast, and wanted her here with me; but now I'm not sure I can afford her. I know guys who could—there are plenty of them in oil, but I'm not one of them. What will people think if I divorce her? All her friends know our marriage is her ticket to US citizenship since she was unable to show she had a real business. How can I bail in front of everyone who thinks I'm living the dream? How can I afford her lifestyle? I would have to make some other decisions about my income if I were to keep her. I hate worrying all the time."*

∽

While disturbed and conflicted by all these recognitions, Charles, like many of us when we do not want to make a new choice but have serious doubts that the existing choice is really what we want, begins to spin yarns, to rationalize:

"No, she hasn't been square with me about her business situation, but that doesn't mean she can't work it a little more, enough for her nails and perfume and shoes—and it might keep her off the bottle some. I know she's sneaking money, but she's probably just worried about her business. No, she didn't exactly indicate she had no ability to support herself, but then I hadn't asked—it hadn't occurred to me. So I suppose that's my fault. After all, she was probably embarrassed to bring it up, given the economy had tanked right at the time she opened her little shop.

"I suppose she could have learned a trade while she was waiting around for customers to come into her shop during those three years. Plenty of courses offered on the Internet, but she probably was just hoping our economy would recover. Foreigners often think like that about America.

"She's just accustomed to spending outrageously because she had it. I need to make her more aware of managing the money; she never had to. She'll learn. She only gets agitated talking about it because all this is new to her.

"Once the 'newness' wears off, we can settle ourselves down more and not go out so much, not spend so much money. I guess if I started back up working again, I could probably make it work—I really do want to 'keep her.' I know she's screwing around, but I've always been out chasing tail in all my relationships—I guess that's the way of it...these modern women. Maybe I will buy her that new car she's begging for; that would make her happy and quiet her down a bit—impress the friends.

"She's talked about putting in more time at her little business, but with us enjoying our time together, that just hasn't happened. And now with football in full swing, we've got the Aggies and the Longhorns on Saturdays and the Cowboys on Sundays, and I like her right here with me—she's getting to know the players and the plays really well."

～

Charles recognizes, to the best of his ability, that he is responsible for making changes if what he's gotten himself into, isn't what he wants. He determines that he wants to "manage" the situation better so he won't worry so much. He likes having a drinking partner every night, feeling popular, feeling he is being "seen" for the first time in his life, not having to go looking for "it," and not being alone. He likes the feeling of control and ownership of knowing his wife won't leave him because he is her "ticket" to stay in Palm Beach. All he has to do is write the checks, and at least a semblance of the good life is before him.

Believing that his buddies in Texas are envious of his whirlwind romance and conquest, he joins in their laughter as they joke with him about his BFGD (Butt F*cking Gold Digger) and how he could have gotten a cheaper deal in Thailand. While a few of them suggest a visit to Florida, he hasn't extended an invite. There is some real money in Texas with a few of his friends, and something tells Charles that could be threatening to his relationship with his Palm Beach darling. He wants to keep her right up close where she belongs.

Charles recognizes he made a choice to be responsible for another adult life besides just his own when he married this woman, for the finances, the caretaking, and the complete responsibility for another grownup and that he did so without discernment. She hadn't disguised the fact that she drank fine scotch like she had a hollow leg and her work schedule was random. He had wanted people to believe she was a successful business woman, that he had really "scored," but it seemed now that most probably knew she wasn't. He'd always supported his wives, but he was earning big money in those days. Now, on a fixed income, he admits to himself he has concerns about what his wife and others would think if he cut back too much on the spending. He *never* wanted to take a job during his retirement. He shakes his head and shrugs his shoulders.

～

When sober, Charles notices some health issues and that his overall sense of well-being appears to be affected. He has awareness of his depleting finances, and moments of unhappiness, as though his vitality is somehow lessening. His unsettled feelings confuse him. His money is disappearing, and he sees little end in sight. He knows he needs to start thinking about earning some real money, but those plans are on hold due to upcoming knee surgery. While trying to help his wife navigate the stairs one night when she was drunk, he took a fall and shattered his ankle and twisted his knee. His wife's friends asked him if she had pushed him away while he was trying to help her. They told him she could really be a bully when she's drunk. Charles can't recall the scene because he was pretty wasted himself, but he doesn't think so. He doesn't want to think about it. He notices he is really missing the golfing he had waited so long to enjoy in his retirement.

Charles begins to explore work options that he will pursue after the operation. He begins to make calls and set up a company. It isn't what he'd planned for his retirement, but it is the way things are shaping up. He can't afford her otherwise. He takes another small step to consider his budget and determine how much he can give his new wife every month for her essentials of care and informs her of his new plan. He has no guarantee that she will abide by that budget because his further discoveries of her actions have shown that to be unlikely, but he isn't going to worry about that now.

No, it hasn't been quite the experience he thought it was going to be, not nearly, but deciding he wants to stay with his choice—Charles chooses to "manage it."

26

A Weakened Relationship
...with the Self

Unhealthy behavior patterns interfere with our heart's desires. This occurs when we tolerate or accommodate our own ill behavior.

In our relationships, jobs, careers, and other situations, we come together to have an experience. We have no idea how things will develop. None of us can know what is to come as we enter a new experience.

Perhaps we feel pleased with an experience taken. Something in our nature wants it, and, at first, it is everything we hoped it would be—it satisfies every reason we accessed it. Some examples may be when we feel certain a new job is a great opportunity for a successful career, or when the school we selected by reputation alone seems a good fit, or when the care provider for our child or aging parents seems to offer us the relief we are seeking. We all know that feeling. Yes, everything can seem fabulous at first with a new experience. It often does.

With active observation, more is revealed

Then something begins to shift—the body senses "something" and is on alert. We start to pay attention. We start to observe. We sober up, preparing to notice what is begging to be seen.

Perhaps things have crept up to a point where we begin to observe that all is not what we had hoped for; likely it was always there available for viewing, but we didn't *want* to see. Now, with active observation, more is revealed in whatever choice was made, and with ourselves. Our body's messages may be informing us that this experience may not be what we want—we sense misgivings, a change in our heart's desire. We may or may not have specific reasons for our questioning—we may not actually know, but we are becoming aware that at least part of the experience has become uncomfortable for us.

When a chosen experience is not correct for us, a dismantling of the illusion of charm occurs. We've all witnessed this. The more life we've lived and the more developed and adept we are at making choices, the quicker the reveal, the quicker the color goes flat. The chemistry—the formula—of us together with that relationship, job, career, or situation that at first seemed like a good decision, ultimately reveals itself as an unsatisfying experience. Yes, our body knows when something is no longer right for us. It may be a big "aha" moment, or it may just be continual messages from the body letting us know.

Maybe we do nothing at first. We choose not to pay attention. It satisfied yesterday, so we assume that it must still somehow satisfy.

Observe with your body. The body doesn't lie

When what you once wanted has begun to show itself as lesser quality or simply is no longer desired, you may find yourself wrestling with the inclination to convince yourself otherwise; but the schism, the split, has begun. All is not what it once seemed, or at least what it once seemed no longer applies; it no longer has the same meaning—something isn't right.

The weight of your choices is becoming heavier and more difficult to bear. Initially, you were light and joyful—almost giddy with delight—but now your laughter is less intense, shallow, or—more often—non-existent. It seems a disconnect is happening within; the body seems to be insisting that this experience is not correct for you any longer.

How about just choosing something else and moving on?

Unhealthy behavior patterns can inhibit our best of intentions

Unwanted and unwell behavior patterns—inherent in our nature— are those inhibiting factors that can disable us from being who and how we desire to be. They are part of us. They come from our genetic history, environments, and our experiences. Some of us have more of them than others. Regardless, they interfere and interrupt our pursuit of ourselves— the pursuit of our true desires.

When we act from these unwanted and unwell behavior patterns and if we do not take steps to evolve, we may render ourselves nearly incapable *at times* of choosing to move from something unsatisfying to something satisfying.

How do my unwell and unwanted behavior patterns restrict my life?

By your invitation and with your full and voluntary participation, when you tolerate and accommodate your own ill behavior, you invite a weakness, an ignorance, and unconsciousness that enslaves your very life force. You inhibit your efforts to live the life you truly desire. Unattended to, these behavior patterns can wreak havoc on your life. And they are worsened and exacerbated when true expression of your desires does not occur.

This is not about anyone or anything else—not your mate, your job, or anything outside of you. None of that matters. You, and you alone, have decisions to make for the life you truly desire, and you may feel trapped. Regardless of how it came about, when you find yourself unsatisfied or unhappy and not living the life you want, that's what you need to know. This is about you and your choices for your life. This is about a weakened relationship with the self.

By your own character, deeds and thoughts, your concerns with image, the cons you do to yourself, and your vulnerability to those external influences that are not in accord with your nature, these unwanted and unwell behavior patterns may render you fearful and impotent. They may cause you to hold to the path you originally chose, even though you now recognize that you no longer find that path satisfying. Perhaps you now recognize that the experience you chose was not one of quality. Maybe with active observation, more was revealed; or maybe circumstances and timing changed. It doesn't matter; you no longer want it. It might be easy enough to reverse or dismantle it, but these behavior patterns contort your thinking so that you will believe that making a change would be problematic at best and possibly your worst nightmare. They may "work you" to keep you from honoring your sensations and your body's knowingness, keeping you from fully comprehending what is before you.

These self-destructive forces keep you questioning and second-guessing yourself—preying upon your concerns about others' opinions and rules and directives—which fuels your hesitation and inability to rely on your own internal authority.

You stay stuck with a choice you made, although it has ceased to satisfy you—sometimes developing a habit of suffering or a habit of denial that forces you to live in a fantasy of what you want that experience to be.

They keep you from moving on toward other more satisfying experiences, although to stay forces you out of integrity—forces you to no longer be responsible or honest—especially with yourself. They obscure your ability to discern how to choose and maintain an involvement with quality experiences and people that bring you the satisfying life you want.

What about your true desires—those hidden yearnings that are trying to come to light, to blossom and emerge? They remain shrouded in darkness. You have disabled yourself from seeing them, accessing them, bringing them forth, and living them. And so your truth—your nature's true desires—still awaits expression...

Unwell behavior patterns impair your senses and clarity in four ways:

First: They muddy your desire and ability to fully comprehend the reality before you. So you seek to avoid recognizing the reality of the experience you are in, and in this way you grant yourself a "pass" at being responsible for making new life choices accordingly.

Second: They distort and steal your sense of responsibility for discernment, even when your body—your truth—is screaming at you. In this way you can pretend something is still a match for what you want, as you create "stories" for all the parts you don't want to give value to. Perhaps you think you partially recognize your reality, and you know that doesn't match what you truly want; but by sheer force of will, you want to make it so. Your body knows—your life reflects the truth—but you mightily justify, defend, and protect your choices and your behavior, and if need be, the behavior of others. You do the "oh well..." and "it will get better..." and "they are this way because..." and "it will be okay if or when..."

Third: They encourage you to pacify yourself so you don't have to give thought to your reality. You continue pacifying yourself, sometimes for your whole life, not making the changes that would remove the discomfort. You involve yourself with near or actual distractions or addictions to drink, drugs, gambling, pornography, shopping, sex, TV—whatever can titillate you and distract you to keep you from experiencing the discomfort. You don't want to experience the value offered in the discomfort, the discomfort that informs you—that lets you know it may be time to make another choice rather than continue to manage and accommodate your false image of the experience before you.

Fourth: They drain and contort and withhold the energy, wherewithal, and sense of comfort to make new choices or change direction, if that's what you want. Just when you've begun to see clearly that you are ready to take new actions to dismantle the old choice and move on toward what you desire, that's when they work to convince you that you can't have it—that you can't figure it out, that it is out of your reach, out of your range of possibilities. They try to steal your desire to follow through. They work to limit or blind you to your options, to restrict or inhibit your ability to open yourself up to possibilities and move your oh-so-tired feet to take new steps of action.

Yes, these deeply ingrained unwanted and unwell behavior patterns create a mindset of confusion and a habit of self-deception, a habit of denying the truth. They reconstruct your perceived desires to accommodate what is before you now—convincing you that you still want what you know in your heart you don't—thus preventing you from taking action away from what you don't want toward better experiences that you desire. They assist you in your denial of reality when you feel compromised, when what is before you does not harmonize with who and how you are. Or they work to convince you that "maybe it's me," that there is something wrong with you that you just can't be satisfied with what you have.

A part of you welcomes these unwell and unwanted behavior patterns; you may find you want to yield yourself to them. You prefer to pretend you can't see reality, avoid seeing reality, or simply create a fictional reality—thereby hoping not to have to make other choices. These may be behavior patterns you have become quite comfortable with, despite the limitations they have imposed on your life. So *how* does this happen?

Managing the disconnect

Perhaps you've always had a good sense of what your true values are, what resonates with you and makes you feel good about yourself. You know what you stand for and what you appreciate and respect in others. You now find yourself in the company of—or in situations where—those values don't exist or are being compromised by you or by others. You may feel uncomfortable or dismayed or disappointed that this is so. Through active observation and noticing, more is revealed; and while you don't want to fully acknowledge it, you are beginning to see it.

If we know we are in an experience that isn't what we want—we don't resonate with it, we don't like who and how we are in it, it doesn't make us feel good about ourselves, it isn't anything we would ever choose if we had "do-overs," it isn't what we want for any reason or no reason at all—and if we stay with it regardless, then there is a profound disconnect. In order to manage this disconnect—to convince ourselves and others that it is okay to stay with the reality before us when we know it isn't what we really desire—we begin to con ourselves.

We get ourselves a big bowl of buttered popcorn, get comfy in a recliner, gather an audience of sometimes only ourselves, and we spin a yarn that in its construction, we—as creative instigators of fantasy—stretch and tease and spark and conjure out a story that replaces the actuality before us. Our tall tales, the "fake lore" we create about ourselves and those people and situations in our lives—the who, how, and what of it all—can rival Pecos Bill using a rattlesnake named Shake to lasso a tornado. We indulge in this folly, often unchallenged, so we can deny our discomfort and justify our actions for making the choice in the first place or for staying with it. Everything before us that we don't want to give value to, we rationalize and excuse. All this we do in order to make our choices appear sensible and valid to ourselves and to others. *That's* how it happens.

Relax—nix the stories and stay in reality; notice, observe

When you know the reality before you isn't the experience you really want, but you aren't yet ready, willing, or able to make a change, you simply are not yet done with the experience. Your nature still has a "wanting" that hasn't yet been fulfilled, that isn't yet saturated. There's no need to play a fanciful and self-destructive "mind game" with yourself and others. It can be simple. Just take that energy you are putting into conning yourself and others, and use it to just keep actively noticing and observing reality. In this way you do not impede your own evolution. An experience is either something you want or don't want. You either like yourself in it or you don't.

Stay if it is so, or take another action if it is not so. No tall tales, no "fake lore." Nix the stories. They don't serve you. Just listen to your body…you'll know. And at some point, when you no longer succumb to those unwanted and unwell behavior patterns because you refuse to deny and excuse and restrict your true desires, you will begin to see opportunities for your fullest expression.

That may well be a moment of genuine liberation.

27

Choices Can Either Nurture or Compromise Our Well-Being

The accuracy of the choice is not as important as what one does with the choice. Does one develop oneself with the chosen experience or not?

Our life may be easier, less messy, and more joyful if we are choosing quality experiences, but it is not only "quality" experiences that offer opportunities to be developmental tools for us. Every experience—both quality and non-quality—has the potential to be used to nurture one's wellness, should that be desired. It is not just about the experience, but more importantly, it is about the character of the individual who is doing the choosing. The more earnest and able an individual is in the desire to grow and develop, the more likely he or she can use any experience to do so.

Experiences Can be Quality or Non-Quality

"Keep Out!"

Many of us have had narrow escapes in situations or relationships. Yes, we saw the red flashing neon "Keep Out" sign complete with skull and cross bones, heavy chains with multiple padlocks, and the ten-foot high barbed-wire fence. But like Peter Rabbit, scrunching and twisting and maneuvering and squeezing himself around in order to scurry on into that lettuce patch or down that rabbit hole, so too, did we. When we truly want something, we will do whatever it takes to get it. It doesn't matter what is standing in front of it. If we want the offering, we figure out a way to get it.

For any offering that others may choose, which we might take a negative view of, some of us may balk at them, claiming them to be soul-sucking happiness stealers. We may say: "Good grief, who in their right mind would choose such a thing?" Even if we saw a slight attraction in one of those types of offerings, we still might think someone would have to have been an *idiot* to choose it; we may even be amazed that someone would actually *stay* with such an experience, believing it to be "wrong" for them. We wonder how they can continue to mute themselves and pretzel themselves around, reconstructing their reality so they can remain in that non-quality or destructive experience.

When one of our friends or a family member is in an experience that appears to us to not be one of quality, we are often right there, urging them to leave it. We tell them: "Oh, that was a horrible choice, a wrong choice for you." Just as we are telling people to leave a non-quality experience, so too, we might also be telling others to stay with an experience that we view as quality—presenting *our* choice as the "right" choice for them.

We might know people who left fabulous jobs and relationships and towns simply because they yearned to move on to something different. When we hear how someone wishes to leave what *we* consider a quality experience, we may judge the individual and the experience. We may say: "Are you crazy? He's a great guy"; "You must not be thinking right; you've got yourself a cherry job"; "There's a waiting list a mile long to get into that school, that program, that doctor, to take that opportunity; don't be a fool." We may needle our friends to give us reasons for their choices so we can evaluate and determine and judge the soundness of their thinking. With our commentary, we may cause them to second-guess their own decisions as to why in the world they would want to leave what we believe is correct for them—that good town, job, mate, situation, or other opportunity. We may do this to our friends and partners; and sadly, we may even do this to our children. We cajole and manipulate and ridicule those we love—and others—about what *we* think are their best choices. We forget to remember that what is important is what *they* think is a correct choice for them at any particular moment.

If they can, people choose for themselves what it is that they want

Our nature wants to evolve; it is compelled to satisfy a wanting. It isn't possible to know others' natures and what compels them to make the choices they do, or how anything ever plays out. We can all too easily become self-righteous and judgmental and indignant about others' choices if we do not deem them to be the "right" ones for them. We may insist that others would have a better life if they would just do what we think is best for them. In extreme cases, we may act like know-it-all bullies. It is not uncommon for us to get our noses in places they simply don't belong, attempting to become their life director.

Sometimes we self-inflict this judgment as well. Perhaps when we have chosen an experience we ultimately come to recognize was not a quality experience for us, we beat ourselves up with negative self-talk, criticizing ourselves for the choice we made. While it may be necessary to disentangle from the non-quality experience, making ourselves feel bad about some bumps along the way as we go down our own developmental path does not serve us well, just as it does not serve others well.

It only causes misery when one has to try to bear and accommodate judgment, even when we do it to ourselves. Where is the humanity in that? Where is the acceptance and tolerance for a life journey in that? An easier, more peaceful life can be ours to live if we can just suspend judgment as we all make our own way as we can.

Outcomes Will Be Unique to Each Individual

Who knows what compels any of us to make the decisions and handle the outcomes of those as we do? Sometimes, as observers, we try to make sense of it. We may hear people ask: "How is it that one person will choose to jump into a pile of manure and just get himself into a bunch of 'you know what' and another person will choose to jump into a pile of manure and come up with a pony? What's up with that? What makes one so lucky and another not so lucky?"

How was it so that one individual found the pony and the other one didn't? On one hand, we may have heard of or seen people who seem to be able to take any experience, quality or not, and extract from it whatever can help them to become the better of themselves. Goodness knows, these are the stories we love to read, to watch, to hear about. These fabulously enlightening stories of people who either walked through life choosing well or people who walked through life choosing or otherwise experiencing adversity, and came out the better for it inspire us.

On the other hand, many of us have known people who have taken either what we would consider a non-quality experience or a quality experience and used it for their destruction, succumbing to a life of suffering and misery. Regardless of the quality of experience they chose, they made a destructive experience out of it.

Outcomes will be unique to each individual. We are not the same. We have the option to choose to make the most of any experience as a tool for our development. And, regardless of what we may observe in others, it may quite possibly be that something is beginning to make a difference, that in his or her nature, something is building…we really don't know.

For those who didn't come out of the womb choosing well or haven't had it exampled in their lives, a fulfilled life is generally the result of development that has been acquired through lots of practice—trial and error, trial and success—over and over again. Those who have more developed skills of self-reliance seem to be more able to make the best of any situation—they tend not to avoid making choices for concerns of possible repercussion or because they shy away from the responsibility of dealing with the outcome. They seem to have an easier time of pursuing their lives with this greater awareness, using every opportunity to refine their skills of better choosing.

Our Own Fulfillment is a Waking Up

Remember Henry in Chapter 3, a once happy reservation doctor? And Clara in Chapter 13, a once happy wife of many years? Both had enjoyed satisfying experiences but had decided to move on. It wasn't as though the actual experiences, as they originally presented themselves, had changed drastically. There were no surprises; more of the experience didn't reveal anything over time other than more of the same goodness. The nature of each of them as an individual—that nature inside us that has a "wanting"—was ultimately fulfilled from that experience. Our "want"—our desire in our nature—to have something else fulfilled can grow beyond what the current experience is providing. We can feel a yearning to move on.

At the point when any experience we are in ceases to be what we want, it will no longer be a nourishing experience for us, even if it once had been. Because we desired it once and found it nourishing, we generally like to believe that it will continue to do so; after all, maybe it was a good job, a good relationship, a good situation. We may even want and hope the experience will continue to be compelling to us, particularly if we have gone to great lengths to act on accessing it.

But then, at some point, we recognize it is not the quality we want for our lives today. Our "want" of a fulfilled and happy life cannot be satisfied in the current situation. Something is not now a match for us. It doesn't matter if the experience is good, bad, pretty, or ugly. It doesn't matter what it looks like to anyone else. It doesn't matter why an experience ceases to fulfill. What matters is what you do once you recognize that all or part of the experience you are in is no longer what you want for your life. Staying in such an experience does not nourish you and can be restricting and even destructive as we saw with both Henry and Clara.

When we find our vitality flagging—our life force diminished—or our health, finances, or overall sense of well-being to be compromised, it may be time to self-assess and self-correct with new movement. Many of us find ourselves in situations that aren't what we claim we want. If we are making strident attempts to "manage" it and stay with it—to *make* it work—then we may want to ask ourselves, "Am I staying in this experience because I want to?" When we consciously choose to remain in an experience and are honest with ourselves about what we are doing, it may be possible it is because we want to—that's simply a choice. If we didn't want it, we would likely make a different choice.

Experiences taken by choice

Experiences taken are not failures or successes; they are simply the way we are doing our life. Really, all relationships and other experiences taken by choice are a success in that regard. We believe they are a match for us when we choose them, and we extract what we desire from whatever is freely given. With choices, our nature has a want—a desire. We move forward seeking to satisfy it—behaving from our truth and responsibly owning our experiences. As we fulfill our desires, we need not view any experience as a mistake. Our own fulfillment is a waking-up. There is greater ease in our lives when we are willing to own that all our experiences—even those of non-quality—can assist us in our development.

We will always have the option to take any experience—quality and non-quality—and use it to become the better of ourselves. But once it has ceased to satisfy—once we are fulfilled from the experience—it no longer nourishes us. It may be time to move on. And we don't know, we can't know what that looks like for another. What we can do is encourage others to trust themselves to figure it out; we can encourage others to develop themselves safely and responsibly.

We can wish them well.

28

The Exchanges We Make

If you want to have a love affair with life, you cannot fool yourself about your responsibility to reality. Doing so interrupts and interferes with the pursuit of the experiences you truly want—the pursuit of yourself.

Our character has the greatest influence on our choices, and the more developed we are, the clearer the lens through which we view our reality will become. A more developed individual not only will likely choose better initially, but upon recognition of an unsatisfactory choice or any sense of compromise or disharmony surfacing, he or she will have better ability to easily take new actions. There exists a level of self-knowing that allows for easier recognition of a mismatch.

Always it is important to call things as they are. In this way, even if the offering is dressed up, even if someone has put lipstick on the pig, we will know not to convince ourselves that what is before us is something other than a pig. We will see it for what it really is. We may still choose it, we may still choose to stay with it, but we won't kid ourselves about it by making excuses and rationalizations and creating stories and managing our image. We won't kid ourselves about the fact that the sum total of the quality of the experience isn't really what we want, and we won't try to accommodate or tolerate our own ill behavior in order to make it okay with us.

Sometimes, when coming out of an experience, it is easy to say that we were scammed. We may claim that others "played us" or tricked us or misrepresented themselves—we may even claim that they lied to us so we couldn't possibly have recognized the true experience. But what's the point? Maybe we didn't discern adequately, but the reality is we made the decision. Instead of assigning blame to ourselves or anyone else, we might say, "Wow, do I ever need to develop my "chooser" so that I have a better quality experience next time." Without sufficient development, we may find we've left ourselves open to being misused, overused, abused, and manipulated.

Remember how Elaine in Chapter 8 came to the point where she liked herself in her choices for her New York experience? She felt she was choosing quality for herself, and therefore she created a vibration—an atmosphere—of acceptability for herself that allowed for expansion to others. When she moved forward with that desired experience, she found "her people"—people with whom she felt good about herself when she was with them. This was foundational for Elaine in developing herself as it is for all of us, and this cannot happen if we define ourselves in an experience as having been victimized or scammed. Simply put, either our choice was not what we wanted (even initially), or it eventually showed itself not to be what we were hoping for.

Owning our choices with our feet firmly planted in reality

If we refuse or are not yet ready to see the whole picture of our reality, then perhaps, with more awareness—through active observing—we can begin to notice a small piece of it. Yes, peek through the window. Bit by bit. Maybe we take a small step so we can view it from another perspective. It's okay. Some of our choices lead us to a better life—and some do not.

We want to simply ask ourselves: "Does this experience bring out the best in me? Do I like myself in it? Is the sum total of my present situation what I want at this time in my life? Am I an individual of integrity in this experience, needing nothing from another?

Charles and His Palm Beach Darling

L et's take a look at the story of the Gold Digger from Chapter 25. The Gold Digger is not a story about love or victimhood. It is a story about an unhealthy exchange. It is about "renting" an individual who agrees to be rented, and then conning and convincing one's self that the exchange is something other than what it is.

Within our society we are all interdependent; this is the ordinary behavior amongst pack animals. There exists a healthy inter-use, a "correct using" by mutual agreement. We call this "healthy inter-dependency."

What we see in *The Gold Digger,* however, is not healthy inter-dependency. Instead, it is unhealthy *co*-dependency, which involves the need to lay the parts of our lives we don't want to do ourselves, onto someone else to do. This can include any numbers of areas, two of which in this case are financial self-reliance and emotional self-reliance.

How is this unhealthy? When joined with another in this type of relationship, each individual assists the other's non-development. In the story, the exchange between Charles and the Gold Digger allows Charles to avoid developing emotional self-reliance—loving and caring for his own self and enjoying his own company—and allows for the Gold Digger to avoid developing financial self-reliance.

Finding our match in a mate is not about finding our "other half"—our complement. That encourages the development of unwanted behavior patterns. Setting up a relationship based on co-dependency limits and hinders a healthy life. If we want to accept personal responsibility for our life, then we'll want to find someone who is a whole individual just as we are—not someone who "fills in the gaps" of who and how we are not, or who wants to use us to "fill in the gaps" of who and how they are not. "You complete me" is not so much a romantic sentiment as it is an indicator; when we set ourselves up to choose our "other half," we are basically saying we are not whole ourselves, that we need someone else to "complete" us. While that might sound great in a movie, it is problematic for a healthy relationship. Not "being whole" means that our own responsibility to be a whole individual does not exist. We attempt to extract from another, what we don't want to create for ourselves. We're not fully self-reliant, loving, capable, and so we rely on someone else to do the parts of our lives that we don't want to develop or take responsibility for doing. And when that other individual can't sufficiently fulfill what is actually our responsibility in the first place, we sometimes blame them.

Misusing ourselves and others

There will always be those who are willing to make the exchange with others who have the money or the need to make it work. Co-dependency is a misuse of another individual and can result in unsatisfying experiences as the participants play "let's pretend" with each other's lives. In the conversation the Gold Digger has with her friend, we hear her say she wants to stay in America but seems to believe she is without options to support herself other than marrying a man with money. She attributes her problems to the fault of others and circumstances. At no point does she entertain taking responsibility for herself, including becoming financially self-reliant.

In marrying her, Charles deflects responsibility for many of his choices onto his wife. With his accommodation of her playacting as a business woman, he continues to prop her up, creating for her a sense of value in her ability to be the consummate party girl in exchange for what he wants. Charles welcomes her dependency, as he needs so badly to please and be helpful, to be a winner, and get his own emotional needs met by some way other than developing himself. But ultimately it will not matter how much gold Charles gives the Gold Digger; it will never be enough. Nor will it matter how much attention the Gold Digger gives Charles; it will never be enough to make him happy. These needs must be met by their owners.

And when we misuse ourselves or others as a lifestyle, our character is at risk.

Even if what we want is not what is in front of us, it is still our truth. When we find ourselves rationalizing and "managing" a decision rather than easily and effortlessly enjoying our choice, something is not correct for us.

Protecting and defending our choices wastes precious life energy

We all see our reality through our own unique lenses. We chose what we want and when we discover that our choice isn't what we hoped it would be—but we want so badly to stay in our "designed fantasy"—we can become attached to our decision. We may try to reconcile our fantasy with our honest reactions to the actual experience. And so the con begins. How otherwise could we take a pass with our responsibility for a life we deeply desire, and not the current one we have settled for?

Contrast that with choosing from our truth, and we see that with the latter approach, there is no need to "effort." Upon re-evaluating choices that once seemed like good ideas, we know—our body knows—if they still resonate with us. We feel no conflict within us, no confusion, no disturbed or unsettled feelings, no incessant worry, no affected well-being, no lessened vitality. With no concerns about image, we have no need to fictionalize our reality and engage in acts of storytelling, performance, or delusion. There is an ease in simply moving on.

As with Charles, we may not want to concern ourselves with the signs that may be reflecting a life not lived in congruence with our truth. However, while our conscious mind may swear we are living our truth, our body will not be fooled. It always has the true experience—*even initially*—but we often invite inner conflict when we choose to ignore, deny, or override its messages in our attempt to distort our reality so that we can convince ourselves that something is true when in fact it isn't.

> *When we misuse our precious life energy to protect and defend choices that are not what we truly want, this efforting can be monumental. A rewarding life is not about protecting and defending our choices; it is about valuing and protecting our very life!*

What about those of us who are using substances? It is far more difficult to deal with reality if we choose to use drugs or alcohol or the sedating effects of food. Under the influences of those substances, we segregate, we put aside, and we deny and don't deal; we are not fully conscious and engaged in reality. People sometimes use them for pleasure, but often their use is a form of self-medication and a tool for avoidance. If the body is numbed and not engaged with reality, it takes a lot longer—or it may actually be impossible—to get the full picture and see clearly. In a non-conscious state, our reality is distorted. For people looking to make choices and changes for a better life, it is definitely a hindrance to do so when using.

When we find our finances, our health, our zest for life, or our overall sense of well-being to be diminished or compromised, we have not chosen well for who and how we are at this moment in time; something is not in sync, and we are deceiving ourselves to think otherwise.

We cannot receive what we are unavailable or unable to give

We are all equipped differently for relationships. It is easier to relax and to be authentic when we are self-reliant, operating from our internal authority—choosing from our truth. It is easier to bless another if he or she chooses to take on a new path and move on. The more developed we are—the more self-reliant, self-caring, and self-correcting—the less attached we are to having another fulfill our needs. This is difficult to do for the less-equipped because if we haven't accessed within ourselves for ourselves, the experiences of intimacy, love trust, and friendship—as a whole, self-reliant individual—we will never recognize these experiences before us.

While some lovely and loving moments may occur, we can never extract from a relationship any quality that we are unavailable or unable to bring to it. When we are not choosing from that place within us that "knows," that *is* our truth, we will never be able to recognize truth staring back at us. Recognition can only occur if something is known to us—has become part of us, within us. When we call an exchange something other than what it is, we delude ourselves. In a co-dependent relationship, experiences of intimacy, love, trust, or friendship do not—cannot—exist. It isn't possible.

Misusing another for our comfort

Without observing sufficiently, it is not possible to discern if someone is bringing "wholeness" into the relationship. If we are not whole ourselves, or if we have no interest in developing ourselves in that regard, we will just be looking for someone willing to do the exchange, strike a bargain or make a deal, someone who is also looking for their complement, their "other half." And when the relationship has run its course and we leave it, often we just go looking for the same thing all over again. We may have a temporary reprieve and find a healthy relationship for a while. But if we have not developed ourselves sufficiently while staying conscious, we will ultimately desire yet another co-dependent relationship where, by complementing and completing them, we get to feel okay about ourselves. We are right there saying "I will do that for you, I will be that for you." In our desperation to find that individual, it won't matter what his or her standards of anything may be because we will not allow ourselves to observe sufficiently—to discern—who and how that individual is; that knowledge and those details are useless. And once together, each participant is invested in generously helping the other to remain unable to meet his or her own needs.

When we choose to misuse our own life experience to degenerate ourselves, we are misusing the self. People can choose to stay unconscious and accommodate their own ill behavior in using another and themselves and possibly devolve because of who they are. It's just a choice, like millions of other choices.

Trusting ourselves

When we make our choices unconsciously (in this case, out of co-dependency), we risk extracting toxic emotions from our experiences—both quality and non-quality—and using those experiences to injure ourselves and others. When we have colluded with another out of need—when we attempt to "own another" by holding them captive to what they lack within themselves—there is always risk. People who "need" share differently from people who do not "need." It is not possible to simply enjoy life in an easy, natural manner free of doubts. How can others be trusted to be genuine when they are not whole themselves—not self-reliant—and need another to "complete them"? More importantly, how can we trust our own selves to be genuine even with ourselves?

Would the Gold Digger still desire her life with Charles if she became self-reliant? We don't know, but we don't see him risking that possibility. No, Charles is job hunting and making plans for his wife to spend her Saturdays and Sundays with him, not at her retail shop where she could earn money. Should the Gold Digger begin to show any signs of self-reliance—signs of sufficient life skills that could take her away from being at Charles' beck-and-call—he could lose interest, and this could put her short-term financial future at risk. She will want to tread carefully should she ever decide to become self-reliant.

When we truly love, we come together with another individual in wholeness. There is no agenda; no questioning of motives; no unspoken bargains, deals or manipulations; no fear of losing, of being "without," of efforts at "managing," of not "being complete" should the other individual move on. Each meets their individual needs independently of the other and simply shares a life together as long as it is desired.

History will keep resurfacing

When we seem to be choosing the same thing over and over again, perhaps it is because we simply are not developed enough to move forward from it. We may never get past it. Perhaps we aren't ready to, we aren't able to, or we just don't want to. But there can be value in our "peeking through the windows" and recognizing the reality that is expressing because the body will continue to attempt to integrate the experience into our whole for our betterment. It will do so until it is fully synthesized—it tries to extract all it can learn from it by attempting to take on a similar experience. If we do not acknowledge the reality of our experience, our history will keep resurfacing in order for us to re-negotiate it. With acknowledgment, we have the fullest amount of information then, and we can move forward into more correct choosing for our betterment.

Many of us may believe that by denying reality—in refusing to discern and acknowledge it—we excuse ourselves from making a different choice or taking a new action accordingly. But the fact that we don't want to own it doesn't mean we don't know it. And ultimately, the life that is actually lived is reflected in our well-being.

Call things as they are

When experiences end because they turn out to be something other than what we truly desired, *consider this:* Instead of focusing on whether an experience was restrictive or destructive for us, we simply acknowledge the truth we discover about ourselves from it. We want to be gentle with ourselves as small bubbles of truth emerge—we needn't ever regret our past. Through conscious development, we can become so practiced at choosing better that the types of offerings we took in the past won't even get a side-ways glance. If we learn the *life* skills of better choosing, history will not resurface for us to renegotiate the experience because it will have been fully integrated and synthesized into our lives. We will not choose that again. We will be done with it.

We are all on a life journey with ourselves. Although we may refuse to acknowledge our reality even to ourselves, or we make rationalizations and excuses and create stories because we are unable to reconcile what we had hoped for from our reality before us, the act of self-deception doesn't really work. Deep inside all of us, we know our truth. Beneath the layers of deception, the guises of society, the common practices of ill-conceived social mores, or the misuse of others for our own comfort, we know. Behind the masks we wear to maintain our public image, we know. It is far better to fully acknowledge who and how we are and the reality before us. We needn't shy away from this. Our truth is part of us—and once "known" to us, we can change our choices if that is our desire. It makes for a more enjoyable life to call things as they are, especially to ourselves. Maybe at this time we will not act to address any changes. That's okay. There's always tomorrow.

A love affair with life begins with well-developed character in the making. You want to be truthful with yourself most of all.

29

Self-Reliance Offers
Greater Freedom of Choice

*Learning to rely on ourselves is key to a more fulfilling and
satisfying life. We simply cannot subjugate ourselves to anything
outside ourselves and know joy. It isn't possible. If we were to do so,
we would give our most precious life away.*

Throughout this book, we have focused on the value of developing
the life skills necessary to acquire self-reliance so that more options are
available for the life we want. This self-reliance is the innate motivation
that, by hook or by crook, we will care for ourselves. That no matter what,
we will figure out how to take any experience we want.

We know that when we are effective in our lives in any way we want,
we set about creating our own access to that which interests us. We are
on our own path; finding the involvements we want. We choose and take
experiences we desire and self-assess and self-correct. We seek out healthy
exchanges with others who have similar natures to ours; we try to stay in
reality and live authentically. We embrace the new and different and odd
and strange experiences that are of interest to us and use them to develop
ourselves. We explore options and bet on ourselves by trusting we will
figure things out as we go along.

Mentioned at the outset were important life skills comprised within a
self-reliant life: healthy self-interest, the capability to discern reality, a curiosity for self-discovery, the ability to operate from our internal authority,

self-management, self-knowing including body knowingness, ownership of our choices and the responsibility for our actions accordingly, self-providing, self-awareness, self-expression, self-assessment, self-correction, and self-care. The natural byproduct that occurs when we act in integrity with those life skills is self-respect.

Without these necessary skills that help us make our desires a reality, we risk putting the life we want in jeopardy. Giving our autonomy to another rather than developing our ability for our own self-care can render us emotionally, physically, intellectually, and financially impotent. When we abdicate responsibility for our self-care to an outside entity or influence, the result will invariably be a compromise of our dream life.

Our life skills of self-reliance can be suppressed or interrupted

While we are born with this natural tendency toward self-reliance, as we learn to make our way in the world, the quality of our internal authority becomes interrupted or suppressed (perhaps by parents or society), and we may find our nature lacking in sufficient self-reliance to pursue the life we want at any given moment. Thus, we become severely limited in our options, leaving us vulnerable.

It could be that some of us were not parented in a way that supported our development in this regard. Some of us were never motivated to be self-reliant because we had learned that we could get what we wanted in other ways, and we were accommodated and enabled—perhaps even encouraged—in this approach. We could "become" what another wanted. We could please another and get our needs met in this way. Some of us might even have had parents or others who wanted us to stay disabled (not self-reliant) in exchange for our life. Some of us grew up seeing exampled how easy it could sometimes be to manipulate with a smile, a compliment, or even a "please" or a "thank you" in order to get whatever we wanted. Then there are those of us who just fell into a habit...that way of being... where we relinquished taking responsibility for any next steps of our own lives, and the outcome of that just somehow became the pattern of our lives. Maybe we even claimed to be afraid when really we didn't want to, weren't able to, or simply weren't ready to take responsibility to become effective in our own lives—acting on what we wanted.

At the core of our being, we each have an inherent belief in our self. However, in our actions of compromise that we might have chosen along the way, we may have traded away that belief; we may have made an exchange. When our innate motivation and determination that prepares us to pursue the life we want is compromised, we have exchanged a life of freedom of choice and autonomy for a life that may require very little self-responsibility. In such a case, we may feel trapped, stuck, and unhappy, claiming to be without the necessary life skills to move into better experiences.

Any one of us who, for whatever reason, does not take responsibility for his or her own self, has only limited options. For example, with financial self-reliance alone, in the absence of family and friends for support, there are generally two possible categories that a completely dependent individual might resort to—reliance on state agencies and marriage. Taking this a step further, we could consider many examples in the arena of life skills that are needed in order to care for ourselves on all levels—to be effective in choosing an action and accomplishing it.

Wanting to be somewhere we are not

Let's take a look at the lives of a few people who are all claiming they want to become self-reliant and mobilize from their own internal authority. They want to have the life skills needed to assure them of having more options for their lives. There is Martha, the widow, who is upset with her dead husband because he never taught her how to manage the finances or change the filter on the furnace or put gas in the car. Then there's Phil, the computer specialist of ten years who wants to change professions and become a chef but is still blaming his parents for his original career choice. And Jocelyn, who, at age forty-five, has been wanting for years to audition on television to become the next famous pop singer but can't seem to figure out how to make that happen, even though she has a spectacular voice. And Matthew, who moved home to work in his father's business but quit after sixteen months and never sought other employment, never moving out of his parent's home—a situation that has become his way of life, even though he says he wants more options.

Becca quit high school, got married, had three children, and now wants to leave what has become an unsatisfying marriage; but she says she can't because she doesn't see how she would be able to support her children. Alice and her adult daughter, Raylene, both love to dance and want to take dance exercise classes together for fun and movement. But Raylene is overweight and Alice would have to go pretty slow at first, so both of them let concerns about looking good keep them from pursuing what they otherwise might enjoy together.

William has stayed at the same low-paying, unskilled, boring job for many years, rationalizing his choice to stay there because his wife doesn't want him to ruin their plans for their retirement in eleven years. And

Jason is concerned about his mother's mental health if he gets divorced. His mother has been obsessively praying because his brother recently declared he was gay. Neither divorce nor homosexuality is accepted in the family's church community and Jason isn't certain his mother can emotionally handle what he desires to do.

A heavy sadness comes with a "life compromise"

What about Andre, Christina, Alicia, Adam, Nigel, and thousands of others who are educated, have good jobs, and have sound finances? They appear successful to others, but—known only to each of them—they want to experience so much more. They all find themselves unable to move forward, even though they have ideas and dreams and desires. These are hardworking, productive people who went out and created careers, had families, did what they believed were all the right things. They were motivated, determined; they took actions. They grabbed the bull by the horns and did what they thought "should be done." But unfortunately, like many of us, they carry a secret within them—a feeling of unrelenting sadness that never goes away. They try—they may stay busy, they may pacify themselves in any number of ways—but this feeling will not yield to their inattention, their negligence.

Some of them believe they are now standing on a threshold whereby they are questioning what changes they need to make to have a more satisfying life; they are motivated to have it, but they can't seem to get past their unknown "interferences." No, these people may not be able to pinpoint why they have the debilitating sadness they do, but their body attempts to communicate to them—with this deep, unremitting pain—their true reactions to their reality they live with every day.

> *When we feel the heavy sadness crushing our life force, it is time to move—even small steps—with actions into new experiences. Even just a slight degree of shifting can interrupt the old habit of self-deception and denial of the truth. This is vital; it may well be time to pursue the life that is deeply desired.*

They could rationalize any number of reasons why they don't know their heart's desires or why they seem unable to move toward any deep aspirations, but that would just be—as often is with the "why questions"—telling stories. The reality is often they have chosen to compromise themselves—subjugate themselves—to something outside of them. They may not even be aware of what that "something" is, but each of them finds his or her self in a "life compromise," and without the life skills of self-authority and self-reliance to move forward. Yes, many of us compromise ourselves, even those who appear to have a treasured life.

All these people mentioned are somewhere other than where they want to be in their lives. All deeply desire to have more options or the wherewithal to pursue those options in order to enjoy a more fulfilled life—a life they want. Imagine the options available to those who previously thought they could only make their way in life by being at some beck and call—by subjugating themselves to anything outside of themselves. The question to ask is this: "Can I get what I truly desire in a way where I won't find myself in a life compromise?"

When somewhere (physically, emotionally, mentally, and so forth) you don't want to be, forget the "why" and focus on *what* you do want and *how* to move toward it.

More options are available to those who are self-reliant

Whose responsibility is it that we each learn to uncover and go for what we desire? At any time, we can request or seek out the life skills we need to develop—that is up to each of us. Many of us have a great job skill, but it can be problematic when we view self-reliance as only a job skill or a talent. We want to accumulate the life skills to be effective at taking the experiences we want *throughout our lifetime*…to become involved in creating our own access—to people, to information, or to any other experiences that will get us moving in a direction we want.

We want to be effective in our relationships and with our communications, to pursue our career interests and manage our finances well, to have the emotional and social intelligence to know ourselves and to get along in the world. We want the integrity to be responsible with our choices and the wherewithal to realize the dreams we desire. When we have the capability to see our reality clearly, we can discern what is keeping us from being effective in our lives. Jobs skills are important, but it is the adequately developed *life skills* that assure us beyond the shadow of all doubt that we will be able to take care of ourselves, giving us the freedom to choose anything we desire.

Anyone of us who decides to live life differently may begin to do so at any time. This motivation to take care of ourselves already exists as part of our nature. No one can give it to us. It exists, is just "in us," wanting expression. We may, however, want to take a hard look at our own past participation.

Could it be that there are those of us who have simply forsaken ourselves, thus emotionally trapping and limiting ourselves with rationalizations and excuses, placing restrictions on our life choices rather than exploring and discovering our own selves through new experiences?

Perhaps no one took anything away from us; perhaps it was we who gave away things of precious value—our trust in ourselves, our self-respect, and our choices for ourselves. We cast them off, and in our own self-abandonment, we left ourselves with only the barest of options.

The question to ask is this: "Do I want to continue to have only limited options?" If not, then what is the price to get those things of value back? With a self-reliant life no one, including ourselves, can be at risk for a forsaken life when we know that—no matter what—we will take care of ourselves. We will figure it out. When we can declare, "I will take care of me!" there *is* greater freedom of choice.

Bring forth what can nourish you

Some of us, after recognizing we are so disabled, so unprepared, or simply just limited in our perspective and therefore restricted in acting on what we want, begin to notice a driving desire to live a more satisfying life, to do whatever it takes. It may start as a slight rousing—an awakening—but it becomes stronger, more vital, as we become more in touch with our nature, with our "true wanting."

Perhaps a song comes on the radio, or you read something that grabs your attention, or one day something is simply different. You don't need any assurances from others that you can do it. Just bring that innate motivation to take care of yourself—that who and how you are—first and foremost to the table. If you have a relationship of integrity with yourself, then if you fall down, you will pick yourself back up, dust yourself off, and carry on. If you feel that motivation rising inside of you, then begin moving, begin to actively seek out that which interests you. We don't know how any new experience taken today will influence and affect our path forward. A new perspective can make everything look different and fresh with new possibilities. Actions taken from our truth nourish us.

When you are ready to become self-reliant, it is helpful to take whatever you were dealt or whomever and however you have become, and use your characteristics—your behaviors—in a way that assists you. It is necessary to begin to liberate yourself; there is no need to hang on to what has been restrictive or even destructive in your past experiences, but rather you can focus on what you can bring forth from them that can nourish you. Stay in reality, declare what you want, and move yourself. Remember, you don't know—you can't know—what treasures, what gems lie in your genetic "bucket," waiting to find their expression in your lifetime.

You want to make the most of everything you can. Your genetics, family history, life circumstances, and experiences exist for you to use on your own developmental journey. Protecting yourself from honestly considering them is not helpful. Every behavioral characteristic has the potential to be a quality experience or a non-quality experience, depending on the amount of that behavioral characteristic and your personal viewpoint and reaction to it. You can stay attentive and fully available to what is presenting in your life. Through comprehension, you can begin to self-correct, owning your reality and your choices.

If you find you've gotten yourself into a pickle, do what you need to do for the short term. That's okay. If you can move forward and break the old patterns, then the action of compromise you are currently living becomes only a temporary tool to get past those prior choices, assisting you as you move on to new choices. Be mindful not to allow any action of compromise to become a lifestyle rather than a tool to develop yourself because misusing yourself or others as a lifestyle puts your own development at risk. Whatever your path forward may require, try to be aware of what and how you are choosing. Maybe you will stay in the relationship, continue to live at home, or stay at a job you don't like while you take some preparatory actions to move to something more to your liking.

A sense of freedom

Amazing transformation can occur by simply recognizing reality, expressing what you want, dispelling what you have settled for, and investing in yourself by taking steps—however small—that move you into experiences that delight and inform you. It may be necessary to take a chance on yourself, even if all you have to offer is your innate motivation to take care of yourself. That is enough to begin. This movement does not have to be difficult. As you access formerly unknown aspects of yourself, those sleeping or not yet experienced parts of you—your truth takes form and surfaces. If you find yourself in an experience that isn't to your satisfaction, you can remember that there are plenty more experiences out there; nature is kind in this regard. This discovery of yourself lasts your lifetime; and the more you can grow to move toward what is satisfying to you, the easier and more rewarding life may become.

Even if you are not sure you are ready to take the steps, just keep actively observing. Maybe you can begin to consider some new possibilities or maybe just do some things differently from the way you usually do. Small shifts and changes can add up; they can offer you a new direction, a new perspective…more of the life you want.

It is natural for us to want to make sense of the world and find a way of life that works for us and makes us feel good about ourselves. We want to respect ourselves—to mobilize from our own internal authority as we tend to our own self-care, develop our own core of healthy self-interest and self-reliance, and not put ourselves at risk of misusing others or being misused. When we acquire these necessary *life* skills, there is an internal satisfaction, a sense of freedom to make any choice we want; we will do whatever we need to do to responsibly take care of ourselves. When we come from this place of integrity—operating from wholeness—we are able to recognize and receive that into our lives. We are free to be ourselves.

When we recognize and give value to our own life in this way and put that into action, the ordinary byproducts are respect, care, and love for all others. It then becomes natural to appreciate that as each one comes to care for one's self, all are cared for.

When we regard our lives in this way, there is no efforting or teaching required for any of us to become tolerant and respectful of the dignity and worth of every individual on the planet. There is humanity in this valuing of our own life and the lives of others.

30

Mac's Story

Mr. Hollywood

Awaken the "gifts" – these gifts that are our true desires. Let them come alive. Through our actions, let them actualize in our life.

I called him "Mr. Hollywood." It was just a joke, but it always brought a smile. Mac and I had been meeting for a "cuppa" (coffee and conversation) every other month or so for about six years. We originally met because he was my instructor for a Wednesday night film class at the city's major film school. He knew the craft of lighting and filming as though it were part of the air he breathed. My classmates and I found him a caring teacher, and the evening raced by in a show of great instruction, tales of his outrageous adventures as a photographer and cinematographer, and overall a really good time.

Mac had a million anecdotes to share about how working in the film industry had played out for him, and we, his students, enjoyed living his escapades through him. I was a real estate developer and finance guy by day—had been for close to fifteen years—and was just sort of exploring ideas for a more creative life; that's why I was in the class. When the semester ended, a few of us guys hadn't quite had enough, so we continued to meet with Mac. Over the years, the coffee club dwindled down to just Mac and me. Every semester Mac had three classes to teach, but he continued to openly state that he really wanted to be out there making more fabulous films. He took a few short sabbaticals to do so, but locally not much was going on; maybe it wasn't the place. Mac was in his late seventies, and he'd had his "run at it," but he was still wanting more. It lit him up.

≈

It all started for Mac when he was serving in the Korean War. He'd barely arrived overseas when someone yelled out to him, "Hey, sailor, you know how to operate a camera?" As Mac was fond of saying, "My destiny was sealed, much to my immense satisfaction!"

After the war, Mac free-lanced in New York City, specializing in photographing fashion models. In one tale after another, he shared his nearly inconceivable adventures about his work for *Vogue* and *Glamour* magazines, as well as other commercial work. We'd leave his class and look up the people he'd mentioned; sure enough, they existed. We thought Mac was some kind of legend, and maybe he was in his own right. My favorite narrative was his account of an evening he spent with Ernest Hemingway. Mac said it was supposed to be just a quick photography shoot, but what with the smoking of Havana cigars and the too many dry gin martinis, they had carried on until four o'clock in the morning when Mac finally headed for home. Apparently both men had engaged in some yarn spinning, with each saga in competition to better the last.

The photography industry was changing, and Mac wanted to move into cinematography. He knew little about it, but he and his wife, Jet, (his "bride" as he called her) headed across country to make their way in Hollywood. While Jet worked as a flight attendant, Mac scrambled to get knowledgeable in an industry new to him. I remember him telling the class how he befriended every gaffer, key grip, and best boy who could help him get things figured out fast. They all knew he was "green," but they saw that he worked hard, was earnest and respectful, and devoured the new information like he hadn't eaten in days. They also recognized his talent.

Visually, Mac knew what the director wanted to have happen—he had brought the photographer's eye to the job. He just wasn't sure how to position the heavy lighting fixtures and cables and install dolly tracks, all for lining up the best shots for the desired effects. But Mac had persevered. He'd had a great run at it, and with Hollywood's finest at that—both in television and in film, awards and all. Mac and Jet had indeed lived the dream. And then it was over.

They (mostly he, as he readily admitted) had blown through the money from the good times like it would last forever. But it didn't, and now he and his bride of nearly fifty years had settled in a quiet bedroom community near a city with a film school, where Mac worked. The lifestyle was affordable with the job, and Mac enjoyed teaching. They vacationed in LA once a year, having a grand time and staying with friends in fabulous digs. Their friends would always ask, "When are you coming back to LA? You belong here with us. We miss you." Mac and Jet would just shrug their shoulders as Mac replied that he enjoyed his work at the film school, but he never denied wanting to be back filming on a set.

Mac and I met for coffee in the springtime, and I was surprised to notice how slowly my friend was moving. He seemed a bit bent over, which was so unlike him. This was a man who was accustomed to carrying forty pounds of gear. He was like the fly fisherman outfitted with multi-pocketed jacket and pants—pockets that held all kinds of treasures for the sport, the craft. Mac had every lens and filter possible and suitcases filled with gear that seemed to follow him without a leash. Like a grade school librarian with spectacles hanging from a chain, Mac always had a camera around his neck.

"So, how goes the life, Mr. Hollywood?" I asked my friend as we settled into our familiar places at IHOP.

In time, he answered in a way we had never spoken before. "Well, Buddy, the school has cut back on my classes to just one class next semester, and maybe none after that. What with students more interested in working with new technology, I'm obsolete there. I still really want and need to work. So, Jet and I are thinking we'll put the house up for sale and move south of Santa Fe. With the proceeds from the house, we could afford to buy a condo there and be comfortable. New Mexico's offering tax incentives to attract the film industry. It's possible I could get the work I want there. With nothing here now, there's no reason to stay. Jet has never really wanted to be here, even though she has made the most of it. "Her people" aren't here. She has one distant friend in Santa Fe, and the weather is mild and she could do her walks and play tennis year round.

"You don't sound particularly excited about moving there. Is it what you want to do?"

"I want to work, and Jet's willing to try out a new community. And I can't just buy a house anywhere for us. Spent it all, I did. Left myself without any options. It was fun, and we aren't on the street, but we need to be careful. Anyway, it's time for a new plan. I want my bride to be happy. And I miss the work. It's in my blood; it's who I am."

"I only met Jet once, but she sure is one beautiful and alive woman. She's no one's patsy, that Jet of yours. She probably wants you to be happy, too. Go for it and see what happens. We can always have coffee on Skype. So what are your next steps?"

"Thanks, Buddy. We've got a realtor lined up to come take a look, and Jet's been busy cleaning things out, but we're moving kind of slow. There's not a lot of energy to leave, but there is absolutely no energy to stay."

～

Three months later I walked into IHOP and hardly recognized my friend. He looked like death warmed over. He had been in the hospital for a stay and was just recuperating and "rejoining the living," so to speak. We talked for a while, and then I asked him what his plans were. He said he and Jet were just finishing up with getting the house ready for the market when he got sick. Again, he commented on how slowly things were going. Jet was the one doing everything to make the move possible, but even she was moving slower than her normally spunky self. He confided that neither of them was feeling very positive about Santa Fe, but the plan was still to go there. He could no longer navigate the stairs at his home, and at least there he could afford to buy a condo and possibly get some work.

"It sounds like you're taking the steps, Mac, however slowly. So, what'd the doc say?"

"I have cancer. But things are under control, and with time I will be able to work again and get us resettled."

"I'm so sorry to hear that. I wish there were something I could do."

Neither of us said anything for a few moments, and then I asked, "In all our years of friendship, I've never put on the financial or business hat with you, but I'd like to offer up some thoughts if I could? If my questions are too personal, just let me know; but I am going somewhere with this conversation. Trust me."

"Sure, Buddy, shoot."

"Mac, I've never seen you like this. I know what Jet means to you; you get teary-eyed just talking about her—have ever since I met you; you love your wife. And your work? You're crazy about it…If you could wave a magic wand and have whatever you wanted, what would that look like? What would really float your boat?"

"That's not a hard question to answer. It's always on the tip of my tongue. I want to be in LA. So does Jet. I want to work in film again, I want to visit with friends and enjoy the warm weather and take my bride where she will be happy. I can hardly stand an idle day without my camera, without a project, without my work. It's my life, my passion. Maybe you've never experienced thinking dawn would never break, wanting so bad to get to your craft, but that's how it has always been with me. I want that feeling back. It's who I am and how I've lived for most of my life. And LA has it; it's there, I know it. I feel it. How's that for a wish list, Buddy? But I can't buy there. Our house in Brentwood is worth over two million at least by now. I pissed the money away—that's a fact. Buying a condo in Santa Fe is the best we can do."

"Hmm…So, do you have a life insurance policy?"

"Yes, I do."

"How much is it for?"

"Half a million. Why do you ask?"

"I see." I nodded. "I'd like to toss a few ideas out; you don't have to say anything if you don't want. But just play along with me here for a minute… Now, we can't debate that I was one of the best film and lighting students you ever taught. And it's you who taught me about how things can be visible but not seen—about perspective, about how filters and lenses can change the way we view things. Just for a moment, forget any preconceived notions you may have, any thinking on your part that could restrict your options. You know what I mean?"

"Okay."

～

"Mac, what if…what if you didn't buy? What if *buying* didn't matter? You rent instead. You go where you want to go, and you rent and check things out. What if you sold everything here—sold your second car, your house, your things—and you and Jet got yourselves out to LA?"

I watched him perk up. "Hmm…and rented an apartment there…? I didn't respond.

Mac began musing. "A nice apartment… We'll be getting proceeds from our house here that could supplement what a condo payment near Santa Fe would be…just until I could get some work." He looked me straight in the eye. "I know I could get work there."

"You've always said you could get work there, that's true…So, what about taking yourself and your bride back home?"

My friend sat there and stared at me. Neither of us said anything for several moments. I'm sure the clamoring of coffee cups and dishes were somewhere in the background, but to me it felt as though time and motion and sound were suspended.

"What if...when it's your time to go and Jet gets that half a million, she's among her friends and her people, and will make her own best decisions then. Mac, all we ever do in life is *rent*. We rent experiences even when we think we're buying; all choice is temporary. And then we die. We all do."

I could almost hear the wheels turning in Mac's head. After a moment, I asked, "Do you want to talk about it?"

"No, not now," he whispered. "I want to sit with it. Buddy, I had never considered for even one moment that it might be possible for me to live in LA and work in film again there. I could actually take my bride back home—to *her* people, to *our* people."

~

The next time I saw Mac and Jet, they waltzed arm-in-arm into the Chateau Marmont on Sunset Boulevard in Hollywood. I was in LA for business, as I too, had moved on to a fabulously creative and satisfying job, inspired by our conversation. We were meeting for an early dinner at one of Hollywood's half-hidden gems that sparkled with old fashioned glamour. When Mac and I spotted each other, I called out, "Mr. Hollywood!" I'd forgotten where I was, and, of course, five men turned my way. As he and Jet strolled on over, I couldn't help notice the change. There they were, dressed to the nines, looking twenty years younger than their age. Mac stood tall in his dark blue jacket complete with silk pocket scarf, his white hair perfectly groomed, wearing the latest fashion sunglasses. Jet looked beautiful, still a mite of a thing, with quick movements and a welcoming smile. Both were laughing. Anyone could see they were in love, and they were happy.

We hugged the kind of hug that good friends do. Dinner on the charming, idyllic garden terrace was the perfect setting as we enjoyed our precious moments together, catching up on the events that had transpired since their life-changing decision to move to LA. They were lovely together, vibrant—so full of life.

~

Maybe because I had a small part in it, I don't know, but I'm just saying...of all of the stories Mac ever relayed, it was his best story. They practically told it in unison, each one adding a part the other forgot to mention. It held me spellbound as they relayed the steps they had taken. The steps of courage, energy, conviction—born of the desire to do whatever it took to get back home so they could recapture and create anew the life they truly wanted. They had been on fire about it since the morning he had returned home from our "cuppa" and presented the idea, in its embryonic stages, to her. They were openly loving and grateful to me.

Jet laughed as she said, "All the miles driving out, Mac was almost immobilized that it was actually happening. He just sat there and could barely move. Buddy, he didn't want anything else; he was just anxious with wondering. As soon as we arrived in town and got settled in with our friends, he just came to life. We scored a fabulous two bedroom apartment that's perfect for us. It is as though we never left. We've had no less than a dozen dinner parties, our date cards are full to our hearts' desires, and we see all the newly released films just like we used to."

Mac then told me of his film work here and there, and how he was again involved with activities at the American Society of Cinematographers' clubhouse. He had a few new mystery book authors to recommend to me, as their morning routine involved Mac sitting in the park and reading his mysteries while Jet walked their beloved spaniel "Bullet" on her five mile loop. Mr. Hollywood and his beautiful bride loved, absolutely loved, their lives.

≈

Eleven months later, Mac passed away at his home. There was no suffering. He and Jet had returned home from yet another fabulous evening of enjoying the company of close friends, and he had a heart attack and died. He had recently been hired as the cinematographer for an upcoming film.

Come to Peace with Yourself

One of the greatest gifts we can give ourselves is the freedom and dignity of living an authentic life—to know our innermost desires through listening to our body. If we listen, it will inform us of correct choosing so that we can create a life of greater ease and satisfaction, a life that is truly our own.

A life experience connected to our innermost desires provides for a vital life force, strong chi, and a greater sense of well-being. Our body has a way of letting us know what it is that we want. Do we want a full-flavored, tasty life or something else of our choosing? We may not have the ready answers, but our nature will always move to further its own evolution; it wants to thrive. Our nature—our truth—compels us, based on the data available to us at any given moment, received from our experiences. We want to welcome that information.

The body will re-energize toward movement of enriching choices; it will be loyal. It will inform us if we will allow it. When we take on new experiences, this exploration and discovery mode shifts our life pattern; and our nature—our body, our whole being—expands itself in its awareness. If we want our life infused with and influenced by greater flavoring in order to increase our life satisfaction, we may want to add more variation and substance while participating in our own access and enjoying the beauty of self-discovery. This needn't be hard work. Each experience taken brings new and different variables into the mix—new and ever-transpiring data. And as the body compounds itself in the awareness from these new variables, it expands in its desire and receptivity to more new experiences.

It doesn't matter that we don't always have ready answers; the body knows what we are responding to, and it can bring its messages into our consciousness for that which supports the expression of our truth. Our job is to simply keep taking on new experiences chosen from our desires today. We are then evolving and changing and growing, recalculating and recalibrating the new data, fine tuning our experiences with better choosing, becoming happier and more fulfilled in our lives.

We not only want to recognize reality, but we want to declare and pursue that which is compelling to us. In order to do this, we want to fully participate in getting access to new information, people, resources, and experiences and be open to recognizing all the possibilities.

In doing so, we may find prejudices and restrictions we are inclined to place around possibilities. As with Mac, who realized he had restricted himself to living only in certain geographic locations by his prejudice to buy instead of rent, so too, our thinking can limit us. We want to become aware of those—free ourselves from any constraints—while we are musing and considering our options so we can clearly recognize which of the many possibilities may be for us and which ones may not. Once we discover greater possibilities exist, we are free to handle that information in any way we so choose, acting on all of it, parts of it, or none of it.

Be at peace with whatever you choose
Some people believe that choosing what they desire in life is just not possible. Many think that if they were to choose what they really wanted, some of their relationships—maybe even with their spouses, children, or jobs—would be at risk. That may be true; it's a logical assumption that

when a change is made, something else will transpire—a shift will likely occur. So, if you decide not to take the actions necessary to satisfy your true desires, that is your choice; it's okay. Regard yourself with the same kindness you would naturally extend to someone else. There is no reason for blame or shame. If you stay in any exchange, it is because you have chosen to accept the exchange. Just call it what it is—stay in reality—and enjoy the peace of the decisions you've made for your life.

Come to peace with your past

We all can agree no one comes to earth the same as anyone else and through birth or circumstances, we all have things we deal with. But, many of us have fallen into the habit of misusing our emotional responses to our life situations to keep us stuck or frustrated, or for self-reproach. When we instead consider allowing our emotions to simply do their job— to inform us of what we like and want and don't like and don't want in any experience—and use that information to become more aware of our experiences, we can begin the process of making new choices that can lead to positive change. Because once aware, it's easier to then ask ourselves, "Okay, what can I do now to better my life experience?"

If you have regrets, be kind to yourself; nothing is gained from suffering. These regrets are just the result of compromised choices made without sufficient awareness and consciousness to make better informed choices. You could not have known to do otherwise at the time; you simply were not developed enough.

If you are able now to look at a choice made in your past and notice—perhaps even see clearly—how you would now choose a different action, then you can celebrate your new awareness rather than lament your previous choice. Our regrets can be tools for knowing better. They can heighten our consciousness for future experiences, as we will then be more able to anticipate the consequences we can accept. This better prepares us for living the rest of our life. If you, as a parent, have regrets about how you raised your children, you might want to try to share those feelings openly in conversations with them and offer your insights. This may encourage healing, and it may also assist them in their own development. At any point, you can begin to create a new relationship with those who are important in your life.

As we further our development and gain maturity, choosing to grow from our experiences, we naturally will have fewer of them that may cause us regret.

Movement is key to making changes

If you find your life worn down, worn out, your chi burned up, it may be time to look at reality and take back your life one small step at a time. As you begin moving forward with small choices and actions toward what you feel is right for you at the time, you may want to abandon the mistaken notion that change is hard.

Change is easier than we have been led to believe. We, as an animated and evolving species, exist by movement and change. Making changes is just a matter of taking one step after another. Sometimes we may need to form some new—or cast off some old—habits. But our very nature compels us to take action to dismantle choices of incorrect choosing for us.

There is no need to cause yourself stress or difficulty. Remember, it is better to tell yourself, "I may not have all the answers for how I'm going to do this; but if I want it, I will figure it out. My body will inform me; I'm not going to allow the mind to interfere." This way may offer the greatest possible sense of ability and ease.

As you explore each experience in your life, simply *consider* whether it supports your sense of well-being or if it diminishes and inhibits it. All movement leads to an opportunity to look at your life from a fresh perspective and choose anew.

Once in a new and different space, even one degree different, your perspective—your way of viewing things—will shift, and new and better choices can be made. Each of these new experiences allows for greater exposure of your truth—your true desires.

Caring for yourself

This is about you and taking care of yourself. You will want to know who and how you are so it is possible to be loyal to yourself. As you come to appreciate how your symptoms are the expression of your body speaking to itself, you will welcome the body's information and avail yourself of its messages. You may want to assess your life and gently and lovingly ask yourself the following questions for the purpose of gaining awareness—no stories, no rationalizations, just simple truths…this is between you and you alone:

- Does my life feel as though it is not my own, and if so, what choices did I make that caused that to happen?

- Do I see when I compromise myself?

- What do I believe I owe another individual or anything outside myself?

- What might happen as I begin to know what truly resonates with me in any given moment? Will I create obstacles from my "guess work" that influence me not to act on what I want?

- What are the difficulties I face if I decide to make changes in my life?

- Have I restricted recognizing the options of what is possible? Are there possibilities beyond my current thinking?

- Will I benefit from living a self-reliant life? If so, am I willing to acquire the life skills necessary to become more self-reliant?

- Will I be happier and more satisfied if I make new life choices for me?

- What actions can I begin to take to assist me in determining what I truly desire?

Becoming whole by coming to our own truth

In our better health—our more complete development—when we choose well, only what belongs to us will feel connected to us and make sense to us. When that occurs, it nourishes us. When we express our truth through our actions in any experience, we have the greatest possibility of being able to recognize truth from others. The correct scenarios for each of us have better opportunities to connect, and we act as our own matchmaker as we responsibly seek out harmonious matches. There is less conflict within our body as we move toward the experiences we truly desire—those that resonate with our unique evolutionary process. We find a wholeness…a progressive beauty, a natural elimination. In this way, our fullest expression of our truth emerges in a well-lived life of our own choosing. Our personal Lioness is alive within us—*is us, our nature*—and we use this body know-ingness to assist us in our discernment and awareness of correct choosing for our lives. When we honor those possibilities for life experiences that seem to resonate with our deepest desires, we come to know greater ease, peace, and happiness.

It can be rewarding to practice the life and love that satisfies, exalts, and delights us until we get really good at it. And then do it a whole lot more. The nature of an individual is stronger than we can ever begin to imagine. It is our partner, our body, our truth. When our "wanting" within us is so strong and we take action from that truth, amazing things open up. Everything enriches everything else, and pathways naturally change and emerge. For those who are bold, for those who dare, or for those willing to simply take a small step, it may be time to wake up and move.

> *If all you can do is crawl...start crawling.*
> *—Rumi*

31

Your Story

Any Field—You Choose

*Our ultimate responsibility is to the life experiences we are seeking.
We are all different, and we each find our way. Uniquely. If we
desire a life of peace and harmony, we will want to be loyal
to the life we choose to live.*

It's very simple really. An individual has the option of choosing any field as his or her playground for doing life. Every field offers a path for the journey.

∽

It may appear, for example, that on both sides of the road there exists a beautiful field—green, expansive, and inviting. You look to one side and see, way out in the field, a beautiful flower, a white daisy. "Oh my, isn't that lovely," you tell yourself. You look to the other side and see, way out in the field, a weed. "Oh my, that weed is really messing up the field. Well, I can fix that," you tell yourself, and you choose in that moment to head down that path, with the intention of pulling that weed so the field will appear flawless. You arrive at the weed, bend over, and pluck that weed out of the ground. You pat the ground and yourself as you feel good about fixing the field so all will be beautiful.

As you straighten up, readying yourself to continue your journey, you gaze out into the distance and see three more weeds, all in a clump. "Oh my, I guess I have another task at hand to do. After all, if I don't do it, who will?" you tell yourself. You mosey on over, kneel down, and pluck those three weeds out of the earth. Again, you pat the ground and yourself for taking on that project that so needed fixing for the benefit of all.

～

As you stand up and begin walking again, you become more observant to your life, to your environment. And what do you see up ahead but a small patch of weeds. You tell yourself, "Oh my. Now this is getting to be too much, but it needs to be done so that all will be right and beautiful. I probably can fix it, and because I can, I should. I wish I didn't have to spend my time tackling that patch, but oh well, I guess I will. I'm here already and if I don't do it, who will?" You sigh deeply, and reluctantly walk over to the patch, kneel down, and begin the hard work of pulling the weeds out to fix the field. You'll miss the picnic that is starting shortly and be late for the evening's plans with loved ones, but it has become a project that needs to be done.

This time as you finish up, you do not pat the ground or yourself. No, you aren't feeling joyful and giving and filled with gratitude for the precious moments of the day. The sun is hot, and you are sweaty and cranky. As you stand and look around the spot you are in, you cry in amazement. "Oh dear, I am standing in an entire field of weeds in an experience I recognize I no longer want. If I stay here—on this path, in this field—I will have spent my entire life surrounded by weeds, distracted in the fixing."

～

There were, and still are, other choices to be made should that be your desire. Remember that you noticed another path—one that from the road led into a field in which no weed was standing and where a beautiful white daisy caught your eye. What if you were to choose that path now, and play out your life in that playground?

You make a courageous but easy decision to change course because you trust that you can figure it out and be responsible however it plays out. As you head down the path in the field with no weed standing, you walk with a lift, a feeling of joy. You find yourself humming a bit as you head toward that flower. Your skin feels alive in the slight breeze and the familiar V shape of a flock of birds above you brings a smile to your face. Coming upon the daisy, you exclaim, "What a beauty!" You kneel down to sense the essence of its stunning presence more closely.

Upon standing you notice three more daisies ahead and coming upon them, you again kneel to embrace more closely the discovery of such delight and interest. Your eyes fill to the brim with tears of appreciation and gratitude for how fortunate you were to have experienced them on your path. You brush away the mist from your eyes. You lift your gaze toward the brilliant red and golden sky of the setting sun and stare with awe at the splendor of reality before you. Oh my. You are standing in an entire field of daisies, non-stop daisies as far as the eye can see. And you declare—every cell of your body declares—joyfully, to the world: "Yes! This is the experience I want now. This is where I choose to live my precious moments of this life I was given!" You kneel down and kiss the ground—this field of daisies—your playground for your life.

I am the master of my fate. I am the captain of my soul.
—*William Ernest Henley*

A Personal Note
and Acknowledgments

This book was in my "wanting" for many years. I felt compelled to write it. That being said however, I found myself stuck in the "get ready, get set" stage, ineffective in moving forward. I knew what I wanted to try to do—to write this book—but I was meeting with "resistance" of my own creation, engaging in major distractions from the pursuit of my own heart's desires, and I felt my life force diminishing as I conned and compromised myself.

Finally listening to what my body was telling me, and after a few seemingly "false starts" for new movement, I began to pursue my life as the active writer of this book. I did an eighteen month "walkabout,"—albeit driving my older Subaru—hosted by nearly a dozen open-hearted friends and family in several states throughout America. Conversations abounded—at an interstate rest area in Tennessee, while reconnecting in Stanwood, Iowa at Ditto's Restaurant and Clarence, Iowa at the American Legion and the public library, as a visiting choir member learning African tribal songs in Portland, Oregon, around dinner tables of friends old and new—and found their way, in parts, into the mix of this book and informed it.

From both present and past, observations and voices that represented an array of experiences—some profound, some hilarious, some extraordinarily painful—were woven and crafted into stories that wanted to be told.

For nearly two months, a warm smile, hot coffee, and my writing space awaited me at dawn on the upper floor of the Vesuvio bar in the North Beach neighborhood of San Francisco, the hangout of Beat-era writers Allan Ginsberg, Jack Kerouac and Lawrence Ferlinghetti. I wore my beret and scarf and was tempted to dye my hair black. If ghosts were alive and encouraging, it was there where I felt emboldened to take greater unconventional and poetic license with the work.

～

Now, what had been waiting to be written came easily as I found myself crossing paths with what I needed, and I knew I was choosing correctly for me. I was living my book, owning each experience, even though—given my genetic predisposition, past environments, and history—my own personal development wasn't always pretty. So goes the surrender to a reality-based life.

Like Forrest Gump who ran and ran until it seemed he was "all ranned out," I wrote and wrote until I was "all wrote out." Three times I thought I was done, and finally one day it was true. Unlike Forrest Gump, however, I did not—and still do not—have a profitable shrimping empire for financing…but I took a risk on myself anyway. I trusted that I would figure it out, that I would be responsible; I always had been.

❧

While each life is a solo journey, I have been blessed with welcomed support from many in the making of this book. You will find in the book, *A Special Acknowledgment to Karen Sontag*, where I express my appreciation for her wise counsel. This book would not be—could not be—what it is, were it not for her wisdom and clarity we can sense on every page.

So too, there is a *Dedication* to my family—my son, Nathaniel Leonoudakis; my mother, Phyllis Hanus; my brothers Tom Hyde and Steven Hyde and sister Peggy Miller-Peterman and their families; and my nephew Ron Hyde. While their inspiration alone would have been sufficient, they freely gave far more than that and their choices to do so have impacted me deeply.

I wish to thank my talented friends and editors, David Miretti and Robert Vernon, for their significant and thoughtful suggestions and the tender care with which they regarded the content. With genuine hearts and a sense of humor, they worked steadfastly with me and brought forth their best. For his creative design efforts on the book's beautiful cover, I offer my warm thanks to Robert Vernon, and for her efforts on the pleasing interior design, my gratitude goes to Val Sherer.

Many (including my generous extended family) brought their skills, time, offerings, and contributions that supported me and enriched this work in its development and birthing. For those who have preferred to remain anonymous, or who may have been omitted by my error, you are closely held in my appreciative heart. It is with thanksgiving that I list those I can in alphabetical order:

Amanda Barrett, Howard Beckerman, Dr. Judith Briles, the Brouhard family – Michael, Diane, Adam, and Nick, Dr. Vicki Burnett, Sabrina Callahan, Ozzie Cheek, Jesse Clark, Tina Collen, Sandy Condra, Vicki Dean, Karen Dennis, Michael Embry, Rebecca Ford, Bill Fox, Jean Franzblau, Trisha Frey, Joel Friedlander, Nick Gillespie, Luis Gonzalez,

Greg Harrington, Kathleen Harrington, Christina Hills, Angela Hyde, Regina Hyde, Tammy Hyde, William Hyde, Paul Kaihla, Bryan Kaplan, Derek Khanna, Tara Kilian, David Kudler, David Lane, Ellie Mae, Marlene McAllister, Peggy Marlatt, Linde Martin, Charlie Mikulewicz, Ron Miller, Howard Monroe, Mike Motta, Deborah Myers, Kim Myers, Nicole Myers, Mike Newport, Stacey Oberhardt, Linda Olsson, Racquel Yurrita Orbegozo, Shannon Parish, Bob Pasqualina, Lynda Phelps, Robert Pimm, Mark Platjes, Christian Prahl, Marilyn Pruess, Jocelyn Rahm, Barry Reis, Robin Roberts, Dr. Roger Roberts, Natia Romero, Dr. Jeffrey Saffer, David Salaverry, Diane Salinger, Joy Sallee, Marita Sallee, Ramona Sallee, Steve Saunders, Ruth Schwartz, Dr. Larry Shardt, Joan Sherman, Jerry Soper, Meredith Spear, Gerry Stellern, Pat Timberlake, Ariana Uffman, Dr. Bonnie Uffman, Geeta Vora, and Susan White.

All of us love the feeling we have when we are effective in our lives, pursuing our true desires. But more importantly, who among us can deny that when this happens and we experience joy and satisfaction, connection, and peace within our own lives, we regard ourselves and all of humanity more favorably? I never dreamed—how *could* I have possibly foreseen—that I would be so profoundly rewarded in this manner for the writing of this book, and I am immensely grateful to everyone for their part in this.